The Mediator

GEN. LAZARO SUMBEIYWO AND THE SOUTHERN
SUDAN PEACE PROCESS

Kenway Biographies and Autobiographies

1. Memoirs of a Biscuit Baron - *Madatally Manji*
2. A Love Affair with the Sun - *Michael Blundell*
3. Tales from Africa - *Douglas Collins*
4. The Illusion of Power - *G.G. Kariuki*
5. Nothing But the Truth - *Yusuf K. Dawood*
6. From Simple to Complex - *J.M. Mungai*
7. The Mediator: Gen. Lazaro Sumbeiywo and the Southern Sudan Peace Process - *Waithaka Waihenya*

The Mediator

GEN. LAZARO SUMBEIYWO AND THE SOUTHERN SUDAN PEACE PROCESS

WAITHAKA WAIHENYA

KENWAY PUBLICATIONS
Nairobi • Kampala • Dar es Salaam

Published by Kenway Publications
a subsidiary of
East African Educational Publishers Ltd.
Brick Court, Mpaka Road/Woodvale Grove
Westlands, P.O. Box 45314
Nairobi - 00100
Kenya.

Email: eaep@eastafricanpublishers.com
Website: www.eastafricanpublishers.com

East African Educational Publishers Ltd.
P.O. Box 11542
Kampala
Uganda.

Ujuzi Educational Publishers Ltd.
P.O. Box 32737
Dar es Salaam
Tanzania.

© Lazaro K. Sumbeiywo & Waithaka Waihenya 2006

First published 2006

ISBN 9966-25-480-3

Printed in Kenya by
Printpak Ltd.
P.O. Box 78354
Nairobi.

Foreword

It is not unusual for a diplomat to defuse an explosive situation, successfully broker a peace deal and watch peace descend on a place that has never known it for decades. It is, however, unusual for a soldier, ideally meant to make war, to venture into intense negotiations and at the end of them, make peace.

General Lazaro Sumbeiywo's success in brokering the Comprehensive Peace Agreement in Sudan, a country that was immersed in Africa's longest civil war for decades, can be said to be a first in many ways. He was no diplomat when I called upon him to try and find a lasting solution to the Sudan problem. But he learnt the art of diplomacy, perfected the craftsmanship of negotiation, walked the tightrope of antagonism and came out with what can be billed as Africa's biggest prize – peace – for a region that desperately needed it.

When I chose General Sumbeiywo for this delicate task, I knew I was not making a mistake. First, apart from having distinguished himself as a diligent military man, he also had a passion for every task he undertook. As many of those interviewed in this book attest to, he was a man who was highly respected by his peers in the military and one who was relied upon by his superiors to execute tasks and translate the wishes of his superiors into action.

This quality was especially evident in his role as the Army Commander, a demanding post and whose duty he went about with remarkable zeal.

Secondly, I knew this man was and still is a committed Christian. Drawing on his faith in God and the confidence of a military man, he would plunge headlong into the onerous task of negotiations knowing that nothing short of victory would satisfy him.

Thirdly, the task at hand required a man who knew the art of war and who also knew how to use that knowledge to attain peace. The protagonists in Sudan were basically military people. On the one hand was the President, Omar Hassan Al-Bashir, a military man, and on the other was Colonel John Garang. It would have required a man who knows how the mind of a military man works to do the task.

Today, as I look back, I am full of satisfaction at what we were able to achieve in the three years it took to hammer out a comprehensive peace deal. I have always stressed on the need for the African continent to nurture peace and for everyone to live in harmony. Right next to us were our brothers and sisters, dislocated by the brutality of war, disillusioned at the prospect of peace and dispirited by the failure of those who attempted to negotiate a peace deal. We could not pride ourselves, as a country, on having peace while our next door neighbours were languishing in bloodshed. It is thus a matter of great pride for me, for Sudan and for Africa in general, that it took an African to do what foreigners could not, and thereby reiterate the fact that solutions to Africa's problems will come from Africans themselves, from the rich recesses of the continent and not from outside its borders.

This book is not about the triumph of one man or one country. It is a tribute to what the spirit of reconciliation can do. It is a celebration of a major breakthrough in the history of the African continent. It is an act of homage to what unbreakable determination can do. More importantly, it is a firm testimony to the indisputable fact that peacemakers are all among us.

Daniel Toroitich arap Moi, CGH,
Second President of the Republic of Kenya
August 2006

Contents

Foreword v
Acknowledgements viii

1 The Call 1
2 Growing Up 7
3 The Army Man 15
4 At Sandhurst 19
5 Back Home 23
6 Meeting Lorna 28
7 The Days of Darkness 31
8 The Making of a Mediator 36
9 The Conflict, the Country 47
10 John Garang 67
11 Machakos 84
12 New President – Retired General 103
13 Where is the Peace? 111
14 The Nairobi Declaration and After 132

Epilogue 144
Appendix 149

Acknowledgements

Telling this story required bringing together key people who were instrumental in the peace process, as well as those who played a central role in Gen. Lazaro Sumbeiywo's life and career.

This book would, therefore, have not been possible without the invaluable assistance of the following: First, the Second President of the Republic of Kenya, His Excellency Daniel arap Moi, who encouraged Gen. Sumbeiywo to document his experiences and who wrote the Foreword for this book. Then there is the late Dr John Garang and the former First Vice-President of Sudan, Dr Ali Osman Taha who urged Gen. Sumbeiywo to tell the story of the process.

General Sumbeiywo's family showed a great deal of understanding and helped him recollect some events that would have easily escaped him. His two brothers, Elijah and Daniel, played a key role in reminding him of the events of his younger days.

There was also the indefatigable team at the IGAD secretariat: Mrs Felicita Keiru, Dr Susan Page, Mrs Virginia Gitau and fellow envoys at IGAD who encouraged Gen. Sumbeiywo to put down his experiences.

Lawyer Desterio Oyatsi and Mrs Margaret Waithaka, the wife of the author, read through the manuscript and made helpful suggestions.

Former Foreign Affairs Minister Hon. Kalonzo Musyoka, who played a key role in the peace process also spent hours with the author and, despite his busy schedules, availed himself for interviews at short notice.

Thanks should also go to Former Chiefs of General Staff, General Jackson Mulinge and General Mahmoud Mohammed who provided invaluable information for the book. We must also mention Major General Ikenye, Lt Gen. A.S.K. Njoroge, the current Army Commander, and many of Gen. Sumbeiywo's former colleagues who were interviewed for this book and who would like to remain anonymous.

The American Reference Centre was most helpful in availing some material used in the book.

Special thanks go to Dr Khalid Mansour, who has written extensively on the problems of Southern Sudan and whom the author met in Nairobi. He offered helpful suggestions and most of his works form the basis of the historical material for this book.

Gen. Sumbeiywo would also like to thank profusely Reverend Mathews Mwalwa and members of Africa Inland Church, Milimani, Nairobi, for the support and encouragement they offered him throughout the negotiations and in the writing of this book.

1

The Call

This was no ordinary call. The Brigadier listened to the instructions coming from his superior, General Mahmoud Mohammed. Long used to being handed urgent assignments at short notice, Brigadier Lazaro Sumbeiywo did not think much about the call.

"President Omar Al Bashir of Sudan is in town," General Mahmoud thundered, "and you are required to accompany him aboard an Air Force plane to Lanet. The Army Commander will be there and the President will inspect a guard of honour."

Lanet is about 140 kilometres from Nairobi. It is part of an expansive Army camp which is located in the picturesque sceneries of the Rift Valley and which is also used as a training college for Army cadets. It is there that the Brigadier was supposed to deliver President Bashir who would inspect a guard of honour as a visiting head of state.

"From there," General Mahmoud continued, "take the Sudanese President to State House to meet President Moi."

"OK, sir, will do." The Brigadier responded. What his boss, however, did not tell him was that he was acting and tasking him on the direct orders of President Moi.

By then, the Brigadier was Director of Military Intelligence, reporting to the Chief of General Staff, Gen. Mahmoud. In his role, he was no stranger to State House and the President. It was not surprising then that he was the one who had been detailed to perform this task. He knew that the presence of President Bashir in the country had something to do with the situation in Sudan, a country that had been at war with itself for seven years then. As head of military intelligence, he had churned out copious reports on the situation in the Sudan, the war ravaging the country between the Government and the Sudan People's Liberation Movement and Army(SPLM/A) headed by Dr John Garang, and given them to the President. He was better informed about what was happening beyond the borders of the country than perhaps anyone else.

On the other hand, Bashir had just overthrown a civilian Government in Khartoum which was led by Sadiq Al Mahdi and complicated the already bad situation in the country. Bashir was only six months into power, a report about which Sumbeiywo had already filed.

That morning of 1989, as he hurried to accompany President Bashir, Sumbeiywo wondered what plans the new military leader of Sudan had in store for the country. But this did not bother him much. For now, his task was to take the visiting President to Lanet and then convey him to the State House, quite an unusual task for a non-politician, much less an army officer in a civilian Government.

After President Bashir finished inspecting the guard of honour, Brigadier Sumbeiywo started on the second part of his mission. As he made his way to the Nakuru State House, everything started clearing up. He got to know that President Daniel arap Moi would be having a "small" meeting with both Bashir and Dr John Garang. The two were the main protagonists in the seven-year long Sudan civil war and their relationship was more or less like that of Jacob and Esau in the Bible.

The meeting had been set up by the Chief Executive of the Lonrho Group, the late Tiny Rowland, who at the time wielded immense powers in the country owing to his network of contacts, both political and corporate, and a nominated MP, Mr. Mark Too, who was also Chairman of the Lonrho Group in Kenya.

Too was a close confidante of the President and was also known as *"Bwana Dawa"* (Mr. Fix it) for his ability to resolve conflicts, fix appointments for politicians and businessmen with the President and bring enemies and warring groups to the negotiating table. Tiny Rowland on the other hand had massive investments in the country and had a particular interest in Sudan where he was running the country's biggest sugar factory, the Kenana Sugar Plant. The prospect for oil was also a driving factor. The rich potential of the South had been blighted by the war there. So long as the place remained bloody, no business could thrive. It was no surprise then that both were involved in this complex and almost odd meeting.

This was the first meeting of its kind between Moi and Bashir. Though Moi was familiar with Garang, the two (Garang and Bashir) had never met face to face in the presence of a neutral party. For years, Dr Garang's SPLM/A had been engaged in a bitter war with the Government of the Sudan. The war was at its peak and despite all the best efforts by Sudan's neighbours to broker a peace settlement, the situation remained hopeless. The coming of Bashir to power had presented a remote possibility for negotiations, even though SPLM/A was bitter that he had overthrown a democratically elected civilian government. It was this offchance for peace that the Kenyan leader and the political operatives were seeking to exploit.

On this day, Rowland and Mark Too had convinced the two protagonists to meet at State House to explore possibilities of a lasting solution to the Sudan conflict. They had agreed to meet the President separately. What they perhaps did not know was that the appointment was fixed in such a way that they both had to be there and that there was a big possibility of them meeting with each other.

As Brigadier Sumbeiywo made his entry to State House, he kept wondering what the outcome of the meeting would be. He had previously met Garang, but this was the first time he was meeting the new Sudanese leader. As Director of Military Intelligence, he had remained close to the Kenyan Head of State. Later, he served as the head of the Liaison Department in the Office of the President for five years. While the awesome power the President wielded cowed many, Sumbeiywo regarded the President with bold deference. He had direct access to him and he understood him in ways many others did not. He knew that the Sudan conflict had occupied the President's mind for many years and that he wanted a speedy resolution to a conflict that was hindering development in the Horn of Africa. But the biggest problem remained how to get the protagonists together and how to hammer out a peace agreement. Now that they had agreed to come to Kenya, there was, at last, a silver lining in the dark cloud of the conflict in Sudan.

There was nothing to show that an extraordinary meeting was taking place. Nor had there been much fanfare at the arrival of the two leaders. They had come in quietly and driven to Nakuru, away from the din and media attention of the City of Nairobi. Still, Sumbeiywo wondered what his role and mission was in this affair. Whatever his President wanted him to do, he would do it to the best of his ability.

Sumbeiywo found Moi standing at the State House door. The President greeted Bashir and then invited him into a room in which the Comptroller of State House, then Abraham Kiptanui, and Mark Too were. Sumbeiywo did not enter the room. His mission, he thought, had been accomplished. Yet, he could not leave until told to do so. He went into a room called "Angola". This was the room that the founding President of Kenya, Jomo Kenyatta, negotiated a peace agreement with Jonas Savimbi, the guerrilla leader who was waging a war against the Government of Angola under President Eduardo dos Santos, in 1974. It was from this feat that the room had acquired its name.

Inside the room, Brigadier Sumbeiywo found Dr John Garang with a coterie of SPLM/A officers. They were patiently waiting to meet President Moi. Not being a stranger to Garang, Sumbeiywo greeted him and engaged him in some small talk. He perfunctorily informed him that he had come with the Sudanese President and that even as they talked, Bashir was meeting Moi.

Garang did not comment. After some time, Moi came into Angola Room and spoke with Dr Garang. Sumbeiywo was to learn later that Moi was trying to convince Garang to meet with Bashir. The guerrilla leader adamantly refused to meet him and Moi was frustrated to the point of desperation. He came from the room looking distraught and beckoned at Kiptanui. He spoke to him in Kalenjin, which Garang could not understand.

"Take this man away. Take him home." Home was Kabarak, a few kilometres from the Nakuru State House, the private residence of Moi. On cue, Kiptanui immediately arranged for Garang and his men to leave for Kabarak. Moi went back to Bashir.

At that time, Sumbeiywo saw Rowland and Too. Sensing some discomfort in the hallowed residence, he ventured to ask; "How is Bashir?" "He is OK," Mark Too curtly responded, "He is with Mzee." No more information was forthcoming.

Whatever was going on in that room was well hidden from Sumbeiywo. But from the body language of those involved and the level of activity, something was not right. Before Garang's departure, Moi had been shuttling between Angola and the meeting room, talking to both Garang and Bashir privately. Now, after spending some few minutes with Bashir, he came out and again called Sumbeiywo.

The Brigadier stood at attention, as he had been doing virtually all his life, and listened to his Commander-in-Chief. " I want you to take care of Bashir as I step out to negotiate with Garang," he told him before adding, "You are both military men. You should relate well."

It was a tall order. He had seen what had happened and he knew he would be dealing with an annoyed and humiliated man. What they would discuss in the interim slightly bothered the Brigadier, but as an Army person, he knew that was an order that had to be obeyed. Bashir had spent many years in the military before overthrowing the civilian Government of Sadiq Al Mahdi to ascend to power. He was a brigadier and Sumbeiywo on his part was also a brigadier in the Army and was well gunned up in the thinking of a military officer. He would, somehow, find a way of striking a rapport with the Sudanese leader. Mark Too was there too to give some back up, should it be necessary.

Sumbeiywo tried to strike up a conversation with Bashir. He found him a cautious man who did not talk much and who, though he could speak English, opted for Arabic with a translator to put across his points. To lighten up the situation, Sumbeiywo tried telling military jokes while quaffing mugs of tea. He was not met with a lot of success. Bashir was taciturn and thoughtful. He talked in monosyllables and, although he did not say it, he did not wish to be bothered by another military officer. Sumbeiywo did not know what to do with him. His remit then was not to discuss a resolution of the conflict, or politics or even anything to do with the fighting in the south of Sudan. It was to "take care of the man" as the President fixed things on the other side. Their discussion was interspersed with long moments of silence as each one of them counted the minutes slowly ticking away on the clock on the wall. As Sumbeiywo was to recall later, there were times the thread of silence unspooled and seemed to tie up all of them in an embrace of solemnity. Suddenly, they all discovered, they had little to tell one another.

After an hour, Sumbeiywo could not take it any longer. He excused himself, left Bashir with Too and got out quietly, entered his car and followed Moi to Kabarak. There, he found Moi and Garang at the garage of his motor vehicles trying to take everything easy. Moi was explaining the features of an old 4-wheel drive that Garang had taken a liking to and he was putting everything he saw in the garage in the context of the war in Sudan.

"Mzee, this is a good vehicle for fighting," he was telling Moi.

"No John, this is an old junk; it is of no use to anybody."

"We guerrillas don't mind things like these."

Later, the two started taking a quiet walk in the serenity of the gardens of the palatial home. They were having what could not be called an animated discussion. It was clear to Sumbeiywo that even here, things were not smooth, only that the two had something to discuss even if it was in an off-hand, taciturn manner. Garang was given to furtive observations and witty comments. As they walked towards the farm he saw green maize and remarked, "Mzee, I like green maize."

Moi immediately instructed someone to bring some green maize. He was also a lover of it and it was never in short supply at the home. As the two sat down to enjoy the roasted and boiled green maize, Sumbeiywo saw an opportunity to ask his question. He wanted to know if Garang and Bashir would have a meeting.

"No," Moi responded, "This is not working."

Moi appeared distraught. And as Sumbeiywo knew him only too well, he knew that his mind was no longer with Garang. He was now trying to find a solution to the conflict elsewhere.

"Go and take care of the man," he told Sumbeiywo in the local language. "It is not working." He repeated.

"What do we do now?" he asked the President. The President kept quiet. Then in a moment of alertness, Sumbeiywo suggested a solution: "Can I take Bashir to the Lake Nakuru National Park? There, he can see some animals and probably relax."

"Good idea," the President responded. His ADC immediately started making arrangements for Bashir to be driven to Lake Nakuru National Park which was only a few kilometres away.

The President was again left with Dr Garang while Sumbeiywo went ahead to "take care" of his special problem. The plan worked. President Bashir had a nice time driving in the park and viewing animals. He did not have to keep talking, so the atmosphere was free of tension.

By the time Sumbeiywo took him back to State House, Garang was long gone. They found Moi at State House and the two went into further negotiations. That day, Bashir did not go back home as it was already late. He spent the night at State House. Sumbeiywo was not to know at what hour Dr Garang left or what transpired between him and President Moi. He did not know then that he had come face to face with the two men who would irrevocably change his life.

2

Growing Up

Lazaro Kipkurui Sumbeiywo was born on July 14, 1947 in Elgeyo Marakwet District, now known as Keiyo, only two years after World War II broke out. Keiyo is a deeply forested area nestling in the undulating hills of the Rift Valley. It is an expansive area that looks isolated but whose one enduring feature is its evergreen nature. Fed by a network of streams, it is a fertile area for agriculture and farming.

Sumbeiywo's father's home was between two villages: Kiptingo and Katalel. These two villages were only a few kilometres away from each other but there was a marked difference between them. Kiptingo was a small holding community of about twenty five households. Half of those households were related to each other by blood. Each family had an average of two wives in each household which also boasted between five and seven children per household. The village bordered a forest called Kessup.

On the other hand, Katalel was sparsely populated. It was inhabited by only eight families of between five and eight children. Each household boasted huge tracts of land and, like in Kiptingo, the people were largely polygamous. They were considered rich and more polished. Those of Kiptingo were "lazy" and they "drank a bit too much", something that their relatively affluent neighbours cited as reason for their poverty. Though they spoke the same language, the two villages led different lifestyles, had slightly different values and the villagers considered themselves a cut above those of Kiptingo.

Sumbeiywo's father, Sumbeiywo arap Limo's real names were Kiplagat arap Kipkatam. He had become an orphan at a very early age and was brought up by his uncle, Limo arap Rogocho. His mother, Sarah Jessang, had been born in Setek area of Keiyo district. She was given the name Taprandich when she reached womanhood. The name means "the one who gathers cattle". But she became a staunch Christian later and was baptised Sarah, the name by which she was to be known throughout the village.

Sumbeiywo was the sixth born in a family of seven. The elder sister whom he followed died young. His birth was heralded by a particular joy. According to tradition, the birth of a baby was a joyous occasion throughout the community. But this occasion was even more joyous. This baby, according to customs, was meant to replace the one who had died earlier. His name would then have to show that he was a replacement.

He was born in the homestead one evening, just as people were retiring to bed. Those days, most babies were born at home, more than in hospitals. Aided by traditional midwives, births were as swift and clinically safe as those done at hospitals.

"What shall he be called?" a woman from the crowd asked.

The people who had now gathered around the homestead were certain what the answer would be. The name would have to reflect the idea of "coming to life" or resurrection.

Jessang looked at the woman, paused before answering and then said, "He shall be called Lazaro."

The crowd gasped. Lazaro? Who was Lazaro? Why would he be called Lazaro?

Knowing the questions in their minds, Jessang explained, "This baby has come to replace the one who has died. Yes, he has risen from the dead. Even Lazaro in the Bible rose from the dead." She was referring to Lazarus in the Bible who was raised from the dead by Jesus.

Jessang was a staunch Christian and when she quoted the Bible and the example of Lazarus, the people began to understand. Still, they could not understand why this baby did not have a nickname. Everyone had to be named either after a dead person or the environment in the local Kalenjin language. Sumbeiywo himself, had a nickname, *Saa sita*, because of his bald head. It was said that when the sun was shining, it would reflect on his hairless head like the sun at mid-day. His other name, Sumbeiywo, meant a thorny bush. *Sumbeiywo* is a protective bush with thorny branches that run in and out of each other. This makes it look like a net. If an animal entered that bush, it would be caught up in the complicated interstices of the branches. When a sheep gets under the thorny shrub, not even a leopard would be able to extract it from the shrub. The shrub would have to be hewn to pieces in order to reach the sheep. Sumbeiywo then was like a protective haven, the place you run to when in trouble. When a sheep or goat was lost, the people used to say, "May it be under a *sumbeiywo*."

Sumbeiywo's father had all his children named after the environment. It was said that he came to work for people around Katalel and that when he married he could not remember where he had originally come from. His children were therefore named after the hills, the forests, the animals and the shrubs.

In keeping with this tradition, Lazaro was also given a name that showed that he had a strong connection with the environment or one that said something about when he was born. He was called Kipkurui, which means, "one born when people are going to sleep."

Sumbeiywo's father joined the Kings African Rifles 5th Battalion in 1922. He served for 12 years, leaving in 1934 as a corporal. The old man, as Sumbeiywo likes to say, conveniently missed both World Wars. During World War II, however, he served as a Warrant Officer or Sergeant Major in the tribal police now known in the country as Administration Police. He resigned from the police to become the Chief of Irong Location in 1952 and later became the Chairman of African Tribunal Court in Keiyo District before retiring in 1965.

His life in the Army was to influence his sons greatly. Life in the forces enthralled the older Sumbeiywo and he wished that his sons would follow in his footsteps. His wishes came true as they started developing a liking for the forces. The fourth born, Elijah Kipkosgei, joined the Junior Leader Company, a military academy intended to produce officers for the emerging independent Kenya. But Elijah was to drop out later, a decision his father did not take lightly. He quarrelled with him incessantly for leaving the Army, until the young man caved in and joined the police force. Determined to make up for his earlier lapse, he rose from a constable to Senior Deputy Commissioner of Police, the number two man in the Kenya Police Force. Upon his retirement, Elijah was to become a Member of Parliament.

But it was Sumbeiywo's mother who was to have a profound effect on his life. She imparted into him strong Christian values which he treasures to this day. "She taught me the value of everything and the need to thank God for small mercies," he remembers.

One of the things she taught him was that one should not eat without giving thanks to God. To this day, Sumbeiywo would neither eat without praying nor get away from the table without giving thanks. He will not start a task without praying and he will not end it without offering thanks.

Like most families then, life was brutal and basic for the Sumbeiywos. Sumbeiywo used to wake up at 5.00 am, fetch water and milk the cows. He would wash his face with very cold water, which was usually trapped in a bamboo pipe called *soiyet* and which was corked with a tuft of grass and left overnight. In the morning, it would be as cold as water from a refrigerator. Every time the water touched his face, he would jerk up and all the sleep he had would disappear. The water was particularly good at waking people up. After this, he would go and fetch water before starting to milk the cows. His father had 70 head of cattle, out of which ten were milk cows and they had to be milked before morning.

After he had milked them, he would have some breakfast. This usually consisted of some tea and the previous night's leftovers. If there were no leftovers, he would take plain tea. He knew then that he would spend the whole day hungry, for the leftovers also served as lunch. After this, he would separate the calves from the cows, take his bows and arrows and take the cows out to graze. The fields were expansive and grassy and because the village was still sparsely populated, there never was shortage for some. He would not be back until late in the afternoon. This is why breakfast was so important.

When he was not grazing the cattle, he was doing other household chores like fetching water from the river. With the other boys, they used to gather twigs to make a carrier with which they carried gourds of water. They also foraged in the forest where they gathered wild vegetables for their meals. This is a chore he did not like. It involved a lot of patience and walking. In those days, one could gather wild vegetables anywhere. There were no strict laws governing private property that prevented one from getting to other people's farms to gather wild vegetables.

"It was a tough job gathering vegetables for the whole family. One required a lot of patience."

Rather than do this, he much preferred grinding the finger millet. This was done using two stones. One acted as some sort of anvil and the other was the grinder. Through repeated back and forth motion on the stone, the finger millet was ground to fine flour. This was usually the flour that would be used that evening for supper. It was a tiring exercise particularly because one had to grind enough to feed the entire family.

But one of the chores that Sumbeiywo remembers enjoying doing most was pasting the floor of their house with mud and cow-dung. This was usually done on Saturdays. The mixture was a smooth paste which, once dry, gave the floor a tidy, shiny look and a smell of freshness. The house was a grass-thatched unit which was shared with goats and sheep. The animals slept on the lower deck while the children slept on the upper deck. Many years later, Sumbeiywo would still remember the bleating of the sheep at night, their snores and the smell of the house as man and animal effected a warm harmony and learned to share the scant resources without ill will. The main house was reserved for the parents but it also served as the kitchen from which family meals were made and served.

The same pattern replicated itself during the school days, only that this time he did not take the cattle out to graze. He attended a primary school called Yokot which was not very far from his parents' house. It was only two kilometres away and this was usually a very short distance for Sumbeiywo and the other boys.

"We would run to school and make it in time. That to us was a short distance," he reminisces. He had to carry some lunch to school. This consisted of the previous night's leftovers. When there was nothing left from the previous night's meal, his mother always made sure that there was some boiled maize. He would eat some and carry others to school, which he would eat during lunch time. Carrying food to class was not allowed so one had to hide it carefully so that the teachers would not notice it.

One day Sumbeiywo carried his boiled maize to school and did not want the teacher to see it. He hid it in the grass in the school compound hoping to eat it during lunch. At lunch time, he ran to where he had hidden the maize. It was not there. Apprehensive that he would not have lunch that day, he looked for it everywhere but could not find it. Then he looked a few yards from where he had hidden it and saw a cow peacefully chewing the cud. Next to it was a cob. He knew the rest. The cow had eaten his maize.

That day, Sumbeiywo went without lunch. When he went home and narrated the story, his brothers broke out in laughter. He still remembers them laughing at him. But from that day, he was very careful about where he hid his lunch.

Sumbeiywo also knew that those who worked hard always had something to eat. Next to the school was a farmer who had a big piece of land. At lunchtime, Sumbeiywo would rush there and speak to him.

"May I do some work please in return for some money?"

"Yes," the farmer answered, "weed the farm and I will pay you some money."

The farm was under maize and the farmer paid Sumbeiywo 25 cents for weeding an area of five steps by twenty-five steps. The money was a lot those days. With it, he would buy himself some soap and sometimes a piece of bread and have some change.

On Sundays, the young Sumbeiywo attended Sunday School at the Katalel Africa Inland Church where he carried a single cob of maize as an offering. It was all he had to offer and it was accepted without reservation. The church was a grass-thatched building which leaked liberally when it rained.

As a young boy, Sumbeiywo marvelled at the composition of Yokot Primary School and the politics surrounding it. It was a new school and the Catholics wanted to sponsor it. However, the Protestants rejected the idea, accusing the Catholics of influence-peddling. One morning, he arrived at the school to find a crowd of about twenty people gathered in the compound. He wondered what was amiss. But he could clearly hear the voice of one old man called Jacob Meto clashing with another whom he identified as Mateo Kisang. The two were well known in the village and were always present at every function.

"This school is not a Catholic affair," Jacob, a Protestant, was arguing in a state of agitation.

"We cannot allow the Catholics to sponsor it. After all, they have sponsored Kaptaren and Iten primary schools." The two schools were not very far from Yokot and the elders felt that the Catholics wanted to control all the schools.

"But you already have Kessup," argued Mateo who was Catholic, "Why don't you want us to have Yokot?"

The debate degenerated into furious acrimony. The two sides could not agree and there was no one to mediate in the dispute. Later that day the school was closed. Young Sumbeiywo and the other pupils were immediately dislocated, their education was cut short.

"Why could they not just agree?" he remembers asking himself. "Why did they have to argue until the school had to be closed?"

There were no answers to these questions. But Sumbeiywo and the other dislocated pupils immediately found an alternative school, Kessup Primary School where they resumed their education. To get to Kessup they had to go through a sharp escarpment and a forest. There was also a boarding school not very far away and people used to get milk from the white farmers who ran the school and inhabited the valley. One early morning as he was going to school, he heard some rustling in the bush and thought that it was an animal. In his hand was a piece of wood for his art and craft work. He knew that if he ran away, the animal would give chase. He had to fight it. Summoning up all his courage, he threw the piece of wood at where he thought the rustling was coming from. He heard a scream as the wood landed on what he came to learn was a man. "Don't kill me", the man screamed, "It is only I." The old man was to remember young Sumbeiywo, a mere boy who had viciously attacked him for scaring him, for the rest of his life.

In 1956, the conflict surrounding Yokot Primary School was resolved by Sumbeiywo's father who was then the Chief of the area and Sumbeiywo went back to the school where he sat his Common Entrance Examination. He was ten years old then. Afterwards he proceeded to the Government African School, Tambach, for his Intermediate School. It was in this school that he developed a talent for sportsmanship, and where he led in most of the sport disciplines. With a towering figure and a big build, he was to nurture sportsmanship into his adult life which was to bring him much respect and adoration.

As was the custom those days, Sumbeiywo had to undergo the most important rite of passage before he could consider himself a man. In 1963, therefore, he was taken to River Senetwa together with other boys of his age to be circumcised. It was an early, freezing morning, long before the rest of the village had woken up. Circumcisions, like births, were not done at hospitals. Boys of the same age were usually gathered together and driven to the river in the morning to start the painful rite of passage.

With the cold waters of River Senetwa gurgling down the valley, the boys were immersed, one by one. With the water acting as the anaesthetic, they were circumcised by a traditional circumciser. At such a time, a boy had to show that he was ready for manhood by bearing the pain with remarkable fortitude. If one cried, he became something of an outcast and a shame to the family. As the circumciser swung the knife to excise the foreskin that would mark a turning point in his life, Sumbeiywo felt the searing pain cut to the bone. He clenched his teeth and felt his whole body melt in a convulsion of pain. Yet the pride of becoming a man surpassed the pain. He looked at the other boys. They had all borne the pain bravely. From then onwards, they were men.

After his Kenya African Primary Education examination, he went to Tambach to begin his secondary school education. This was in 1963. Now a proud high school student, he was almost disillusioned when he learned later that although Tambach had been upgraded to a secondary school, the teachers and the books were the same as those they had used in primary school. Despite protests, nothing changed. There was also a teachers' training college within the school whose students used to get preferential treatment. By then Sumbeiywo was the games captain. One day, there was a fight between the students and the teacher trainees. They fought with plates and spoons and only when the fight was over did both sides realise that they had wasted their lunch.

When things did not improve at Tambach, the students tabled a list of demands. They wanted new teachers and they wanted new books. They were ignored. They went on strike, which was led by Sumbeiywo. The strike was peaceful and it involved boycotting classes until the school administration met their demands. But the administration had no such intentions. Instead, police were called in. They did nothing to the students but when more reinforcements were called in, the students sensed danger and packed and left.

During the strike, the District Commissioner visited the village of Kiptingo over a boundary dispute. The administration wanted to align the forest boundary and the reserve. Sumbeiywo, feeling that he had something to contribute to the meeting, rose to speak. He proposed that instead of the forest being extended, the people should be allowed to move into the forest and settle. The DC looked at him and growled,

"Haven't I seen you somewhere?"

"Yes, you have," responded Sumbeiywo, "I was at Tambach School."

"Mmh" the DC said in a knowing, sarcastic voice. He was a member of the school board and he knew exactly why Sumbeiywo was home and that he was one of the ringleaders of the strike.

Much later, they were to be called one by one to be grilled. Sumbeiywo and three others, Isaac Chepkwony, Joseph Kimemia and Joseph Barsolai were suspended for a whole term. But when they came back, things had changed dramatically. There were new teachers and there were new books. Now they could call themselves secondary school students. But Sumbeiywo had already lost the prestige of being the Games Captain. However, after one term, the school saw his value and reinstated him.

One of the new teachers at the school, by the name Lee, was a member of the Peace Corps who had done military training. He started showing the students how to march. Sumbeiywo was enamoured of the practice. When some members of the Army came to give a lecture at the school, Sumbeiywo was seized by an urge to join the Army. He would learn a lot from the lecture. He knew the difference between an officer and a service man. So when he was asked to join at Form Three, he graciously declined. He had rather wait until he finished his secondary education. After his Form Four examinations in 1967, he went to tend to his father's small shop at Kipsoen Centre in Keiyo. The shop was close to Yokot Primary School.

One morning, his brother, Elijah, who was then the District Intelligence Security Officer came to the shop. He looked excited.

"I know you have always wanted to join the Army," he told the young Sumbeiywo. "Take these 200 shillings and go to Lanet. They are recruiting."

Two hundred shillings in 1967 was a lot of money. It could last one a long time. Without further thought, Sumbeiywo closed the shop, went home and announced the decision to his father who gave him another 100 shillings and told him : "Go".

From his home to Eldoret, which was the nearest big town, Sumbeiywo hiked a lift in a lorry transporting vegetables and potatoes. He ensconced himself between the sacks and endured the long tortuous journey through the valleys and hills of Elgeyo Marakwet to the relative urbanity of Eldoret town. From there he took a bus which took four hours to accomplish a journey of about 170 kilometres to Nakuru. Off to Lanet he went, to start his new life in the military, a life that would dramatically change the way he related with other people.

3

The Army Man

On reaching the Army camp, Sumbeiywo proudly announced himself to the duty officer.

"I have come for selection."

The duty officer looked at him and wondered what he was talking about. It was then that he was told he had gone to the wrong barracks. In his excitement, Sumbeiywo had found himself at the Kenya Rifles 5th battalion while the selection was being conducted a distance away at the Sergeant Leakey Barracks, later to be renamed Armed Forces Training College.

At the barracks, he was received by Captain Bartilol, a distant relative of his who served in the 5 KR and who was later to become Kenya's champion in steeplechase. A captain was a very senior person then and Sumbeiywo was to learn a lot of handy tips from Captain Bartilol. "That is one man who taught me about determination and endurance."

Having been an athlete, Sumbeiywo had no problems coping with life in the army. In that place, one's name, as Sumbeiywo was to learn later, was almost irrelevant. The recruits were known by numbers. His was number 21. With this number, his name was momentarily forgotten. You answered to this number, you identified yourself by the number and you called yourself by the number. This was a different kind of life, but it was the one he had chosen.

From 2,000 people, only 100 were left. This number was to be trimmed later with many falling afoul of written and physical tests. At the end of the recruitment, only 60 were accepted as cadets. Sumbeiywo was one of them. Although nothing could have been better news than that, Sumbeiywo knew that being a cadet was not anything to be proud of. "You are not a soldier, you are not an officer, you are not a civilian," he was later to remark to himself, echoing what he had heard, "You are nothing."

That first night after he took his attestation on January 31, 1968, to say that he will serve in the Kenya Army, he wondered what his examination results would look like. They were not yet out and to be fully accepted in the army, one had to have at least a Division Two. Though he was not worried about making the grade, he knew that anything coming between him and the army would be a great disappointment. The examinations vindicated him. He was clearly above the minimum requirement and he plunged headlong into the army. He was cadet No 3316.

He was to realise that the army was also a test of nerves for him. Those who were training them did not have a lot of education and were a constant vexation to those who had. Pronunciation was different and unschooled. There was one tutor called Captain Stephen Ngerechi who was trying to teach them how to choose a line of advance. He could not explain what choices there were. Because they had pamphlets, the recruits politely sought to tell the tutor what the choices were. He listened and blurted; "You know nothing, you are nothing and I am teaching you." In the training, he was to learn, one was reduced to an almost infinitesimal element. The commissioned officers knew it all, even when they were wrong. For one to succeed, humility was key.

Because Sumbeiywo was considered brighter than many of the others, some tutors had a dislike for him. He was lean and tall. The drill Sergeant, Major Kipsambu used to tell him, "You stand there as if you are looking for honey." This was said on account of his height. Traditionally, tall men were said to be good honey hunters because they could spot the hives from afar and up at the corner of the tallest tree.

For some reason, the sergeant major always picked on Sumbeiywo and his friend John Lebo, for ridicule. "You come from Majengo and you were sired by policemen." Majengo is the name given to filthy squalid slums and to be told that you are from such an area was to underline your misery and worthlessness. The army people had a particular dislike for policemen. To be told you had been sired by a policeman was to endure a bitter insult. John Lebo was to rise to the rank of brigadier before he retired from the army.

The initial days at the army were marked by mistrust between the recruits, and especially the bright ones, and the instructors who were considered dumb and unpolished. One weapons instructor called Sergeant Abdullahi, could not pronounce the word 'squad'. Instead he would say "cat, stand easy." This was said even when the squad was sitting down. One day, he started his lessons with the words; "Today, we are going to teach you the general purpose machine gun. Because you don't understand, we will break them into numbers; First, strupping (for stripping), cleaning and assembling." The recruits could not laugh because to do so was to invite punishment. But they later had plenty of laughter in their barracks, long after the lessons were over. For some reason, it never occurred to Sergeant Abdullahi that "machine gun" was not one word but merely the name of a gun.

Waking up at four, being given a huge loaf of bread and steaming hot tea and being told to fall in even before you had taken the first sip, taught the young recruits how to sleep with one eye open and to eat hot meals in the fastest time possible. Up to this day, Sumbeiywo eats very fast, to the extent that his family complains that it makes them look like gluttons because long after he has finished, they are still at the dining table.

But this did not even faintly prepare them for what was in store in the Army. One day, when doing the long drop exercise in which one was dropped at a far away place and asked to trace one's way back to the camp through map reading, Sumbeiywo and his partner encountered a heard of buffaloes. They had only water, blankets and a rifle with no live ammunition. The two young men now had to trace their way back to the college, a distance of about 30 kilometres.

It was dusk then and they could make out the shape of the animals from a distance. The animals stood in the middle of the road and stared straight at them. The young recruits stared back. Animals and men stood their ground. "We knew our end had come," he was to say later, "We were only 20 metres from them and we knew that if they charged, we were finished." Although no one could say it, the thoughts of the two cadets went back to the homes they had left and to the death that now awaited them. Buffaloes are dangerous animals. When they charge, they do not stop till they gore their victim to death.

As they stared at the animals through the moonlight, the recruits knew that it was just a matter of time before the animals charged. As still as rocks, they knew if they started moving, they would provoke the animals. It was better to wait for their reaction than provoke it. The best they could have done was to climb a tree if the animals charged. But they also knew that you do not play such games with a herd of buffalo. Once a buffalo charges and you climb a tree, it waits for you at the bottom until you climb down. Some are known to push the tree by violently leaning on it in the hope that the victim would fall.

After about twenty minutes in a state of suffocating patience, the animals began to move away. The young recruits wiped a thin film of sweat from their brows in an almost coordinated pattern. They waited for another twenty minutes and once convinced the animals had gone, started walking back to the camp. Many years later, they would talk about this episode in excited tones. It was, they believed, a mark of bravery to have encountered dangerous animals during training and survived.

This, however, was not the worst of the nerve-testing episodes. It is said that those who claim they are not bothered by small things have never spent a night in a room with just one mosquito. One day, when the recruits were doing defence exercises, they were left around Lake Nakuru National Park. At night, a swarm of mosquitoes descended on them. They bit them mercilessly so that by morning they were swollen all over. Sumbeiywo was convinced that training had become a punishment. He debated with himself whether to leave the army and regretted not having accepted an athletics scholarship he had been given to the University of Massachusetts in Boston, USA. Were it not for the captain in charge, who encouraged him to stay on, he would have left the army in 1968.

In many ways, Sumbeiywo was a loner. After the strike in secondary school, in which he was suspended, he had adopted an aloofness that bordered on mistrust for other people. He loved his own company and he trusted only his soul and his conscience. One day, the captain in charge of the cadets asked him; "Why don't you socialise,"

"I don't find it interesting," he responded. "Is there anything wrong I am doing?"

"No," the captain responded, "But as an officer, you should interact."

"As an officer, I will interact," he responded, "on social issues, I would like to keep to myself."

As such, Sumbeiywo did not have a close friend. He was cooperative but chatted with very few. He, however, remained distinctive especially in sports and drill where he gained immense respect from his peers.

A few months later, the cadets were scheduled to appear before a commissioning board. One lot had appeared earlier and had already been sent to the Mons Officer Cadet School in the United Kingdom. Sumbeiywo's lot had to wait. That wait robbed him of his seniority because the lot that had gone earlier, though not necessarily the best, would obviously pass out before them.

The period before the commissioning was usually a tense one for the cadet officers. They waited for their fate patiently not knowing whether they would be dropped or whether they would be given a commission. Many were those who were denied a commission and tearfully packed their bags to go home and face an uncertain future. Those commissioned were sent to academies out of the country.

When the recruits appeared before the commissioning board at Harambee House in Nairobi in 1968, they were 43. Thanks to an intense sieving process, only 23 were commissioned and six were selected to join Royal Military Academy, Sandhurst in the United Kingdom. Sumbeiywo was one of the six. The rest were Peter Ikenye, Tom Wanambisi, Titus Tuum, John Ngare and Sam Kilonzo.

4

At Sandhurst

The Royal Military Academy – Sandhurst – is one of the most prestigious military training centres in Britain. Known as simply Sandhurst, the Academy boasts of rich alumni of famous and powerful people. Prince Harry of Wales attended Sandhurst where he received his commission on April 12, 2006. His brother, Prince Williams, also attended the Academy. All British officers and many from elsewhere in the world are trained at Sandhurst.

Formed in 1947, the Academy straddles the border between the counties of Hampshire, Berkshire and Surrey. It is marked by a small stream known as the Wish Stream after which the academy's journal is named.

Sandhurst is the dream of every cadet. In fact, at the time Sumbeiywo joined, it was equated to a university and those who graduated from it were admired and placed on a higher pedestal than the rest. Going to Sandhurst was the culmination of Sumbeiywo's determination to become an army man. The commissioning course took 44 weeks.

Sumbeiywo was leaving the country for the fist time in his life, travelling on a plane to a far away land. It was something that disconcerted him for a while. But he still remembers that day when he got into the plane for the first time to fly away from his motherland. It was like he was living one dream at home to pursue another. Those days, not many people travelled out of the country and for him to have achieved this feat was as glorious as it was prestigious. Moreover, he was pursuing his destiny, so he felt emboldened to move on, leaving all that he had loved behind. One of them was his then girlfriend. Before he left, he went in search of her to break the news. He did not know how she would take it but he had to tell her and deal with the consequences later.

"I will be leaving for the UK shortly," he announced to the disbelieving girl.

"For how long?" she asked incredulously.
"For 44 weeks."

The girl looked at him and was evidently lost for words. She tried to speak but words could not come out of her mouth. To leave for two years was one thing, she must have thought. To be in a far away country was another. Both these options were apparently unimaginable to her. She continued looking at him then managed to curtly say, "You go well, I cannot wait for you."

"Thank you," he said, turned and left. It was as short as that. He had experienced the end of something and, in a way, the beginning of another. He was sad to lose her but he was also thrilled to join an elite group of officer cadets in one of the most prestigious academies in the world.

On the day he was to leave, the mood in the village was that of jubilation. There was also anxiety that he was leaving to go to the white man's land. But the people were proud of him. He was one of the very few who had literally broken out and flown out of the country.

At a time when the white man was still a mystery and somewhat an object of adoration to a people who did not even know where he lived, the people in Sumbeiywo's village regarded his impending departure as a supreme mark of distinction.

They composed a song for him.

Chumbin wee, chumbindenyo chumbindetab koroni
Kialeen Ane chumbin ne leel,
Kaka chumbin kabisa
Kipkurui wee Kipkurui nenyo
Kipkurui nebo Kapsumbeiywo
KialeDen ane chumbin ne leel
Kaka Kipkurui nenyo

Loosely translated the song says:

White man our white man who is of this land
I thought he was a white man
But he is a true white man
Kipkurui the son of Sumbeiywo,
We thought he was a white man;
But it is our Kipkurui.

Before he left, he visited his brother Elijah in Kericho, who threw a big party for him. In his father's homestead, there was only a modest feast. Then escorted by military officials, Sumbeiywo left for the UK.

The first months at Sandhurst were not easy but young Sumbeiywo displayed patience for the Academy's trying endurance-building programmes. Being black, one of the very few at the Academy, he had also to endure some harassment from other cadets. One day, a junior white cadet kicked him when they were running. He did not know why he did that but he immediately turned and punched him. He was arraigned before the Commander and, although he tried to explain himself, he was made to do extra duties. The junior cadet was not punished.

At Sandhurst, Sumbeiywo distinguished himself as an enthusiastic sportsman, winning many medals in many disciplines. Together with another Kenyan, Tom Wanambisi, who was later to retire as a full colonel, Sumbeiywo was a member of the colour party which meant carrying or escorting the royal flag or the national flag. It was a prestigious thing.

But Sandhurst also had its trials and uphill moments. At one time, his strength was tested beyond his wildest imagination. While he thought that the mosquito incident that left him all swollen when he was a recruit was the worst thing that could happen to him, the four-day exercise for the officer cadets at the college left him stumped. It was an exercise that required one to keep going for four days and four nights without stopping. "For four days you sleepwalk, you knock into each other, you learn to sleep while walking." He recalls. It was one of the biggest endurance tests he had ever taken. Still, he never felt the temptation to give up. Everyone fell in neatly and took the test in good stead. After the test, they were given a two-day break out. But no one left the camp. They slept through the two days, too tired to go anywhere.

At Sandhurst, Sumbeiywo continued with his aloofness. The other recruits thought he took life a little too seriously and did not want to joke with him beyond what he could permit. One night, he remembers, a Kenyan who was also a good sportsman got drunk and started disturbing him at night. He wanted to sleep as he had sporting competitions the following morning. The Kenyan was making a lot of noise preventing those who wanted to sleep to do so. Irritated and unable to take it any longer, Sumbeiywo woke up and punched him. The other recruits, who had not been bold enough to take action, encouraged him to punch the man thoroughly. He sobered up and ran away. The following, day Sumbeiywo participated in his athletics and took a silver medal in hurdles and a bronze in the relay. The drunk who was to do long jump did not make it.

In the final year at Sandhurst, Sumbeiywo was to take a silver bugle for being the best athlete and broke the 440 yards hurdles record in 1970. He also won the gold in long jump. To this day, his record as an athlete is prominently painted on the walls of Sandhurst Military Academy.

All that time, news from home came through letters from relatives. Sometimes though, it took a long time. Events in the newly independent Kenya were still unfolding and the Kenyatta Government was going through its own hiccups and trials. In 1969, while in Germany performing field exercises, a colleague, Jack Chemos Psirmoi, took Sumbeiywo aside and whispered, "There is trouble at home. Mboya has been killed." Sumbeiywo was taken aback. Tom Mboya was Minister for Economic Planning and Development in the Kenyatta Government. A flamboyant orator, he was one of the most eminent ministers who had risen from the ranks of fiery trade unionists into one of the most mercurial politicians. He was gunned down outside a pharmacy in Nairobi. His death sparked off riots in Nairobi and Kisumu and drove a wedge between the members of the Gikuyu community, from which the First President, Jomo Kenyatta, hailed and the Luo community of which Mboya was a member.

Psirmoi was agitated. He seemed to see in that piece of news one of the most disappointing things to happen to a new government and he feared that it would portend doom for the country and for the recruits in foreign lands too. "What will happen to us now?" he kept asking. The ever cool officer Sumbeiywo responded, "No, let's wait. We will be told."

As it turned out, nothing happened to the cadets and nothing happened to the government. The riots were quelled and the cadets went on to finish their two-year training, receiving their commission on July 30, 1970, at Sandhurst and returning home later that year.

5

Back Home

As an officer at home, Sumbeiywo was posted to the Kenya Army's 1st Battalion Kenya Rifles at Lanet as second lieutenant. He was given the number 17398. This meant that he was the 398th army officer in Kenya.

In his first few days as an army officer he purchased for himself a vehicle, a Volkswagen Beetle with the registration number KLH 996. He bought it for Shs 21,000 from an Asian doctor who initially refused to accept the money until they went to a statue of an Indian god. At its feet, the doctor counted the money and certified it right, blessed the money and pocketed it. The Beetle was Sumbeiywo's.

He was one of the very few people who had a vehicle in his home village those days. This prized possession was to lead him to an interesting encounter. His friend then, Micah Cheserem, who was later to become the Governor of the Central Bank of Kenya, came to him one morning with a request for help.

A couple is getting married today, he told Sumbeiywo. They are stranded a few kilometres away from here. Could he help them?

Being the only one who had a car, Sumbeiywo could not refuse. He was supposed to pick them from Eldoret and take them to a place called Nyaru, a distance of 20 kilometres. He had no problem with this. But when he arrived, he was shocked to see who the bride was. It was a strange twist of fate. He looked at the bride, who looked back at him. They did not have to say anything. It was a wordless encounter but it flung him back in time to the years before Sandhurst. The bride was his former girlfriend who had refused him before he went to Sandhurst.

"I was shocked, she was shocked," he recalled, "but we both accepted things the way they were." Sumbeiywo gave the bride a ride to Nyaru even as he pondered on the fact that his life and that of his former girlfriend had taken distinctly different paths.

At the 1st Battalion Kenya Rifles at Lanet, Sumbeiywo learnt a lot from his platoon sergeant, Kugo. Though he was his junior, they got on well. Sumbeiywo was commanding 36 men among whom were three corporals and one sergeant. He was fast promoted to a full lieutenant and immediately registered for his captain's examination. His commanding officer was Lieutenant Colonel Mahmoud Mohammed, who later became the Chief of General Staff with the rank of full General and with whom Sumbeiywo would work with for a long time later.

There has always been a quiet mistrust between officers who trained at the Royal Military Academy, Sandhurst and those who went to other colleges like Mons Officer Cadet School. The School, located in Aldershot, 40 miles from London in the South of England, was viewed as a little inferior to Sandhurst. Mons was a six-month cadet school and it usually trained officers on short courses. This is where National Service and Short Service officers were trained. In 1972, however, the functions of Mons OCS were transferred to Sandhurst and the college was subsequently closed. Because Sandhurst was like a university with an intensive two-year training programme, officers commissioned there almost always carried themselves with an air of superiority. The Sandhurst elite regarded' themselves as better officers. The other officers mistrusted them but deferred to them in a silent recognition of their "superiority". But Sumbeiywo sought to debunk that myth.

"I did not feel that I was different," he says, "I wanted everyone to get along." The Sandhurst elite were usually judged pretty harshly. When they did something wrong, they were ridiculed. Quite often, the Sandhurst elite were kicked out of the army because they could not cope. The ones who were left were eventually frustrated because of harbouring higher ambitions than their capabilities could cater for.

Sumbeiywo related with the other officers well and rarely, if ever, did he make them feel inferior. But those who worked with Sumbeiywo in the days after his return from Sandhurst recalled seeing a supremely confident but humble man. While the others carried their badges on their sleeves, Sumbeiywo was down to earth. Because of his rapprochement, he became the black sheep of the Sandhurst elite. They felt he had betrayed them by refusing to be different. However, this humility did not mean that the officer would suffer fools gladly when other officers gave wrong instructions or appeared not to follow the teachings of the force as handed down to the new officers by their superiors.

At one time during manoeuvres in Naivasha, Sumbeiywo disagreed with a member of a British training team known as Batken. The name of the officer was Colonel Harbage and he was a Mister know-it-all. He had a low opinion of the Africans and he believed that no one had any right to challenge him. One day, Colonel Harbage watched in a furious state as a company performed some new manoeuvres he had never seen before and which had actually been taught at Sandhurst. In that company was Sumbeiywo. Colonel Harbage lost his cool and shouted at the officer leading the squad, "Take your f***ing company back!" Sumbeiywo could not take that kind of insult. One of the officers in the platoon was Augustine Njoroge who was later to rise to the rank of Leutenant General and who, by the time of writing this book was the Army Commander. He recalled that the other officers did not know how to deal with a *Mzungu*. They revered him and took everything lying down. But Sumbeiywo had trained with them at Sandhurst, knew them and did not fear them. He was also newly arrived from Sandhurst and had been taught the latest manoeuvres. Harbage was still relying on the old tactics. Sumbeiywo immediately challenged Harbage, pointing out that the manoeuvre was correct and according to the book. The officer had never been corrected by a black person. He got into his Land Rover and left for what Sumbeiywo thought was to report the impetuous officer to the commanding officer. He never did. But that marked his first nasty encounter with the British soldiers.

Though he was never overly aggressive, Lieutenant Sumbeiywo was a stickler for fidelity and diligence. At one time in Nakuru, they were practising shooting at the rifle range. The officer in charge, a Major Haiga, set a rule that whoever shot below a certain number would walk back to the camp instead of being driven, a distance of over ten kilometres. The officers accepted this without question. Those who failed to make the target complied with the prescribed punishment. They walked. But when Major Haiga failed to make the target, he got into his Land Rover and drove instead of walking.

The following day, he set the same rule. But Sumbeiywo told the other soldiers who failed to make the target set not to walk. They should all drive back to the camp. Major Haiga was not amused. He accused Sumbeiywo of causing a mutiny and he quickly reported him to the commanding officer, Lieutenant Colonel Mahmoud Mohammed. Lieutenant Sumbeiywo was summoned. But he took his sweet time to appear before the commanding officer. He first ensured that all rifles were back at the armoury and that everything was in order. When he announced himself before the commanding officer, Lieutenant Colonel Mohammed was livid: "When I call you, you should come running," he thundered.

"Yes sir, I should," responded the lieutenant, "but I had to ensure that all the rifles were at the armoury." He was questioned on his action whereupon he admitted telling the soldiers not to walk. Major Haiga sat by and listened quietly. This was an offence for which one could be court-martialled.

"If the Major thought it was a good rule, he should show by example," explained Sumbeiywo to his boss, "But he did not. He got into his Land Rover and drove."

"Is that so, Major?" queried the commanding officer.

"Yes, it is true, sir," the Major responded. The commanding officer once again turned to the lieutenant. "Why did you tell the soldiers not to follow an order?"

"It was not a lawful order," he insisted, "If the Major cannot walk, why should the other officers do?"

Lieutenant Colonel Mohammed realised that he would get bogged down in the labyrinth of force's orders and the semantics of what was lawful and not lawful. He sought to bring the matter to an end. "Give him three days special duties," he commanded. This was a slap in the wrist. Lieutenant Sumbeiywo did not serve the three days nor was the commanding officer keen on having him serve them. He was sent off with the rest of the officers to Rumuruti Rifle Range meet where his team won the young soldiers camp.

This was not the last time the young lieutenant would have brushes with his superiors. During another athletics meet, he was to order the bus to leave the officer in charge of the group, Major Onesmus Wanyoike. Major Wanyoike had started drinking at lunch hour and as the hours ticked by, there were no signs that he had had enough. Sumbeiywo, who by then was a captain, ordered the driver to take off. They left the Major drinking in the mess. Sumbeiywo reported to the commanding officer that he had left his superior. Major Wanyoike arrived much later, and he never revisited the issue.

Lt Colonel Mohammed liked men of principles. When he first met Sumbeiywo right after he graduated from Sandhurst, he immediately saw something that told him that he was closer to the soldier he had always looked for. There was also another officer, Tom Wanambisi, who was also a brilliant soldier. But it was Sumbeiywo that Mohammed would become enamoured of.

"He struck me as a brilliant officer. He had a lot of confidence and he was thorough," Mohammed describes him. As they got better acquainted, the two men became closer. "I saw this man getting closer to what I expected of an army officer. He was a good organiser and a disciplined officer."

But his principles, though admirable, also put him on a collision course with his superiors. He was frank and a bit abrasive. As an adjutant in North Eastern Province, he found his principles clashing with the intentions of his superior. The District Intelligence Officer in Garissa had a bar. He went to the commanding officer of the 1st Battalion who was still Lieutenant Colonel Mohammed, asking for a favour. He wanted 10 crates of beer. The beers were duty free and therefore cheap. The commanding officer called in Sumbeiywo and asked him to give the DIO the beers. In the army, one does what one is ordered to do first and asks questions later. Captain Sumbeiywo gave the officer the beers. Later the same day, he went to the commanding officer: "Sir," he told him, " I have done what you told me to do. But I want you to know that I did it against my conscience." The commanding officer looked at the captain before him. He could not hide his shock.

"Lazaro," he told him, "this is the last time I am asking you to do such a thing." Lieutenant Colonel Mohammed had realised that the captain was guided by his own conscience. "I may not be a very good Moslem," he told him, "but you are a good Christian." From then onwards, there was mutual respect between the two officers and they developed a tight bond as they marched through their army career together. "Because of his principles, he sometimes would annoy," remembers General Mohammed, "he was unchangeable."

So rigid were his principles that some of the other soldiers thought he was unnecessarily harsh. At times, General Mohammed would intervene when he realised that Sumbeiywo had become too hard on the other officers.

"Sometimes I had to tell him to be softer. I would remind him that he was dealing with human beings who sometimes made errors," he admitted.

But he was not for turning. He would tell me, "But sir, you are the one who gave the orders and they have to be followed." And I would sometimes back down." This, however did not affect their personal relationship. Sumbeiywo was the quintessential army officer, a man a boss could trust and one who would carry out and enforce orders without any fear. "Between me and Lazaro," General Mohammed fondly says, "there were no secrets." Now going to his seventies, there are many things that General Mohammed may not remember about Sumbeiywo. But he proudly says that 90 per cent of the Sumbeiywo that people know is what he moulded. " I can proudly say that I moulded Lazaro. I saw in him a great man."

6

Meeting Lorna

The athletics meets were regular. They accorded Sumbeiywo a lot of time from the barracks. But they turned out more than just medals and cups for Captain Sumbeiywo.

There was a young lady he used to see often at the meets. She was working in the Municipal Council of Nakuru as secretary to the Director of Social Services. Three things about her immediately bowled Sumbeiywo over. She was humble, she was beautiful and she appeared very well organised. She was fully involved in the organisation of the games. Her name was Lorna Birir. Much later in 1970, he was to be introduced to Lorna by an officer who was a friend to Lorna's friend. From the first introduction, there was no turning back.

The daughter of a humble evangelist from Eldama Ravine, Dishon Kimutai Birir and Zipporah Tungo, Lorna entranced Sumbeiywo with her charm and understanding of things. Through frequent meetings, they become familiar with each other and started dating.

Lorna insists that it was Sumbeiywo who took her in by his qualities: "He was a disciplined, honest and a handsome man." In all her life, she had never met anyone remotely like him. Tall and athletic, the purposefulness in Sumbeiywo as he went about his duties was to prove a key attraction for Lorna.

Lorna on the other hand had the glamour. As the daughter of an evangelist she also had the religious pull that was so attractive to Sumbeiywo then and which was to prove a major strength in the family that they were to bring up.

Both Lorna and Sumbeiywo shared something else. They had parents who were all-important in their lives and who had greatly contributed to their formation. They made a perfect couple.

In 1971, Sumbeiywo paid the customary visit to Lorna's home to announce his intentions to marry her. By that time the two had completely made up their minds about each other. However, Sumbeiywo's work prevented him from being present when the actual negotiations for the wedding were being conducted. He had been posted to the North Eastern Province, hundreds of kilometres away from home. He was a mortar officer and could not leave his unit, 1st Kenya Rifles, where he was on detachment. It was his parents and his brothers who conducted the negotiations on his behalf and they worked out just fine. In 1972, he married Lorna.

Much later, he was to say that he had realised quite late in life that he had devoted too much time to his career. As adjutant, a mortar officer and a trainer of the shooting team, the workload proved too much for the captain. He went down with an ulcer that was to plague him for years. It was a combination of too much work, stress and lack of enough sleep. Much later, he was to undergo a knee operation that almost put paid to his athletics hobby. But he took over shooting, a discipline in which he excelled as well.

Even as captain, he commanded a company in Nyali Barracks, Mombasa. This was a task normally reserved for Majors. But he was later to learn that being good in the army meant answering the call of service at times when one least expected it. In 1977, Captain Sumbeiywo was left in Garissa as the Company Commander and Adjutant. His battalion was trooping the colours at Jamhuri Park for President Kenyatta. The parade adjutant then was a man called Captain Bedford Githinji. Unexpectedly, he heard the voice of the Battalion Commander, Colonel Mohammed, on the radio ordering him to immediately come to Nairobi. When he arrived he was told that Bedford had lost his voice at the parade. He had to take over as Parade Adjutant. He was unlucky that day. Kenyatta was late for an hour and the parade was left baking in the sun, doing light drills to keep the men busy. Meanwhile, the public was fidgeting, having become impatient. The army had to keep them entertained but they also had to ensure that they do not tire themselves out before the main event. More importantly, Sumbeiywo had to ensure that he also did not lose his voice like Bedford before the parade did what they were there to do. Kenyatta did eventually come and Sumbeiywo commanded the parade efficiently.

When he was later promoted to the rank of Major, Sumbeiywo was put in charge of personnel and administration. But he was to last for only six months after which he was posted back to the Department of Defence as military assistant to Chief of General staff, General Jackson Kimeu Mulinge. It was a completely new office. Sumbeiywo had to act as the Aide-de-Camp to Mulinge. This, he recalls, was the most trying job, "You have to act like a Major but think like a General."

His new role meant that he was always close to the Chief of General Staff. He maintained the diary of the General, wrote speeches and made reports while travelling with him. He usually found himself in the office long after 10 o'clock in the evening. But he and General Mulinge formed a tight relationship that was to change his life dramatically.

The mutual respect that developed between the two men was to continue long after the two had left the army. "He was one of the most diligent officers we had," General Mulinge recalls, "the other was Major Peter Ikenye who was also based at the Army Headquarters." Mulinge, who upon his retirement went into politics and became a Cabinet Minister in Moi's Government, served as the Chief of General Staff for 16 years. Major Ikenye retired from the Army at the rank of Major General.

Though Sumbeiywo was much younger then, Mulinge recalls that his opinions were always sought and respected. "He did not drink, he was a hard worker, he was available every time and his opinions were literally sober."

One thing that was acknowledged but never loudly voiced within the army was that Sumbeiywo was the force behind Major General Mahmoud Mohammed. According to General Mulinge, Sumbeiywo was such a loyal officer and an indispensable pillar to the administration of General Mahmoud Mohammed that the man had a lot of respect for Sumbeiywo and entirely relied on him to execute his wishes and commands. For, although an excellent commander and a good soldier, Mahmoud had one handicap: his low education. He was a self-taught officer who respected the judgement of his colleagues, a living testimony to the fact that education was no handicap to those who had a talent for leadership. Sumbeiywo's influence on Mahmoud started being felt when he was the adjutant at 1 KR. The unit was doing extremely well both professionally and in athletics. The officers knew that whatever made it tick had to do with the combined efforts of Sumbeiywo and his boss. Later, the officers started noticing a tight bond developing between Major General Mohammed and Sumbeiywo. As Mohammed moved, he took Sumbeiywo along. He took him to Gilgil when he was moved there and came back with him to Nairobi when he was transferred. When he went to the Air Force, he went with Sumbeiywo and when he became the Chief of General Staff, the supreme head of the armed forces in Kenya, he again took Sumbeiywo as Director of Military Intelligence. The other officers knew that if there was one person Mahmoud valued, it was Sumbeiywo.

"In fact, he loved him. The two were inseparable," concedes Major General Ikenye, who was also one of the officers with whom Sumbeiywo worked closely at the Army Headquarters.

7

The Days of Darkness

The year 1982 started like any other in the army and in the country. President Moi had been in office for five years and things were running all right. But towards the middle of the year, things took an unprecedented turn.

Major Sumbeiywo was still Military Assistant to the Chief of General Staff that year. He was desperately trying to set up an appointment between the Director of Special Branch, the arm of government dealing with intelligence, James Kanyotu, with General Mulinge, the Chief of General Staff. They wanted to discuss some unconfirmed reports that there was a mutiny in the offing in the Army.

On the day they were accompanying the President to the Nyeri Agricultural Show in Central Province, 150 kilometres from the capital city, Major Sumbeiywo managed to wangle an appointment. "Let's meet on Monday." Kanyotu told him. It was a Friday, July 30. The Army was in training in Lodwar, Turkana. The two men could retire to their rural areas while the Major remained in Nairobi to monitor the Army's progress in Turkana. When the Army called the exercise off at 1.00 p.m. that Saturday, Major Sumbeiywo saw a chance to take a break. He also drove to Nakuru to meet his family. The following morning, his brother, Elijah Sumbeiywo, who was then the Presidential Escort Commander, was scheduled to come home for breakfast.

Major Sumbeiywo was still asleep when he heard the phone ring at 5.30 am. "Elijah must be so hungry he cannot wait for morning," he remarked to his wife.

"Are you still asleep?" the voice on the other end of the telephone asked petulantly.

"Oh yes I am. It is a Sunday, after all," Sumbeiywo answered.

"Don't sleep. The government has been overthrown."

"By who?" Sumbeiywo asked in what might have sounded as a sarcastic tone but which was nevertheless serious.

"By the Army," Elijah answered.

"Forget it. The Army is in Lodwar."

"Yes, but can you meet me at Kabarak? Drive in your civilian vehicle and wait for me at the gate." A different world was unfolding for this Army man. This was a national crisis that needed immediate attention. Kabarak was where the President was. It was also a place in which he loved spending his weekends.

Elijah instructed him to bring extra soldiers along. He put one in front of his Peugeot 204, three at the back and two in the boot. The soldiers had all been ordered to cock their rifles so that if anyone stopped them on the way, they could shoot them down.

At Kabarak, Major Sumbeiywo found Moi talking to the head of the Special Branch in the province, Mr Kimetto and the Rift Valley Provincial Police Officer, Mr Mbijjiwe. They were trying to analyse who had carried out the coup.

Moi was still unfazed by what had happened. He would not leave the house even at the insistence of the officers who feared that the house might be bombed. "If I have to die, let me die in my house," Moi insisted. Finally, the Rift Valley Provincial Commissioner, Mr Hezekiah Oyugi, arrived and, together with Elijah Sumbeiywo, they took Moi by the arm and convinced him to leave. He sat in front of Sumbeiywo's Peugeot and, followed by some heavily armed bodyguards, was driven around his farm in Menengai as they waited for word about the situation. They then drove to State House Nakuru. Inside the palatial house, Lazaro Sumbeiywo noticed Moi's ADC, Major Peter Ikenye, talking on the phone. He was speaking to the Deputy Army Commander, General Mahmoud Mohammed. Sumbeiywo approached him and asked him: "Who has done this?"

"I don't know but I suspect it is my Gikuyu friends." (Ikenye was from the Gikuyu community, some of whose members were thought to be uncomfortable with Moi's Government.)

"Don't be judgmental," Sumbeiywo cautioned, "We will soon know the truth."

By 10 am, they received word that the Voice of Kenya which had fallen to the rebels had been recaptured. The President could have gone on air immediately using an Army vehicle which had broadcasting facilities. But as fate would have it, the vehicle had had an accident.

The President meanwhile was calm and at one time was laughing, saying, "These people are joking." It later emerged that it was the Air Force personnel who had carried out the coup.

The President was convinced by his aides that he should travel to Nairobi immediately. But his ADC, Major Ikenye, was uncomfortable. There were still two Air Force planes that had not returned to base and he feared that they would spot them from the air and attack. He convinced the President to buy time. The President respected his ADC's advice and agreed that it was wise to wait.

The journey from Nakuru to Nairobi only started when word went out that the planes had landed in the Nanyuki Airbase. It was a tense journey. The President travelled in a long convoy which included armoured vehicles. The General Service Unit wanted to meet him half way, but Ikenye persuaded them to remain in Nairobi to avert confusion whereby some exchange of fire could result.

"The GSU might have, on seeing the Army convoy, thought that the military had captured the President," he recalls, "everything had to be kept controlled and clear." When the President's convoy reached Rironi, about 15 kilometres from Nairobi, there was a huge crowd that had gathered there. He ordered the car stopped and came out from the hatch. He addressed the crowd. The crowd was ecstatic. They clapped and shouted.

Later when the President addressed the nation, the head of the Presidential Press Unit, Mr Wamatu Njoroge, wept uncontrollably. It was an emotional moment. By that time, the Chief of General Staff, who was still in Machakos, had been sent for. He had to pass through the Nairobi National Park then straight to the Defence Headquarters.

Meanwhile, Moi was insisting on driving through the streets of Nairobi to reassure the people. But Ikenye had word that there were three Air Force men holed up somewhere on Moi Avenue, the main avenue in the city, and could perhaps harm the President. But Moi insisted on taking the tour. When he saw the huge crowd that had formed along the streets, he insisted on coming out. He ordered his ADC to open the hatch of the limousine. Ordinarily, he would emerge from the hatch to acknowledge greetings from the people. He was aching to be seen and to demonstrate that all was well.

"It is not safe to open the hatch," his ADC replied. Moi was insistent. But Ikenye knew of the Air Force officers waiting at the Kenya Cinema along the avenue and who would almost certainly snipe at the President. He did not want to tell the President about the looming danger. He held on to the line that it would not be safe to open the hatch. Luckily, Moi relented. It was the first time that Major Ikenye had engaged his Commander-in-Chief in an argument. But he knew that he was right. The hunt for the fugitive army officers was still on and as long as they had not been captured, it would not be safe for the President to make public appearances unshielded.

The following day, the three Air Force men were flushed out of Kenya Cinema on Moi Avenue, the very location around which the President wanted to stop and greet the people. This was a welcome vindication for Major Ikenye.

Hours lunged by. The country was still trying to come to terms with what had happened, the army was in a state of heightened alarm and clearly, there would be a great deal of reorganisation to be done. On the day after the attempted coup, Sumbeiywo and his boss slept in the office, trying to work out a normalisation programme and keeping an eye on the situation. It was not the last day they would find themselves in the office in the wee hours of the morning.

The abortive coup was to have a dramatic affect on Major Sumbeiywo's life and career prospects. He realised that overnight, things could change for the worse and that though the coup had been crushed, life would never be the same again within the army and the country.

The first thing to change was his station in the army. The day after the coup attempt, General Mulinge called a meeting of all the service commanders. Already, scores of rebels had been arrested. Major Sumbeiywo was handed the task of writing all the instructions on how they would be dealt with. A meeting was called with the aim of reforming the Kenya Air Force and disposing of the cases. The Army Commander, General Mahmoud Mohammed, who had played a sterling role in crushing the coup, was appointed the new Air Force Commander, replacing Major General Peter Kariuki. Major Sumbeiywo was promoted to Lieutenant Colonel in charge of personnel at the Air Force.

" I was sad to see him go," reminisces Mulinge, "but he was going on promotion, which was a good thing." According to General Mulinge, there were two officers due for promotion, Major Ikenye, ADC to the President, and Major Sumbeiywo, who was his Military Assistant. There was a vacancy for Lieutenant Colonel and there was an opening for further studies in London. As the Military Assistant to the CGS, Sumbeiywo was given the priority to choose what he wanted. He chose promotion and off he went to the Air Force. Besides, recalls Mulinge, his services were very much wanted in the Air Force. Major Ikenye proceeded for further studies in London.

In his new role, Sumbeiywo was supposed to deal with all the cases of the rebels, draft all the court martial proceedings, jail, reform, recruit and think about how the future Air Force would look. This, Sumbeiywo acknowledges, was one of the most trying moments of his career. It was a new service for him and together with 15 other officers from the army, they brought to life a new Air Force, the old one having suffered almost mortally from the coup attempt. The fallout claimed quite a few senior officers. The then Air Force Commander, Major-General Peter Kariuki, was jailed for failing to suppress a mutiny, and Senior Private Hezekiah Ochuka who had led the mutiny, was sentenced to death.

In 1986, General Mulinge retired as the Chief of General Staff and was succeeded by General Mahmoud. Sumbeiywo left the Air Force and joined Mahmoud as Director of Military Intelligence, a unit he built from scratch. Its work was to collect and collate intelligence within and outside the country, brief and advise commanders. In 1993, the President asked him to establish an external intelligence service. The service was supposed to gather hostile information on Kenya and identify areas of interest to the country. His official title was Director of the Liaison Department based in the Office of the President. Unbeknown to him, this was to propel him to a completely different course in his career. He visited many countries and established key links that saw the Government of Kenya play a critical role in the affairs of neighbouring countries. He found himself playing key roles in negotiations, sometimes with senior foreign government officials. Some of these events would be precursors to the monumental role that was ahead of him.

In 1996, for instance, an Australian pilot named Fraser was arrested in Somalia. Sumbeiywo was approached by a Somali who knew where the pilot was being held. If he agreed to pay Shs 2 million, the pilot would be released. He agreed to this request but on one condition: that the Somali leadership be brought on board in the negotiations. At that time there was war in Somalia with various factions fighting against each other. Using the pilot saga as a route to broker peace between the Somalia factions, Sumbeiywo managed to bring the Somalia leaders to Nairobi. By that time the pilot had been released and handed over to the Australian High Commissioner. But Sumbeiywo saw this as a perfect chance to broach the subject of peace in Somalia. The ice had thawed and he wanted to take maximum advantage. Using his closeness to the Head of State, he organised for a meeting between Moi and the Somali leaders.

Led by Hussein Aideed, the Somalia leader then, they met at State House and President Moi brokered a peace agreement in which they all agreed to go to Mogadishu, make peace with the militia and incorporate other Somalis in future meetings. The agreement was contained in a document called the Nairobi Undertaking. This was a momentary success but the war in Somali did not stop. It was to continue for many years afterwards. But it gave Sumbeiywo a snapshot of what his life would be like afterwards.

On the day Sumbeiywo was called to accompany President Bashir to State House, Nakuru, he was to remember this incident vividly. In many ways, it was a dress rehearsal for the critical role he would play in resolving the conflicts in the region.

8

The Making of a Mediator

It was an early morning at State House, Nairobi in July, 1997. As director of Liaison Department, Sumbeiywo watched the convoys snake through the tree-lined driveway of State House, Nairobi. Present were President Yoweri Museveni, President Isaiya Aferworki of Eritrea and Meles Zenawi, Prime Minister of Ethiopia. There were also two very important figures: President Omar Bashir of Sudan and Dr John Garang, the leader of the Sudan People's Liberation Movement and Army (SPLM/A). They had all gathered in Nairobi to discuss the possibility of peace in the Sudan region.

As Sumbeiywo watched the men of power conglomerate at State House, he again remembered that incident in 1989 when Bashir and Garang went to State House Nakuru, refused to shake each other's hands and sent clear signals that peace was not on the agenda at the time. But as the war in Sudan raged, it was becoming urgent that the presidents of the countries neighbouring Sudan accelerate the peace process. The region, they rightly argued, was lagging behind as a result of the conflict in the region and an urgent solution had to be found.

A small door for peace had, however, opened six years after that incident. In 1994, representatives of the Sudanese Government and the SPLM/A had signed the Declaration of Principles (DOP). The DOP was supposed to constitute the basis for resolving the conflict in Sudan. It was considered a road map to peace.

But there was a problem. Garang insisted on what he called "Zero Interim Period", meaning that he was more in favour of a split between the North and South than unity. His insistence, however, did not bear fruit, but all the same he signed the DOP. All the others agreed that what DOP had come up with was a proper diagnosis of the conflict. Bashir did not agree to sign the DOP as the document through which everything else could be negotiated.

Among other declarations, the DOP stated that all parties to the conflict fully accept and commit themselves to the position that the history and nature of the Sudan conflict "demonstrate that a military solution cannot bring lasting peace and stability to the country; that a peaceful and just political solution must be the common objective of the parties of the conflict and that the rights of self-determination of the people of South Sudan through a referendum must be affirmed."

The document detailed the need to cater for the diverse nature of the Sudanese society and listed maintenance of unity in Sudan as one area that should be given priority. The DOP made it clear that complete political and social equalities of all peoples in the Sudan must be guaranteed by law and that extensive rights of self-administration on the basis of federation, autonomy, etc, to the various peoples of the Sudan must be affirmed. A secular and democratic state, the document also stated, must be established in Sudan and freedom of worship and religion "be guaranteed in full to all Sudanese citizens".

It was not a long document but it dealt with the conflict areas that had paralysed the Northern and Southern parts of Sudan and locked them in a furious war. The SPLM/A appended its signature on the document on May 20, 1994, in Nairobi. The Government on the other hand did not, until 1997 at a summit in State House, Nairobi. This was the document that was to guide future negotiations between these two parties.

****

In spite of the DOP, it was clear that there was no political will on the part of the Government of Sudan to resolve the issues. The war had raged on and the Heads of State gathered in Nairobi that morning were clearly becoming frustrated. They feared that the IGAD member countries would not achieve significant development if the crisis persisted. They also understood the problem in the Sudan as one that would best be solved by the people of Sudan, aided by the regional powers who were also being adversely affected by the war.

That July morning of 1997, Moi had managed to bring Dr Garang and Bashir together again. This time, it was hoped that the two would at least make some headway in the direction of peace.

The Presidents went into a closed door meeting in which they were locked for hours. When they came out, no one was talking to each other. Each President came out on his own and headed to his delegation. The meeting had turned rowdy. Bashir looked agitated as he followed Moi. They went straight into his office in which they stayed locked for another hour.

Something had gone seriously wrong at the meeting. Because Moi did not brief the Kenyan delegation, they were all in the dark as to what had really happened. Sumbeiywo was to learn later that the Heads of State had threatened to invade Sudan if Bashir did not resolve the crisis and negotiate according to the Declaration of Principles. Bashir went wild. He fumed and fulminated that the Presidents were pressuring him to negotiate with rebels and criminals.

Bashir had never regarded the SPLM/A as anything more than a rebel and criminal outfit and the thought of sitting down with them was, at the moment, proving too big for him. Moi tried to calm him down. Bashir threatened to walk out and the meeting broke up.

As the elder statesman, Moi guided Bashir to his office and tried to make him see reason. "These young men (meaning the relatively young Presidents of Uganda, the Prime Minister of Ethiopia and the Eritrean President) mean what they are saying. They will do this to you and this will only stoke the conflict," Moi told Bashir. When he considered those words, he feared that the Heads of State whom he considered excitable could as well make good their threat. Bashir calmed down and decided to play along.

When he came out of Moi's office, he looked relieved. It was as if a heavy load had been lifted from him. Back to the drawing room, the Heads of State agreed to establish the IGAD Peace Process for Sudan. Special envoys were appointed. Lazaro Sumbeiywo was appointed Kenya's Special Envoy to the Sudan Peace Process. Because Kenya was the chair of the IGAD subcommittee, Sumbeiywo was appointed the Chairman of the Technical Committee, while the then Foreign Affairs Minister, Kalonzo Musyoka, was the chair of the Council of Ministers. With that appointment, the long road to Sudan peace process began and life once more changed for Sumbeiywo.

What this meant was that he would, from now onwards, play an integral role in the search for peace in Sudan. In many ways, this was different from what he had been trained to do as a military officer. But because he had served in the role of a military intelligence officer, it would not be such a daunting task for him to be Chairman of the technical committee.

There was, however, a monumental question: Why had Moi decided on Sumbeiywo? First, the army officer was well versed with on the conflicts of the region, as Director of Military Intelligence and later head of the Liaison Department, he had immense intelligence on what was happening beyond Kenya's borders.

Secondly, Moi needed someone he could trust. He was close to Sumbeiywo and he knew the man had an independent spirit. As Major General Ikenye was to remember, "The President wanted a man who had the zeal and the energy to execute what he wanted. Sumbeiywo had it."

Thirdly, the combatants in the conflict were all military people. President Omar Hassan Al Bashir was a military officer who had overthrown a civilian government and John Garang was a hardened guerrilla leader who had led the life of a military General. The task at hand would be better handled by someone who understood the mind of a military General rather than a diplomat who might be bogged down by the niceties of diplomatese.

Moi's involvement with Sudan was so passionate that he wanted a man who would translate his desires into action. In the early years of his presidency, he had started giving Southern Sudanese slots at the Nairobi University to educate and train their professionals. Even before Bashir came onto the scene, he had started pursuing a peace deal with President Jaffar Numeiri who unfortunately was overthrown before any such dream could be realised. In Sumbeiywo, he had a tool for his mission.

Moreover, the war in Sudan had affected Kenya adversely. During the course of the fighting, millions of displaced Sudanese had spilled across the northern border, eventually settling in different parts of the country. Kenya was also playing host to Operation Lifeline Sudan, one of the world's longest running multi-billion dollar international aid operations. It was all in the benefit of Kenya and the region that a solution was found to the conflict.

But how would Sumbeiywo, a man not trained in mediation do it? With all the skills of a soldier, where would he get the faintest diplomatic skills to navigate the eddies and currents of such a delicate process? As it turned out, Sumbeiywo had to throw in everything he learned from his father, who was a chief and a mediator and everything he learned from watching elders arbitrate in disputes.

Largely, he knew he would have to employ what he now fondly refers to as the African conflict resolution mechanism. In the olden days, mediation was in the blood of African elders. They would sit under a tree whenever there was a dispute, listen to all sides of the conflict, ask the necessary questions and rarely, if ever, did they fail to get a solution.

They did not know how to read or write. But they would carry sticks or leaves. Every time a point of importance was made, it would be marked by either a stick or a twig. The old men had extraordinary alacrity and wisdom. They remembered every point made, did their deductions and passed an agreeable judgment. These ranged from land disputes to family or clan quarrels to the very delicate cases of pregnancies and marital problems. The court of arbiters was present in every community and its word was law.

Later, when the white men came, these courts were replaced by government courts which essentially dealt with crime and handed out punishments as opposed to resolving or arbitrating conflicts.

As Sumbeiywo uneasily took the role of the chief mediator, this picture of the African courts kept replaying in his mind. He remembered that distant day when a conflict involving the school he was attending played itself out right in front of his eyes. He could see Mzee Jacob Meto and Mzee Mateo Kisang arguing over who should control Yokot Primary School. He remembered painfully the closure that resulted and how, much later, his father resolved that conflict.

"Conflict resolution then," he says with an air of satisfaction, "involved listening to everyone. Even the dull have their story to tell." But his assignment here was different, much more complicated and one which was enacting itself in a completely different age. Though he was no stranger to SPLM/A or the Sudanese leadership, having interacted with them previously and offered them his office when they needed a venue for talks, he knew that his calling would be different. Nevertheless, he knew that conflict resolution followed more or else the same patterns everywhere. As it turned out, the African conflict resolution mechanism was to help him greatly straddle the spokes of the conflict.

After the Heads of State meeting and the establishment of the IGAD Peace Process for Sudan, Sumbeiywo did not waste time. He convened a meeting right after the State House summit and drew up points from the DOP to be discussed by the Sudanese Government and the SPLM/A. Together with the other envoys, they travelled to Northern Kenya to meet the SPLM/A leadership and then to Khartoum to meet with government officials. Time was of the essence.

But if anyone thought that it would be easy to negotiate the contentious issues using the DOP, a huge surprise was lying in wait. Both sides felt that they could drag on the conflict a little longer and even win the war using military might. The government had the army and SPLM/A was funded and trained well enough to give as much as they took. There was therefore deliberate grandstanding on nearly everything. Whenever the envoys discussed an issue with either side, they rigidly stuck to their different positions. "The position taken by one side would be the right opposite of the one taken by the other," Sumbeiywo observed, much to his frustration. Garang, for example, insisted that everything be negotiated as listed on the DOP. But the Government wanted to start from the bottom with the issue of a ceasefire. After much swinging back and forth both sides agreed to go by what was listed on the DOP.

Along the way, booby traps were exploding. The differences in the two sides were openly flaring up into serious confrontations and threatening any chance for proper, fruitful negotiations. One meeting held in 1998 in Addis Ababa ended in disarray when the SPLM/A declared that the boundary of the South be moved because it was not in accordance with the existing boundary as at the time of independence. However, the people of Nuba Mountains in Southern Kodorfan and Blue Nile objected. They said they would continue fighting if the border was moved. These two regions were later to become major headaches for the negotiators and mediators.

The Government of Sudan had not yet come to the realisation that they could end the conflict by negotiating. They believed in fighting, and try as the envoys might, they invariably came back empty handed. The start was slow, the frustrations were immense and the envoys were still working under a loose arrangement that precluded the presence of a secretariat. It was not until 1999 that the IGAD Secretariat was established and given a proper mandate to carry out continuous negotiations on the conflict.

However, in 1998, Sumbeiywo left the country for the United Kingdom to do a course in International Relations. This course would come in handy in the not too distant future. A new envoy, Mr Daniel Mboya, was appointed to take over. Sumbeiywo had interacted with Mboya at the IGAD subcommittee level and he was positive that he would steer the Peace Process well. Sumbeiywo was now out of the process and he did not hope to return to it.

****

It sometimes amazed and always pleased Sumbeiywo that, in spite of everything, he was a military man. That hiatus in which he was thrust into diplomacy and mediation did nothing to blight the fire of the army man within him. As one of the most senior military officials in the country, his star was fast on the rise. He had established the Liaison Department and steered the Directorate of Military Intelligence expertly. In his brief role as Kenya's special envoy to the Sudan peace process, he hoped that he would achieve what other people had failed to achieve and bring peace to the Horn of Africa.

It was not a surprise, therefore, that when he came back to the country, he was appointed the Commandant of the Defence Staff College on September 19, 1999. Usually, this was a stage to a bigger destination. Commanders of DSC went on to become even more senior in the Army. On November 1, 2000, Sumbeiywo was appointed Army Commander designate and took over fully as Army Commander on December 1, 2000. This was a powerful and demanding position.

When he looked back, he realised that the appointment carried with it a Herculean responsibility. He had been out of the army for quite a long time and the army he was now returning to was not the one he knew. In his assessment, it was somewhat run down. Many officers were complaining, especially the ones who felt that professionalism was going down. There were many matters requiring the commander's attention, which had piled up in the former commander's office. They ranged from lack of training and lack of equipment to shortage of staff.

New regulations had been promulgated which had demoralised many officers. One of them was the dropping of written and practical examinations for officers as a basis for promotion. The army was now insisting that academic qualifications were the biggest determinants of promotion. "The army was becoming an elite unit," one officer wryly noted, "the best army officer was not necessarily the most senior."

Servicemen were also being allowed to leave at will instead of requiring them to stay in the army for set periods. The officers' messes had also been closed and officers were now paid allowances as compensation. Lack of a hall made it difficult to assemble the officers in case of a parade. There were also cases of misappropriation of funds and resources involving some officers which were not being dealt with militarily. Some of the most serious cases had been handed over to the Police Criminal Investigations Department. This was not practical. The CID did not have the machinery to penetrate the army and deal with these cases.

Lieutenant General A.S.K. Njoroge, the Army Commander at the time of writing this book, and who was then Brigadier General and Chief of Personnel and Logistics, has an almost flawless understanding of the way the army was being run then. He recalls vividly how matters were when Sumbeiywo took over as Army Commander. "It was a bad time. Officers were openly disobedient to their seniors and there were those who would challenge court martials in civilian courts. The army also had many untouchables who had powerful godfathers in high political circles. These ones could do anything, get away with it and challenge their seniors to do their worst."

This was not surprising. Kenya then was a country in which people held senior positions depending on who they knew in high offices or what community they came from. This political patronage had seeped into the military in its most destructive form.

As Lt Gen Njoroge remembers, there was no one courageous enough to discipline errant officers. The Army Commander, then Lieutenant General Adan, was a hostage to those forces and because there was no telling who was who's godfather, there was little even the senior army officers could do. The army was hurtling down a precipice.

"Sometimes you would question a junior officer," Lt General Njoroge recalls with a tinge of bitterness, "and the officer would threaten you. If you threatened to sack him he would say, 'you might go home before me.' Sometimes when this would happen the senior officers learnt to stay away from the sacred cows.

Officers would take imprests and not repay them. Money would be allocated to the Army and then redirected to other extraneous causes. The army then was in perpetual want. There was no training being carried out, the uniform supplied to them was of low quality and sometimes goods that were never supplied were listed as having been issued. And life went on. Morale was scraping the barrel.

Then came Sumbeiywo. What does one do with an Army that is threatening to run out of kilter? How does one deal with an outfit into which unprofessional behaviour and indiscipline had eaten like cancer? Even a professional soldier like him was unnerved at the state in which he found the Army.

Serious reforms were needed. Sumbeiywo realised that this was a cross he had to bear. At that time, General Jeremiah Kianga, who was later to succeed Sumbeiywo as the Army Commander, was appointed his deputy. Lt General Njoroge was appointed Chief of Operations and Training. This combination worked wonders. Sumbeiywo immediately embarked on redirecting the Army. Because everyone knew that he was close to the President, even the demigods that had instilled fear into their seniors knew that a new era had dawned. (Jeremiah Kianga was later promoted to full General and appointed Chief of General staff.)

Sumbeiywo came with a lot of confidence and fixity of purpose. "He was sure of himself and he knew he had all the support he required to reform the Army," Lt General Njoroge avers. He started using the Armed Forces Act which allowed for courts-martial and started a subtle programme of retirements. Those who refused to be court-martialled were sacked without the General caring about whom they were allied to. But no one went home without knowing the reason for which they were being sent home. There was fairness and justice and the Defence Council always ratified his decisions. Discipline was key in the running of the Army and having risen through the ranks in both the Army and the Air Force, restoring discipline did not present major difficulties for the General. Within no time, the Army started changing. He and his deputy embarked on a programme that they called Zero Tolerance. Those who were there at the time were to remember those days when a new Lt General arrived and completely changed the way things were done at the Army. Sumbeiywo earned himself the name ZT, meaning Zero Tolerance. On their radios, the officers called him Zulu Tango. He chaired meetings to make the officers understand where the Army was going or coming from and the two began what they were calling the guillotine method: If you do not fit, you are chopped off. This was a policy that General Kianga would continue after he succeeded Sumbeiywo.

"The two officers paired very well," Lt General Njoroge remembers, "they were respected, feared and admired."

Soon, the changes Sumbeiywo had instituted started being felt. The Army was better kitted, there was re-emphasis on training and the so-called "untouchables" were sacked. When he started sacking the demigods, there was trepidation. The senior ones loved it but many could not believe it. "How can he sack these people," it was asked in low whispers, "he will get into trouble." Everyone knew what trouble was. It usually came from a call from a senior politician to the Army Commander and it almost always resulted in a transfer or a deployment. Long used to this method of doing things, the Army officers who could not believe that things could change waited for Sumbeiywo to "get into trouble."

He did not. Instead, his shock therapy worked wonders. More resources started flowing into the Army and the Army suddenly had everything it needed. A training programme was put in place and the control of resources in the Army was placed in able hands. This earned Sumbeiywo more respect than fear. He victimised no one, but he brooked no nonsense either.

Even the senior officers had to learn to work with a different kind of boss. They had to learn to think independently. Sumbeiywo detested officers who presented a problem to him with no solution. He was, however, hugely supportive of those who made decisions and only sought his consent to implement them. Because the army had lived through a period of micro-management for far too long, many officers still feared making decisions or bringing forth proposals. At one time, Lt General Njoroge introduced the practicals of a training programme on manoeuvres called the manoeuveristic doctrine. This was a departure from the attritions doctrine which mainly relied on a unit staging frontal attacks on the enemy. Manoeuveristic doctrine taught more tactical ways of combat in which the unit sought out the weaknesses of the enemy and exploited them. This way a smaller army could defeat a larger one simply by being tactical. Most of the officers thought that the head of training would be in trouble for enlisting the support of British soldiers to teach Kenyan soldiers the new doctrine. But when the proposal was tabled to Sumbeiywo, he supported it enthusiastically. He even accompanied Lt General Njoroge to the field to see how the training was being done. This served to show the others that there was a new man at the Army and that he was operating differently from the rest. Zulu Tango was on the march.

****

The year 2000 was a critical time. The country was entering a dramatic phase. In less than two years, the 24-year reign of President Moi would come to an end. Barred by the Constitution from running for another term, Moi was set to retire by the end of 2002. In the twilight years of his presidency, he wanted to leave everything in order. Sumbeiywo on his part wanted to accelerate reforms in the Army and had thrown all his commitment to the cause.

One early morning in 2000, however, he heard the hotline that connected his office to the President directly, ring. It was not unusual for the President to call him, particularly now that he was the head of the Army. But that morning, the President's voice was urgent.

"Lazaro," the President said in a calm, collected voice, "I want to give you a job and I do not want you to refuse." This was it. He would be off to a new appointment even before he had completed the one he had been assigned. He was a bit taken aback by the prospect of starting a new mission. But he quickly remembered that his work was to serve the nation in whatever capacity.

"Your Excellency," he responded, "you are the Commander-in-Chief and there is no way I could refuse a task from you."

"No, this has nothing to do with the military," the President said, "I want us to negotiate peace in Southern Sudan."

General Sumbeiywo did not expect this. Since he left the peace process he knew that the envoys had not achieved much success. They had held several meetings in the country but the peace process had nearly stalled. No major concessions had been made and it looked like the entire process was foundering.

Now, the President was telling Sumbeiywo that he needed him back in the peace process. As he sat back in his high-back chair at the Army Headquarters, he pondered what that meant. The President had not finished, "and Lazaro, I want us to do this between six and 12 months." Quite evidently, the President did not want to leave office with the issue of the Sudan conflict hanging and had been intensely frustrated that nothing much was being achieved. But Sumbeiywo also wondered if the President knew how monumental the task he was charging him with was.

"And one other, thing."

"Yes, Your Excellency," the General deferred.

"You will do this in addition to your duties as Army Commander. I am doing this because I know you are a Christian."

Now fully surprised, Sumbeiywo ventured, "Your Excellency, can I come so that we discuss this further?"

The President, clearly unwilling to prolong this matter answered curtly, "You will receive instructions."

Sumbeiywo really wanted to persuade the President to either appoint someone else to the peace process or relieve him of the Army command. He saw a combination of both tasks as mission impossible. The Army desperately needed him and, judging by the urgency in the President's voice, the peace process also required him. He kept wishing that the President would change his mind. The President did not. Two days later, a letter arrived from the office of the Chief of the General Staff detailing Sumbeiywo's appointment as Special Envoy to Sudan in addition to his duties as Army Commander.

It was a traumatic time. He could not go against the wishes of his Commander-in-Chief. In any case, he had left him no choice. He informed his family and, together with his wife, they fasted for three days. His Church, The Africa Inland Church, incorporated his prayer into the church bulletin for the entire period of the peace process.

But before he could embark on the task, he had to see the President and make him understand about the intractability of the sides involved in the conflict. Unless the parties agreed to negotiate under him, it would be pointless to go on, he told the President. He asked to see Bashir and Garang so as to ask them if they would accept him as the mediator.

Off to Khartoum he went. He had a letter from Moi to Bashir. The Sudanese President had no problem. Garang too had no problem accepting Lt General Sumbeiywo as chief mediator.

"I put myself in the arms of the Lord," he says, "peace had to be found."

Moi's insistence that Sumbeiywo return to the peace process was borne out of the great faith he had in the man. As recalls Kalonzo Musyoka, who knew the man well and one with whom he would closely work together on this initiative, "Though an Army General, Sumbeiywo was a brilliant diplomat, widely travelled and also widely accommodating of leadership and ideas."

These were qualities that were to greatly aid the Minister through the winding road of the negotiations, "He kept me thoroughly briefed. He was excellent in this."

As Sumbeiywo then undertook the task for the search of the elusive peace, Musyoka knew that the process was in able hands. "I had no doubt that something would come out of it." But given the complexities of the sides involved in the conflict, one could not afford to be too optimistic. But Musyoka recalls that while he as Minister was apprehensive of what the outcome would be, there was not an iota of pessimism from the man who would steer the peace process for well over three years and hammer out a deal.

9

The Conflict, the Country

There is a proverb in Sudan that goes, "When God made Sudan, He laughed." The people of Sudan do not know exactly why God laughed. But as Deborah Scroggins writes in her seminal novel, *Emma's War*, some say God laughed with pleasure and others because of the gigantic creation He had made.

For Sudan is the largest country in Africa, covering an area of 2.5 million square kilometres, the size of Western Europe. It boasts of nine neighbours: Kenya, Ethiopia, Eritrea, Egypt, Libya, Chad, Central African Republic, Uganda and Democratic Republic of Congo (DRC). It also has access to the Red Sea in the eastern part.

But Sudan is also a patchwork of diversity. Sharply divided by geography, culture, race, ethnicity and religion, it has been a cauldron of conflict for 34 of its 46 years of independence. Its inhabitants like considering Sudan as the frontier between southern Black Africa and the Arab nations of the north. The people of Egypt and Israel knew it as the land of Cush and later as Nubia. The Greeks and the Romans called it Ethiopia, which means "The Land of the Burnt-Faced ones." After the Muslim conquest of the middle ages, it was named 'the Sudan'. Today, it is simply called 'Sudan'. It has a population of 36 million people and its capital city is Khartoum. Until the signing of the Comprehensive Peace Agreement in 2005, its official language was Arabic.

Through the Sudan, the Nile River snakes into the deserts of Egypt into the Mediterranean. Soon after it crosses the border into Sudan, the White Nile disappears into the Sudd, a 130,000 square kilometre swamp and which is the world's biggest. The Nile is the lifeline of Egypt and a critical feature in Sudan's life.

The geography of Sudan has contributed to a dichotomy in which lies some of the roots of the conflict that saw the country plunge into a two decade bloody conflict. The Northern part of the country is an arid desert that, in good times, could receive only a week of rainfall a year while the south enjoys tropical climate. It is wet, lush, and has fat livestock and rivers teeming with fish. It could receive up to nine months of rainfall.

Only one tenth of Sudan's land is arable. Meadows and pastures cover 24 per cent while forests and woodlands cover a mere 20 per cent of its surface.

With the exception of the Nuba mountains in Southern Kordofan, the Northern people were mostly Arabic-speaking and Muslims. The southern part is inhabited mainly by dark-skinned Africans who are a medley of Christian and traditional religions. Christians account for only five per cent of the dwellers of the South while those who profess indigenous religions account for 25 per cent. The North is mainly inhabited by Sunni Muslims who account for 70 per cent of the believers.

The difference in endowment has, throughout history, created conflict in the Sudan. There are three areas that have always felt, and indeed have been, marginalized. They are the Abyei Area, the Nuba Mountains and the Southern Blue Nile. The Abyei area is occupied by the Ngok Dinka, and, to a lesser extent, the Messiriya, the Nuba Mountains by the Nuba people and the Southern Blue Nile is the home of the Funj, the Ingessina and other peoples.

The people of Abyei, the Ngok Dinka and the land they occupy were part of Bahr El Ghazal province of Southern Sudan when the provincial boundaries were drawn up. In 1905, due to difficulties of administering the Alor Dinka, the Ngok Dinka and the Twic Dinka from the Upper Nile, the Anglo-Egyptian Administration ruling over Sudan transferred their administration to Kordofan Province in the Northern Sudan.

However, in 1952 the Anglo-Egyptian administration asked the Alor, the Ngok and the Twic Dinka whether they wanted to return to Upper Nile and Bahr El Ghazal respectively or if they preferred to remain in Kordofan. The Chiefs of Alor Dinka chose to return to Upper Nile and the Twic Dinka chose to return to the administration of Bahr El Ghazal provinces. The Ngok Dinka's paramount Chief, Deng Kuol Arop (Deng Majok) decided it was in the interest of his people to remain under the administration of Kordofan, believing that by so doing, his people would receive more and better social services and security.

But he was wrong. When the first civil war broke out some of the young men of the Ngok Dinka fought on the side of the South wanting to return the administration of their area to Bahr El Ghazal.

On the other hand, the people of the Nuba Mountains have always been part of Northern Sudan. In the first war of 1955-1972, the Nuba people fought on the side of the Central Government of the Sudan to preserve the unity of the country. But in the recently ended civil war, they closed ranks with the South to fight against the Central Government. Like the Southerners, they were agitating for equality of treatment as citizens, equality in social and economic development, preservation of their cultures, land and religious freedoms and rights. Their problems were similar to those of the people of Southern Blue Nile who also had been marginalised by the central government.

The history of Sudan is, in many ways, a study in the subjugation of one people by the other in terms of social, political, religious and economic equalities. The lighter-skinned desert peoples have always been drawn to the South by its promise of water, natural wealth, slaves, ivory and gold. But the darker-skinned Africans have always resisted the Arab intruders who used to overrun their villages, enslaving their people and taking away their livestock.

Indeed, slavery has been one of the critical marks that defined the early history of Sudan. Thousands of Africans were captured from the lands of Southern Sudan by Egyptians and Arabs. Women and children were seized in raids and later traded in or sold. The Arabs, who spread out in the deserts of northern Africa, specialised in slave trade and used religion to back the trade. They argued that while Islam did not condone enslaving Muslims, it supported enslaving pagans as the ultimate penalty for their unbelief. Muslims then considered slavery just because, in Islamic thinking, it exposed the unbeliever to Islamic civilisation.

However, slavery was not a distinctive institution of Sudan's riverine North, nor was it always North-South based. Before the unification of Sudan, an eminent Sudanese scholar and former minister in President Numeiri's government, Dr Mansour Khalid, noted that raids were common among Northern Arab tribes mainly for purposes of concubinage, paramilitary activities or domestic chores.

On the other hand the tribes of the South – the Dinka, Shilluk, the Nuer, the Anuak and others – lived in rudimentary homesteads, herding cows, farming and fishing. They lived in typical African kinship where clan and family bonds defined their societies. They lived from day to day, carrying out their duties, raiding one another, making peace, but referring to no central head. With the arrival of slave hunters and their firearms, these tribes were exposed to weaponry with which they attacked the villages of their enemies and divided up the loot with the providers of weapons.

Historians record that the coming of Islam is what fundamentally changed the nature of Sudanese society and facilitated the division of the country into North and South. Though Christianity had arrived earlier, coming to the Nuba community as early as the sixth century AD, it was Islam that was to become more predominant in the coming years. According to tradition, a missionary sent by Byzantine Empress Theodora arrived in Nobatia and started preaching the gospel about 540 BC. Nobatia was one of the states that had emerged as the political and cultural heirs of the Meriotic kingdom which had been established after the Cush were driven from their land to set up base at Meroe. Under the aegis of Coptic missionaries from Egypt, conversion of Christians began and spread under the watchful eyes of Nubian kings who accepted the form of Christianity practised in Egypt and acknowledged the spiritual authority of the Coptic Patriarch of Alexandria over the Nubian church.

The emergence of Christianity re-opened channels to Mediterranean civilisation and renewed Nubia's cultural and ideological ties to Egypt. The church encouraged literacy in Nubia through its Egyptian-trained clergy and its monastic and cathedral schools. The use of Greek in liturgy eventually gave way to the Nubian language, which was written using an indigenous alphabet that combined elements of the old Mereotic and Coptic scripts.

The Christian Nubian kingdoms prospered and gained in military might, but all this changed when Islam came. Its spread is said to have begun shortly after the Prophet Muhammad's death in 632 AD. By that time, he and his followers had converted most of Arabia's tribes and towns to Islam. This, Muslims maintained, united the individual believer, the state and society under God's will. Islamic rulers therefore exercised temporal and religious authority backed up by the sharia law which encompassed all aspects of the lives of the believers.

Within a generation of Muhammad's death, Arab armies had carried Islam north and east from Arabia into North Africa. Muslims imposed total political control over all the territories they conquered in the name of the *caliph*, the Prophet's successor. Historians record that the Islamic armies won their first North African victory in 643 in Tripoli, Libya. But the Muslim subjugation of all North Africa took about 75 years. The Arabs invaded Nubia in 642 and 652 and destroyed its cathedral. Even though the Nubians put up a strong defence forcing the Arabs to accept an armistice, the spread of Islam was not halted.

Contacts between Nubians and Arabs were established long before Islam came to the scene. The Arabisation of the Nile Valley had began years before and it took about 1,000 years to be fully accomplished. It was mainly attributed to the fact that Arab nomads continually wandered into the region in search of fresh pasturage and Arab seafarers and merchants also traded in the Red Sea ports for spices and slaves. Intermarriage and assimilation also rapidly facilitated Arabisation. Indeed, slave trade was a cardinal precept of commerce between the Arabs and the Nubians. This practice was to spread further into the region.

About the time the Ottomans brought northern Nubia into their orbit, a new power had risen in southern Nubia. The Funj had supplanted the remnants of the old Christian kingdom of Alua and in 1504, a Funj leader, Amara Dunqas, founded the Black Sultanate at Sannar. This black sultanate was to become the keystone of the Funj Empire. The Funj state included a loose confederation of sultanates and dependent tribal chieftaincies drawn together under the suzerainty of Sanna's *mek*, or Sultan. At the peak of its power in the mid-17th century, Sannar repulsed the northward advance of the Nilotic Shilluk people up the White Nile and compelled many of them to submit to Funj authority. After this victory, historians record the *mek* Badi II Abu Duqn (1642-81) sought to centralise the government of the confederacy at Sannar. To implement this policy, Badi introduced a standing Army of slave soldiers that would free Sannar from dependence on Vassal sultans for military assistance and would provide the *mek* with the means to enforce his will. This was a wrong move. It alienated the dynasty from the Funj warrior aristocracy which in turn deposed the reigning *mek* in 1718 and placed one of their own on the throne of Sannar. The Funj dynasty continued to expand when they took control of much of Kordofan. But buffeted by heavy demands on the defence of the sultanate, the Funj's resources began to decline.

****

Over in Darfur, the homeland of the Fur, Islamisation started occurring on a large scale between 1682 and 1722 when the sultan imported teachers, built mosques and compelled his subjects to become Muslims. In the 18th century, several sultans consolidated the dynasty's hold on Darfur, established a capital at Al Fashir, and contested the Funj control of Kordofan. The sultans prospered from slave trade on whose traders they levied taxes and export duties on slaves sent to Egypt. They also took a share of the slaves brought into Darfur. Naturally, some household slaves advanced to prominent positions in the courts of sultans, and the power exercised by these slaves provoked a violent reaction among the traditional class of Fur officeholders in late 18th century. The rivalry between the slave and traditional elite caused recurrent unrest throughout the next century.

Darfur is mostly semi-arid plains that cannot support a dense population. There is, however, one area in and around the Jebal Marra Mountains which is the exception. It was from bases in these mountains that a series of groups expanded to control the region.

The Daju, inhabitants of Jebel Marra, may have been the dominant group in Darfur in the earliest period recorded. How long they ruled the region is uncertain, for little has been recorded on them, save a list of kings. Tradition, however, has it that the Daju dynasty was displaced, and Islam introduced about the 14th century by another group called the Tunjur, which was thought to be of Arab origin. The first Tunjur king is said to have been Ahmed el Makur, who married the daughter of the last Daju monarch. Ahmed ruled the area with an iron fist, reducing many chiefs to submission. Under him, the region prospered. His great-grandson, the sultan Dali, is a celebrated figure in Darfur history. He was a Fur on his mother's side. He divided the country into provinces and established a penal code which, under the title of Kitab Dali or Dali's Book, is still preserved and differs in some respects from the Quranic law. His grandson, Soleiman, disrespectfully called Solon, (which means the Arab or the Red), reigned from 1596 to 1637. He was a great warrior and a devoted Muslim, and is considered as the founder of the Keira dynasty. Soleiman's grandson, Ahmed Bahr, who ruled from 1682 to 1722, made Islam the religion of the state and increased the prosperity of the country by encouraging immigration from Bornu and Bargimi. His rule extended east of the Nile as far as the banks of the Atbara. But this system of dynasty was to create a major friction. Each successive king wanted their sons to be heirs and in cases where one king had many sons, they wanted each of the sons to rule in turns. But once on the throne, the sons attempted to make their own sons heirs which in turn led to an intermittent civil war that lasted until 1785. Major internal divisions occurred which badly affected the prosperity of Darfur.

During this period, one of the most capable of the monarchs was Sultan Mohammed Terab, one of the sons of a former King, Ahmad Bukr. He led a number of successive campaigns and, in 1785, led an army onslaught against the Funj but did not go beyond Omdurman. Here he was stopped by the Nile and could not get his army across the river. Unwilling to give up the project, Teirab remained in Omdurman for months and the army started becoming disaffected. Some stories have it that Teirab was poisoned by his wife at the instigation of some disaffected chiefs and the army returned to Darfur. The throne did not go to his son. Rather it went to his brother Abd al-Rahman. It was during Rahman's reign that Napoleon Bonaparte was campaigning in Egypt. In 1799, Abd al-Rahman wrote to congratulate Bonaparte on his defeat of the Mamelukes. Bonaparte is said to have responded to this by asking the sultan to send him by the next caravan 2,000 black slaves upwards of 16 years old, who were strong and vigorous.

His son Mohammed-al-Fadhl succeeded him but was for some time under the control of an energetic eunuch called Mohammed Kurra. He, however, ultimately wrested himself from him and became independent, his reign lasting until 1838 when he died of leprosy. Al-

Fadhl devoted himself to the subjection of the semi-independent Arab tribes who lived in the country, notably the Rizeigat, of whom thousands he killed. In 1821, he lost the province of Kordofan which in that year was conquered by the Egyptians. An army sent to reclaim the province was routed by the Egyptians whose grander intention was to conquer the entire Darfur, but who encountered difficulties consolidating their hold on the Nile region and had, therefore, to abandon those plans.

When Al Fadhl died in 1838, one of his 40 sons, Mohammed Hassan, was appointed successor. He was a religious but an avaricious man. In 1856, he went blind and for the rest of his reign his sister ZamZam was the *de facto* ruler of the sultanate.

Beginning the year Hassan went blind, a Khartoum businessman al-Zubayr Rahma began to set up operation in the land of south Darfur. He set up a network of trading posts which were defended by well armed forces. Soon, he had a sprawling state under his rule. This area was known as Bahr el Ghazal and had long been the source of the goods that Darfur would trade to Egypt and North Africa. These goods mainly consisted of slaves and ivory. The natives of Bahr el Ghazal paid tribute to Darfur. When Hassan died in 1873, the succession passed to his youngest son, Ibrahim, who soon found himself engaged in a conflict with al-Zubayr. But al-Zubayr had the critical support of the Egyptians to whom he had become an ally and with whose cooperation he embarked on conquering Darfur. The resultant war ended with the kingdom being destroyed. Ibrahim was killed in battle in 1874 and his uncle, Hassab Alla, who had sought to maintain the independence of the country, was captured in 1875 and moved to Cairo with his family.

Under the Egyptian rule, the Darfurians were restive and mounted a number of revolts. In 1879, the British General, Gordon, who was then governor of the Sudan, suggested the reinstatement of the ancient royal family. This was not done. When a new governor, Slatin Bey was appointed, he attempted to defend the province against the forces of the self-proclaimed Mahdi Muhammed Ahmad who were led by a Rizeigat sheik called Madibbo but was obliged to surrender in 1883. Darfur was then incorporated in the Mahdi's dominion. His rule was, to many Darfurians, as bad as that of the Egyptians and the region plunged into another state of constant warfare. This eventually led to the gradual withdraw of Mahdi's forces from Darfur. Following the overthrow of the Mahdi's successor at Omdurman in 1898, the new government of Sudan, which as an Anglo-Egyptian venture, recognised Ali Dinar, a grandson of Mohammed-al-Fadhl, as sultan of Darfur. Under Dinnar, Darfur enjoyed a period of peace and a *de facto* return to independence.

However, in 1916, during World War I, Ali Dinar allied with the Ottoman Empire and declared war on Britain. This was crushed and the Sultan was killed. Darfur's independence was lost and it was incorporated into British-ruled Sudan, subsequently becoming part of the Republic of Sudan on the country's independence in 1956. After independence, it became a major power base of the Umma Party, led by Sadiq al-Mahdi. In 1994, Darfur was divided into three federal states within Sudan: Northern (Shamal), Southern (Janub) and Western (Gharb). Northern Darfur's capital is Al Fashir, Southern's is Nyala and Western's is Al Junaynah.

Darfur was to suffer its own special problems under the Sudanese Government. It became the scene of a bloody rebellion in 2003 against the Arab-dominated, Sudanese government. Two local rebel groups, the Justice and Equality movement (JEM) and the Sudanese Liberation Army (SLA) accused the government of oppressing non-Arabs in favour of Arabs. In response, the government mounted a campaign of aerial bombardment, supporting the onslaught with a ground attack mounted by an Arab militia, the Janjaweed. The militia, which the government supported, committed major human rights violation, including mass killings, looting and systematic rape of the non-Arab population of Darfur. They frequently burned down whole villages driving the survivors to flee into refugee camps mainly in Darfur and Chad. By 2004, 50,000 to 80,000 people had been killed and at least a million displaced. Darfur, like Southern Sudan, was the scene of a major humanitarian crisis. But in terms of human rights violation, Darfur has been a special case of a completely traumatised people and a tragedy of stupendous proportions that enacts itself daily even as peace in Southern Sudan was being sought.

****

Even after the abolition of slave trade, the colonial legacy bequeathed Sudan left it badly fragmented. This was exacerbated by its relations with Egypt and later the British. Modern relations between Sudan and Egypt began in 1820 when an Egyptian army under Ottoman command invaded Sudan. In the years following the invasion, Egypt expanded its area of control into Sudan down the Red Sea coast and towards East Africa's Great Lakes region. The 64-year period of Egyptian rule, which ended in 1885, left deep marks on Sudan's political and economic systems. But in 1898, Sudan again fell under the combined control of Britain and Egypt. This was a direct result of a man called Herbert Kitchener's (later Lord Kitchener) efforts to start the reconquest of Sudan. In 1892, Kitchener became *sirdar*, or Commander, of the Egyptian army and implemented Britain's decision to reconquer Sudan from the Arabs. This decision resulted in part from international developments that required that the country be brought under British supervision. In many ways this was out of fear that if Britain did not do so, another power would gladly conquer Sudan and take advantage of its instability to acquire territories previously annexed to Egypt. By the 1890s, British, French and Belgians had laid claims on the Nile waters. Further, Britain wanted to establish control over the Nile to safeguard a planned irrigation dam at Aswan. In 1895 the British Government authorised Kitchener to launch a campaign to reconquer Sudan. Britain provided men and material while Egypt financed the expedition. This Anglo-Egyptian assault to reclaim Sudan accomplished its mission in 1899. This was also the year an Anglo-Egyptian agreement restored Egyptian rule in Sudan as part of a condominium (or joint authority) exercised by Britain and Egypt. Egypt then was a quasi-protectorate of Britain. Britain by then had become deeply involved in Egyptian matters but it was not until 1914 that it declared Egypt its protectorate.

Britain then took over the management of South Sudan leaving the North under nominal Egyptian rule. The British saw Southern Sudan as a buffer in which it would protect some central interests, key of which were Christian values and beliefs, English language and its legal tradition. In fact, the British encouraged the presence of missionaries and deliberately isolated the South from the North.

From the beginning of the Anglo-Egyptian condominium, the British sought to modernise Sudan by applying European technology to its underdeveloped economy. It also injected a strong dose of liberal English traditions. But all this was concentrated in the urban areas. The remote and undeveloped provinces like Equatoria, Bahr al Ghazal and Upper Nile received little official attention until after World War I. What little attention they got was in the form of efforts to suppress tribal warfare and the slave trade.

The British justified this policy by claiming that the South was not ready for exposure to the modern world. In fact, they allowed the South to only develop along indigenous lines by closing the region to outsiders. As a result, the region remained isolated and backward. A few Arab merchants controlled the region's scanty commercial activities, while Arab bureaucrats administered whatever laws existed. Christian missionaries, mainly the Verona Fathers, operated schools and medical clinics and provided limited social services. Later, the British authorities were to expel the few Arab merchants doing business and the Arab administrators in the South and reinforced its ban on Northern Sudanese entering or working in the South. This served to sever the south's last economic contacts with the North.

The colonial administration also discouraged the spread of Islam, Arab customs and the wearing of Arab dresses by the Southerners.

At the same time, they made efforts to revitalise African customs and tribal life that slave trade had disrupted. In 1930, the British issued a directive stating that blacks in the southern provinces were considered a people distinct from the northern Muslims and that the region should be prepared for eventual integration with British East Africa (present day Kenya, Uganda and Tanzania).

Meanwhile, being predominantly Muslim, Egypt encouraged Islam in the North while the British continued to concentrate economic and social development in the North. In time, disproportionate political and economic power came to be centred more in the North. The South felt left out and the two region's cultural and religious identities became too fractious. The stage was set for discord.

In 1947, Britain realised the inevitability of independence and embarked on fusing the separately ruled regions. It gave political power to the Northern elite at the expense of the South. This immediately sowed the seeds of war in the emerging independent State. For Southerners, independence merely meant a change of masters of one colour to another. At issue here was the control over state power. Peter Nyok Kok, a lawyer by profession and a native of Southern Sudan, observes that it was felt that a section of the Sudanese controlled the state power by inheritance from the British colonial authority to the exclusion of other social and ethno-regional groups.

The Northerners merely took over from the British and started defining the new nation according to their Arab-Islamic identity. The bulk of government officials appointed to replace the British ones came from the North. In 1956, the Legislative Assembly appointed a committee to draft a national constitution. At the end of it, only three of the 46 members were from the South. The Southern delegation walked out after its repeated call for a federal constitution was outvoted.

Before that, the Southerners had been excluded from the epochal agreement on January 10, 1953, between the Egyptian Government and all the Northern political parties on self-determination for the Sudan to be preceded by self-government. Many felt that the Southerners were excluded not because they did not have a political party as it was claimed, but because their representatives felt that self-determination and independence should be delayed until "backward areas of the Sudan catch up with the North."

Even before independence in 1956, a violent conflict had broken out, fuelled by the apprehension of the Southerners that independence held nothing new for them. There were riots and a bloody rebellion ensued. Rumours that the army's southern corps would be disarmed and transferred to the North led to a mutiny that ended with over 300 people, mostly Northerners, dead. Two years after independence, the Army, led by General Ibrahim Aboud, seized power. The military regime suppressed opposition and imprisoned politicians, trade unionists, students and communists. Aboud created the Supreme Council of the Armed Forces to rule Sudan, a body that contained officers affiliated with the Muslim brotherhood. He also launched a controversial programme of "Islamisation" which was targeted at the South through aggressive proselytism. In February 1964, he ordered the mass expulsion of foreign missionaries from the South. He then closed Parliament to cut off outlets for Southern complaints.

Aboud was not a consensus seeker. From the outset, he was hostile to the South and accentuated the economic marginalisation of this part of the country which further entrenched the uneven development that started with the colonial masters and which was one of the critical factors fuelling the hostility between North and South. 96 per cent of industrial establishments were based in the Northern and Central Sudan, 44 per cent of these were located in Khartoum alone while 97 percent of the labour force was concentrated in north and central Sudan, with 62 percent coming from Khartoum.

Of the 205 banks in Sudan before the outbreak of a vicious civil war in 1983, 15 were in the South, Khartoum had 78, Central region 46, Northern region 25 and Darfur region 11. There were also striking disparities in education. Northern region had 37 academic secondary schools, Central region 60, Khartoum 55, Kordofan 18, Darfur 11 and the three Southern regions had a total of 15. From 1974 to 1984, the average annual admission to the University of Khartoum was 1,700 students out of which 22 on average were Southerners.

Sudan then boasted a relatively developed centre in the north-central riverine Sudan and an undeveloped periphery represented by the Southern Sudan, the Nuba Mountains, the Western Sudan and the Southern Blue Nile. These disparities were wrought by the British in the 50 years of colonial rule. When they realised what they had done, they hastily embarked on trying to make up in the South. This yielded the Zande Cotton Scheme, the Yirol Oil-Mill and a number of intermediate schools were started. But this was too little too late.

Neither Aboud nor the succeeding regimes bothered to correct this anomaly, in fact, they perpetuated the uneven development. Aboud's Ten Year Plan of Economic and Social Development (1962/63-1970/71) had five objectives:
1. to attain an appreciable increase in the real incomes per head through a satisfactory growth of the total national production,
2. to promote the broadening of the structure of the Sudan economy,
3. to achieve a considerable increase in the export and import substitution,

4. to further improve social conditions and services including general and technical education, and
5. to create sufficient opportunities of productive employment.

The latter objective was the maintenance of a relatively stable price level. Nowhere was the problem of socio-economic disparities among the regions recognised or singled out for redress. Thus the disparities between the centre and the periphery widened.

By 1964, the Northern and Central Sudan boasted of major development in irrigation schemes, infrastructural constructions and over 37 import substituting factories and industries. Most of these were located in the Khartoum area. On the other hand, the peripheral Sudan only had token schemes over the same period, key of which were the Wau fruit canning factory in the South, dairy products scheme at Gazalagawatzat and an agricultural scheme in Darfur. Most of these schemes failed and the government allowed them to wither on the vine.

In the area of education, the Aboud regime expanded secular education in the North in the academic and technical fields and expanded organic schools in the South as part of a larger policy of Islamisation and Arabisation.

Repression forced thousands of Southerners into exile in the neighbouring Uganda, Kenya, Ethiopia and the Central African Republic. Cut off from their country, the refugees came together and formed opposition organisations, the most significant of which was the Sudan African National Union. SANU petitioned the United Nations and the Organisation of African Unity to intervene, arguing for self-determination and a peaceful solution to the Sudan problem.

As SANU emerged as a political force, a Southern Sudan military movement was taking shape. It was known as Anya-nya, meaning snake poison, and was composed of mainly former soldiers and police officers from the 1955 mutiny. It materialised from the bush one day to ecstatic support from the Southerners. SANU was, however, suspicious of Anya-nya and initially condemned its violent tactics, it favoured rapprochement over violence. But they were to be proved wrong. Aboud responded with a crushing military campaign which drove over half a million Southerners into exile. The war, however, intensified with Anya-nya fiercely locked in an armed conflict with government forces.

The government stubbornly refused to recognise that its failure to incorporate the Southerners into the political and economic mainstream of the nation was the root cause of the problem. Following the brutal repression, even SANU started seeing conflict as the only language the government could understand. It started organising guerrilla attacks. By 1963, a fully fledged civil war had broken out.

In 1964, Aboud was overthrown by a Northern civilian uprising. Power changed from the military to civilians with Sirr al Khatim al Khalifa becoming Prime Minister to head a transitional government. A small door of peace opened with some Northerners extending an olive branch to the Southerners. The new civilian regime, which operated under the 1956 Transitional Constitution, tried to end political factionalism by establishing a coalition government. But the people did not easily warm up to the reappearance of political parties because of their divisiveness during the Aboud regime. Two political parties emerged to represent the South: the Sudan African National Union (SANU) founded in 1963 and led by William Deng and Saturino Lahure (a Roman Catholic priest) and it operated among refugee groups and guerrilla forces. The other was the Southern Front, a mass organisation led by Stanislaus Payasama that had worked underground during the Aboud regime and which functioned openly within the Southern provinces. They presented the best option yet for peace between the North and the South.

But a round-table conference in Khartoum failed to bring a political settlement. The Northern politicians were not prepared to meet the Southerners half way. The Islamists and Arabists were dead against the granting of any sort of autonomy to the South. The Muslim brothers saw the problem as a simple one of Christians versus Islam and they were more in favour of the latter.

The war not only intensified, but it also drew in other countries which started taking sides openly, some of them supported Anya-nya, while others openly supported the government. Israel, for instance, became a financier of Anya-nya, and so did the rebels from the Democratic Republic of Congo. Israel shipped weapons captured from Egypt in the Yom Kippur war of 1967 in the hope that this would encourage the Government to limit its assistance to mid-east nations. Israel also established its base in Uganda and started training and supporting Anya-nya. Meanwhile, Ethiopia also gave sanctuary to the rebels from where they launched their attacks.

Khartoum immediately responded by strengthening its alliance with Egypt while the United Arab Emirates, Algeria, Saudi Arabia and Kuwait also started providing the Government with arms. The biggest financier of the government was, however, the Soviet Union.

As the war raged, another coup d'etat was executed in 1969 and General Jaafar al-Numeiri came to power. This was at the height of the Cold War and because Sudan straddles the Nile and has access to the Red Sea, it was a potent battleground in this War. Numeiri courted the Soviets and other communist countries and also allied himself with the Arab cause in a bid to contain Israel. After he brought Sudan into the Arab Federation with Egypt and Libya, Israel's support for Anya-nya peaked. Similarly, Soviet military and financial assistance also increased. Prospects for peace were dim. Sudan had all of a sudden become the battleground in which the Cold War players were flexing their might.

In 1971, an abortive military coup dramatically changed Sudan's domestic political landscape as well as its international allies. The coup was engineered by the Soviets and Numeiri immediately changed alliances and started warming up to the West and most Arab states. Relations with the Soviet bloc deteriorated. Consequently, the Soviets terminated their support for the government and without its biggest financier, the army weakened and Numeiri realised that he could not continue with an unpopular war against a determined rebel group. He started gravitating towards peace.

This led to an agreement signed with Emperor Haille Sellasie of Ethiopia in which both leaders agreed to cease assisting each other's separatist movements. Later that year, Numeiri signed an agreement with President Idi Amin of Uganda, ending Uganda's support for the rebels in exchange for a similar arrangement with Anya-nya. Amin ejected Israelis from Uganda, Ethiopia ceased offering Anya-nya sanctuary and the movement started a slow process of withering. Numeiri could now push forward his agenda for peace, knowing only too well that a weakened Anya-nya had no choice than to sail along. With little opposition to ending the war in the South and a fearsome monopoly of power, Numeiri accelerated peace efforts in 1971.

Meanwhile, Anya-nya mutated from a disorganised, disparate group plagued by ethnic and personal rivalries into a more unified political force. Colonel Joseph Lagu seized authority, united its officers under his command and declared the formation of the Southern Sudan Liberation Movement. The unity proved invaluable in the peace negotiations that began in Addis Ababa later that year.

Enjoying full command, Lagu convinced his followers to accept Numeiri's proposal for peace "within the framework of one Sudan". An agreement that included power-sharing, security guarantees for Southerners and the granting of political and economic autonomy to the South was hammered out. Under the Agreement, former Anya-nya soldiers were to be included in the national army in proportion to the national population. Six thousand Southerners were to be recruited into the army's Southern command, an important security provision. Later to be known as the Addis Ababa Agreement, the document was signed in the Ethiopian capital in 1972.

For some time, peace prevailed. There was excitement. Sudan, the biggest country in Africa was going to become a mighty force in the continent and the Middle East. Numeiri supported the Camp David Accords between Egypt and Israel and as a result, the United States poured aid into Sudan making it one of the biggest recipients of American aid after Egypt and Israel. Numeiri's government borrowed more than 21 billion dollars from the International Monetary Fund and the World Bank and the Arab countries of the Gulf started financing some of its biggest developments. International businessmen started investing heavily, constructing the world's biggest sugar factory at Kenana, south of Sudan, and an Anglo-French consortium brought the world's biggest digger to Sudan to construct the Jonglei Canal. This was a grand scheme that was going to use water from the Sudd to irrigate Northern Sudan and Egypt. It would create an initial 200,000 acres in the South and semi-nomadic tribes would be settled on the reclaimed land. The project, which would cost 75 million dollars, was intended to bring together Western technology and expertise and Arab money to exploit Sudan's natural wealth. Several industrial projects interlinked with agriculture were either initiated or completed. Sugar and textile industries took the bulk of these initiatives. The road network was improved and many master plans to develop a more comprehensive roadwork were put in place. As notes Khalid Mansour in his book, *Numeiri and the Revolution of Dis-May*, a much more ambitious network was envisaged in the master plan and a few sections were initiated. A master plan for transportation on both rail and road and a 25-year plan for agriculture development, sectional plans for industry, a plan for storage and another for river transportation was put in place. All these plans were financed through technical assistance from Kuwait, the Federal Republic of Germany and other friendly countries. The road network included the completion of the Medani-Sannar-Kosti road and the Port Sudan-Khartoum road to pass through Kassala. In addition, work was initiated, according to the master plan, in the West, White Nile, Blue Nile and the Southern Gelabat on the Ethiopian-Sudanese borders.

The Sudan railways also received a lot of attention. Being the only effective transport network linking different parts of the country, it was also one of the oldest in Africa having been started in 1905. It linked nearly 6,000 kilometres of railroad in different parts of the country. As Khalid reports, the railway system had increasingly deteriorated in the late 1960s owing to outmoded methods of operation, lack of maintenance and ill-defined worker-management relations among a host of other reasons. The only extensions that had been introduced in the system since independence were carried out in the Abboud era. This included the first railway linkage between North and South-Babanoosa-Nyala in western Sudan in 1959, Sennar-Damazin in the Blue Nile in 1958, Babanoosa-Wau (south west) in 1962, and Girba-New Halfa in eastern Sudan in 1962.

The years of promise, as Mansour, who served in the government as Foreign Minister, calls them, also witnessed a complete revolution in the field of telecommunications. A microwave network was established to link different parts of the extensive Sudan, with a view to integrating it with the African telecommunication system. The network within the Sudan extended from Khartoum to Sannar via Madani, to continue at a later stage to Kassala. Another one stretched from Khartoum to Port Sudan via Atbara, to be extended to Halfa and eventually to be linked to Aswan-Cairo. A third network was to go out from Khartoum to the Southern Sudan to link the Arab and African worlds. Further, a satellite station was completed in 1974, linking Sudan with the outside world. In all the main cities of Sudan, other satellite stations were constructed, helping to improve both telephone communications and TV transmission.

But the most promising was the master plan for agriculture. The sector registered impressive records of growth with the areas under crop increasing by three-and-a half million acres. Major agricultural projects, of which some had been on the drawing board for years, were put in motion. Those projects included the Rahad Scheme, which involved three provinces and brought 300,000 acres into cultivation, in which cotton and groundnuts were grown along a fifty-mile canal linking the Blue Nile and the Rahad River. The 180 million pound project was financed by the International Development Agency, the Arab Fund for Economic and Social Development and the Kuwaiti, Saudi, Sudanese and US governments. The scheme included plans to accommodate some 14,000 families and provide employment for 90,000 workers. The Kenana Sugar Plant also stood out as one of the biggest plants during the years of promise.

Alarmed by the cost of imported sugar and attracted by the prospect of increasing its foreign currency reserves, the government authorised the British company, Lonrho, of which Tiny Rowland was chairman, to undertake a feasibility study. Plans were drawn for the world's largest sugar plantation irrigated by a complex canal system. The scheme included a refinery to yield some 30,000 tons of sugar a year, expanding its capacity to one million tons. This was enough to satisfy much of the Middle East market. To finance these projects, the government had borrowed nearly 300 million dollars, 42 per cent of which came from Arab countries, while the rest came from the World Bank Western and European countries and the African Development Bank.

With this impressive development plan, Sudan was in a clover. The Americans started showing much more interest in South Sudan. The American ambassador to the United Nations then, George Bush, who was later to become US President and who at the time was also a Texan oil man, visited Khartoum and advised Numeiri that remote-sensing intelligence had showed that oil might be found in the south-eastern part of the country, especially the triangle of land located in the Sudd region between Bentiu, Nasir and Malakal. In 1974, the American oil company, Chevron, was granted a licence for oil exploration.

In spite of all the hope the early Numeiri years inspired, Sudan's attempt at rapid development was to founder on the rocks of corruption and a rigid government that allowed apparent success to get into its head. Within a few years, the hopes for a prosperous Sudan started fading and its claim to being the breadbasket of the Arab world degenerated into a chimera. Numeiri became an autocrat, intolerant of dissent, playing his ministers against one another and serially dismissing those ministers that were perceived to be too independent or disloyal to the regime. Corruption crept in and discontent from some Northern hard-liners that were unhappy with Numeiri (whom they accused of ceding out too much authority to the Southerners) started being felt. They also felt that the Agreement had failed to grant Islam a special place in the nation's affairs and instead lumped it together with Christianity for a competition of place. They rubbished the Addis Ababa Agreement and mounted stiff opposition to Numeiri. In 1976, a coup was mounted by Sadiq Al Mahdi, former Prime Minister and a hard liner but it failed. This was the third uprising, the other two having been carried out in 1970 and 1975. They were all backed by Libya.

The coup had a profound effect on Numeiri who felt that his power base had been severely challenged. He feared that a fourth uprising might well succeed and he therefore decided to appease the hardliners. He introduced a policy of reconciliation in an attempt to win over the North and increase his power base. He encouraged the conservatives to come from exile in exchange for top Government positions. This process led to the appointment of opposition leaders and the hardliners to prominent positions. Among them were members of a group called the Ansar movement which was an organisation of radical religious fundamentalists and who followed the conservative teachings of the Mahdi who ruled Sudan in 1880s. The Ansar movement believed in the sharia law, insisting that a good Muslim nation should have the sharia law as the bulwark of its legislation.

The sharia law provides for such punishments as amputation, stoning and flogging. Under it, unbelievers, who include Christians and members of other religions, may not rule over the believers. This meant that the sharia law closed off all the highest echelons of the government to non-Muslims. Effectively, this meant that the Southerners had no hope of ascending to the high places of power.

Numeiri then appointed members of the Ansar and the Muslim brotherhood into top government positions. Hassan al-Turabi, Mahdi's brother-in-law and the leader of the Muslim brotherhood, was appointed the Attorney General. Turabi embarked on a process of making Sudan's laws more Islamic.

In 1977, the hardliners, led by Mahdi, demanded that Numeiri review the Addis Ababa Agreement, especially its provisions for security, border trade, language, culture and religion. Numeiri obliged and gave in to many of the hardliners' wishes. The Southerners protested but they had already been squeezed out of the government. Resentment was now at an all time high.

In 1978, matters became thoroughly complicated when Chevron struck oil north of the town of Bentiu in an area inhabited by the Nuer and the Dinka. The area is located on the north-south border and the oil was located at a spot known as Pan Thou, or "thorn tree" in the Nuer language. In a move seen as an attempt to appropriate the oil by the Northerners, Chevron and the government insisted on changing the Dinka name of the place to Heglig, the Arabic name for the same tree.

The oil was to prove one of the biggest bones of contention in Sudan. Under the Addis Ababa Agreement, the Southern regional government was to receive the revenues from any minerals or other deposits found on Southern land, agricultural and commercial activities. The government could not countenance this, it wanted the provisions changed. This was slightly difficult. In 1978, Numeiri and Turabi attempted to change the boundaries between North and South so that the area in which the oil was would belong to another province called "Unity." The South went wild. Riots erupted everywhere and the government backed down. But the seeds of mistrust and tension sown by the government's recapitulation on the stipulates of the Addis Ababa Agreement were fast germinating.

But Numeiri subtly went on with his oppressive measures. He, for instance, replaced Southern troops with Northerners in Bentiu, the area of the oil deposits. In the Bentiu area, a movement calling itself Anya-nya II emerged and clashes broke out in various parts of the South. In 1983, a battalion of Southern soldiers stationed in the town of Bor mutinied over a pay dispute with their commanders. At the same time, grievances of the Southerners were rising and Numeiri was becoming increasingly apprehensive that half of the southern Command was controlled by former Anya-nya soldiers. At the same time, southern troops of the 105th battalion refused orders to lay down their arms and be transferred to the North. They feared that they would be taken to Iraq to join other Sudanese contingents fighting in the country's war against Iran and leave the South vulnerable to an all-Northern unit. Numeiri ordered an attack on these soldiers. Colonel John Garang, a Dinka army officer, was sent to quell the mutiny and led the Southern unit on that mission. He never went back. He and his

Sumbeiywo as a Major in the Kenya Army and Military Assistant to Gen. J.K. Mulinge.

Lorna in a 1970 picture when she met Sumbeiywo in Nakuru.

Sumbeiywo in 1985.

Sumbeiywo (Left) in France in 1969 during an athletics meet. He was then studying at Sandhurst.

Sumbeiywo & his wife, Lorna at Married Quarters, Moi Air Base in 1985.

Sumbeiywo with his wife Lorna, when he was a Brigadier in the Airforce.

Left: Sumbeiywo and his family outside Married Quarters at Moi Air Base in 1983. Missing from the picture is Gideon. This Peugeot 204 is the one that was used to evacuate former President Moi from his farm in Kabarak during the 1982 coup d´etat.

Sumbeiywo and daughters (L to R): Flora, Rose, Anne and Joan in 1992.

Sumbeiywo, Lorna and sons Paul & Gideon (standing in front) in 1992.

Sumbeiywo & Lorna at a church service in Thika Military camp.

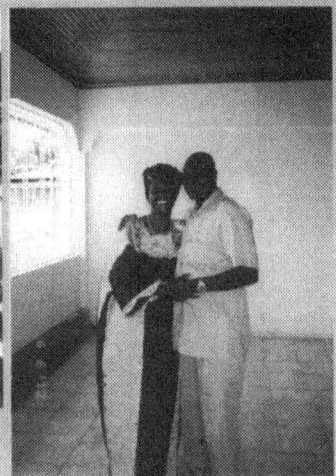
Sumbeiywo & Lorna in a happy moment.

Sumbeiywo & larger family, from left: Mary, Bilah, Catherine, Jonathan, Rosaleen, Lazaro, Elijah and Lorna (lying down).

Sumbeiywo & Lorna at Kahawa Officers' Mess.

Sumbeiywo, trying his hand at mechanics.

(L to R): Bishop Silas Yego, Sumbeiywo and Lorna at a graduation ceremony at Scott Theological College, Machakos in 2004.

A youthful Sumbeiywo in a reflective mood.

Sumbeiywo during a fund raising at St. Peters on the Hill Church, Moi Air Base. With him is Rev. Paul Lantey.

The Lekwelet, in which Sumbeiywo and siblings used to carry water gourds.

unit fled, taking weapons and equipment and inspiring a succession of desertions and mutinies in the South throughout that year. They found sanctuary in Ethiopia from where Garang started urging the Sudanese to rise up against Numeiri's government and founded the Sudan People's Liberation Army (SPLA). At that time the Ethiopian Government was locked in a war with Eritrea and it thus welcomed the mutineers as it saw in the rebels a mirror image of its own problems with the famine and the civil war already raging in that country. In any case, after Haile Sellasie was overthrown by a Marxist military regime, Sudan resumed its support for Eritrea. The Ethiopian Government therefore was only too happy to help the rebels fighting the Sudanese Government.

Feeling the heat, Numeiri stiffened. On June 5, 1983, he issued "Republican Order Number One", abrogating the Addis Ababa Agreement and returning regional powers to the central government. This effectively destroyed the South's autonomy and carved it into three powerless administrative provinces. It also transferred the South's financial powers to the central government and declared Arabic, not English, the region's official language. The order also abolished direct secret ballot elections for the southern regional assembly and dissolved its powers to veto central government laws. It cancelled the sections of the Addis Ababa Agreement that guaranteed local control of the armed forces in the South and transferred this responsibility to central government.

In a further heave towards authoritarianism, Numeiri officially transformed Sudan into an Islamic state, decreeing in September 1983 that sharia law "be the sole guiding force behind the law of the Sudan." This was despite the fact that one-third of the population was non-Muslim. This is also what the hardliners in the cabinet had all along been agitating for. They were thrilled, but the Southerners were livid at the abrogation of the Agreement. Violent protests erupted again and Southerners coalesced around SPLM/A. John Garang emerged as a potent force against the government.

Undeterred, Numeiri continued with his assault on the constitution and the Addis Ababa Agreement. He dichotomised the country between the believers (Muslims) and the infidels (the Southerners) and used sharia to subjugate them. He often accused his fellow Muslims of being drunk and womanising whenever they fell foul of him. Petty thieves had their hands amputated, but the bigger thieves of state coffers went scot-free. As Mansour reports, "he launched his new era of religious puritanism by pouring millions of gallons of alcohol into the Nile." To Numeiri, alcohol was the greatest vice and those who refrained from it were seen as the true Muslims. In Islam then, drinking was a lesser offence punished only by flogging. But according to observers, Numeiri wanted to use it to intimidate the people and keep the Southerners at bay. On the other hand, adultery is a cardinal offence punishable by death. Because of its severity, the sharia dictates that four valid witnesses be produced before indictment, all four having seen at the same time the "vile" deed. To circumvent this, Numeiri invented what he called "attempted adultery". But drinking was easier to detect and Numeiri could choose those he wanted to humiliate and punish at will. This usually happened to his opponents.

In one such incident, when a Regional Minister told Numeiri something he did not like, the Minister was accused of being drunk. The allegation was denied by the accused and the doctor that examined him confirmed that the Minister was sober. Numeiri insisted that his private doctor examine the Minister. Needless to say, the doctor declared the Minister drunk.

Numeiri went ahead and declared a state of emergency and the imposition of martial law later that year. This followed months of civil disturbance, strikes, riots and demonstrations. The first to go on strike were university professors, judges and doctors. The doctors threatened to resign if they were not given a pay rise. Numeiri rejected their demands and they resigned *en masse*. Numeiri, however, issued an ultimatum that if they did not report to work within 72 hours, they would be prosecuted for high treason. The doctors called his bluff. He dissolved the doctors union and arrested the ring-leaders and accused all Sudanese doctors of being Libya's puppets. The engineers and accountants threatened to join the doctors. Fearing an escalation of the crisis, the kind that drove Abboud's regime out, Numeiri, ever the sly politician, decided to lie his way out. He ordered the release of the doctors and, receiving them in his palace, lied to them that he had never issued any order for their arrest and told them that they were free to return to their work and trade unionism and promised that their demands would be met. That was not to be for he thereafter declared a state of emergency and imposed martial law. "In order to protect the faith and the fatherland from schemes of schemers and the mischief of Satan," he announced while declaring the martial law, "and in order to protect the gains of the believing people and fulfil my national duties and constitutional responsibilities, issued Presidential Decree Number 258 (1984) announcing the imposition of martial law throughout the country." He also declared that the Southerners who were fighting with John Garang were enemies of God and development.

The country was in a state of paralysis. Meanwhile, John Garang, who Numeiri never passed an opportunity to vilify, was amassing serious opposition against the government.

10

John Garang

Dr Colonel John Garang de Mabior was born on June 23, 1945, into the southern Dinka Nilotic community in the village of Buk, in Bor County. At a time when education was not a priority to members of the community, Garang immediately went to school, attending Bussere Intermediate School in nearby Wau. Reflecting on those very early years, Garang told the Sudanese national TV in January 2005, "It was only chance; no one in my village could even read."

Garang spent the 1960s as a refugee in socialist Tanzania where he attended high school with Yoweri Museveni, Uganda's President and Paul Kagame, Rwanda's President. He later attended Grinnel College, a liberal arts school in Iowa, America, on a scholarship. Immediately after graduation in 1971, he joined the Anya-nya rebel movement and rapidly gained a reputation as a man wedded to the cause of Southern Sudan. But he did not have adequate time to see much of the action as, shortly after that, Joseph Lagu signed the Addis Ababa Agreement. He did not like this very much. Nevertheless, he joined the Sudanese Army at a time when the army was shunned by educated Southerners. In 1977, his superiors sent him to the US officer training school at Fort Benning in Georgia. He persuaded the army to let him stay on and he earned a doctorate in Agricultural Economics from Iowa State University. His thesis was on the agricultural development of Southern Sudan.

When he founded the SPLM/A, he insisted that the Southerners had a right to self-determination and that their multi-ethnic and multi-religious nature had to be respected. Unlike Anya-nya, John Garang's SPLM/A defined its objectives carefully, arguing that the issues they were fighting for went beyond Southern autonomy. There was the bigger question of self-determination, the need to transform the whole Sudan into a multi-racial, multi-religion and multi-ethnic democratic state. This found favour in many Southerners and gave SPLM/A much support from all those who felt that the government had become too authoritarian, too discriminative and too Islamic. Numeiri had pushed things beyond a point of no return.

When a people feel oppressed for a long time, with no one to speak for them and having all decisions taken by other people for them, nationalism displays itself in the clamour for self-determination. In some of its most useful instances, self-determination addresses the central problem of inter-ethnic relations, inequalities of power, economic and political rights and the right to express and live one's faith. In this context, it insists that human beings cannot be at home with themselves unless they have self-determination. It rests on the premise that people want to speak for themselves, rather than being spoken for. For, as Michael Ignatieff observed in his book, *The Warrior's Honour: Ethnic War and the Modern Conscience*, where ethnic minorities have been subjected to genuine tyranny, where language and culture have been genuinely suppressed, national revivals, even nationalist uprisings, are both inevitable and justified.

However, as Ignatieff again observed, the problem with this kind of nationalism is not the desire for self-determination itself, but the particular "epistemological illusion that you can be at home, you can be understood, only among people like yourself." But the Southerners fight was not premised on this. It was a product of a visceral desire to determine their own destiny, to control their own wealth, and if not so, to have it shared equitably, to be treated equally and to have their values respected, not subordinated to others that the government considered superior.

The Southerners then felt that the fight for equality was an integral part of their destiny. Self-determination, as we shall see later, would form a key bone of contention in the peace process.

Garang assembled his people to fight for these rights. He avoided fighting the war on a religious front preferring to concentrate on the trampled rights of the Southern Sudanese. An inscrutable man, Garang inspired both fear and loathing. As he steered the SPLM/A, he survived several attempts on his life from both within and outside the movement. Those who met him described him as a cunning, proud and purposeful man. Gill Lusk, deputy editor of *Africa Confidential* and a specialist on the Sudan told the BBC, "He is a man with charisma and his leadership qualities are obvious. He is very much a professional military man." To others, Garang came through as a proud and aloof man. As he immersed himself into guerrilla warfare in Africa's longest civil war, he probably became detached and taciturn, a man seeking wise counsel in solitude and from his inner self.

"It's rather difficult to warm up to the man," a Sudan specialist, Petey Moszynki, was quoted as saying by the BBC, "he has this cold outlook, giving you this idea that he is above everybody else."

Among his people, Garang has been described as one who has a terrific sense of humour and has acquired notoriety for his intelligence, determination and grand ideas. "Did you ever see a government pray?" he would often ask his troops, eliciting rounds of laughter, "A Government never goes to church and it never goes to mosque."

His admirers used to say that he was a man who had always known how to juggle a stone and an egg without losing his sight on either. It was these qualities that he brought to SPLM/A. He rallied his people to the cause of Southern Sudan and plunged them into a war whose cause they all understood but whose end nobody could tell.

As Garang honed SPLM/A for the long war, the god who is said to have laughed when he created Sudan smiled at the country once again and intervened to bring new change. For, in 1985, another military coup was staged. Lieutenant General Swar al-Dhahab ousted Numeiri and opened another small door for peace. The process to resolve the crisis started chugging along. Egged on by popular pressure, the SPLM/A joined other political parties, trade unions and the government to the negotiating table. In 1986, the parties signed the Koka Dam Declaration which called for a peace process spearheaded by a National Constitutional Conference.

But even to the conference, the issue of sharia proved too hot a potato. It was left to an incoming civilian government which was headed by Sadiq-Al Mahdi. In his book, *Intervening in Africa, Superpower Peacemaking in a Troubled Continent,* Herman Cohen, the former US Assistant Secretary of State for African Affairs recalled how Mahdi was adamant on the question of sharia: "Sadiq told me that no Government in Khartoum could ever repeal sharia law and expect to get re-elected." Sadiq however "froze" but did not revoke sharia law and offered to hold a constitutional conference to establish a more representative democratic system. But this had immediate ramifications. The fundamentalist National Islamic Front headed by the Islamic scholar, Hassan Al-Turabi, quit the coalition government of Mahdi protesting at what it saw as the weakening of Islamic rule. Mahdi himself complained about Garang's failure to accept whatever little he was doing (like stopping amputations and allowing non-Islamic provinces to opt out of sharia).

Under Mahdi, the government continued to sink into turmoil with successive governments collapsing for failure to agree on social, economic and peace initiatives. There was clearly no path towards peace. Meanwhile, SPLM/A was consolidating its strength, having acquired the backing of Libya, Uganda and Ethiopia. It was now controlling almost the entire South. The government was feeling hemmed in. Forced to confront the enormous losses it was undergoing and the inexorable cost of war, the government was by 1989 willing to negotiate with SPLM/A which also understood very well that any victory by them, should there be any, would be a pyrrhic one. Garang gave Mahdi preconditions for peace, including the convening of a constitutional conference and the expulsion of the hardliners of the National Islamic Front from the cabinet. Mahdi obliged and SPLM/A immediately declared a ceasefire. Mahdi on his part extended a further peace overture to SPLM/A and stopped referring to the organisation as terrorist but an "armed movement."

However, when everything appeared headed for the way of peace, the gods frowned on the country once again. On June 30, 1989, another coup was staged by Brigadier General Omar Hassan Ahmad al-Bashir. The people behind the coup were the hardliners of the National Islamic Front who had been shunted aside by Mahdi. Bashir immediately cancelled all prior arrangements for peace that had been put in place. The proposed constitutional conference was jettisoned and started consolidating political power by destroying the opposition.

Bashir established himself as a hardliner within weeks of seizing power. He imposed a state of emergency, did away with the cabinet and created the Revolutionary Command Council of which he was the chairman and which acted as the cabinet. The RCC revoked the transitional constitution of 1985, abolished Parliament, banned political parties, detained all political party leaders and closed newspapers.

Leaders of student groups, professional associations, unions and political leaders were arbitrarily arrested, incarcerated and often tortured and killed. In one fell swoop, authoritarianism was brought back and the war intensified.

Bashir was not interested in peace, often stalemating talks at the slightest opportunity. Two sessions, in Addis Ababa in August 1989 and in Nairobi in December that year, failed because the parties could not, once again, agree on the contentious issue of sharia law. The NIF fuelled the fires of extremism, holding that where sharia was concerned there were no two ways. It was either the sharia or the highway. Bashir further escalated the war by committing new resources for the army and declared that soldiers fighting in the war were martyrs fighting the Holy War against those who were opposed to God's law (sharia). Bashir courted Arab countries by regularly harping on Pan-Arabism and the purity of Islamic values in his speeches. For this, he was rewarded handsomely. Iraq soon started providing arms and the ties with Libya which Numeiri had banished were restored with Tripoli bringing in armaments and oil. Later, when Iraq started feeling the pressure of the Gulf War, Bashir turned to another Arab ally, Iran for support.

Motivated by what they saw as *jihad*, the army vowed not to give up any inch of the soil to the Africans and government officials rushed to their allies abroad to plead for assistance for what they called "winning back Arab towns captured by African infidels." On the other hand, Garang and SPLM/A refused to recognise Bashir as President because the military coup that brought him to power had ousted a democratically elected leader, Mahdi, and they denounced the military junta as "running dogs of Islamic fundamentalism". On their part, the government dismissed Garang as a communist and an agent of Ethiopia, the neighbour with whom the Sudanese Government had been locked in a bitter war as a result of its support for Eritrean rebels.

Garang fought on and SPLM/A became the sharpest thorn in the side of the government. But its ability and success was too dependent on other forces rather than those within it. In May 1991, the collapse of the Mengistu regime in Ethiopia, which had provided SPLM/A with an operational base, military and financial support, dealt a severe blow to SPLM/A. The new regime was composed of rebel groups which were backed by the Sudanese government. They were hostile to SPLM/A and Garang was left with no choice but to evacuate his military base. More than 200,000 Sudanese refugees escaped from their camps in Ethiopia back to Southern Sudan. The government, sensing the likely annihilation of rebellion, became more brutal. In May 1991, the Sudanese Air Force bombed Southern Sudanese refugees as they fled their camps in Ethiopia.

This, however, did not daunt Garang and SPLM/A. They fought on, but as the pressure from the government mounted, SPLM/A's top command was soon to realise that the army had a more formidable challenge than that mounted by the Sudanese Government itself. Several SPLM/A commanders began questioning Garang's leadership resulting in a serious split in its ranks which was led by Gordon Koan, Lam Akol and Riek Machar. Some accounts of the split held that the Sudanese Government managed to infiltrate SPLM/A and effect fissures that would seriously undermine Garang's leadership. Riek Machar from the Nuer ethnic group especially played a key role. (The Nuer are a warlike community in Southern Sudan and they, and the Dinka from which Garang hailed, had had a violent history.) Nuer are the second largest tribe after the Dinka and their complete way of life revolves around their livestock.

Machar founded SPLA-United, taking with him a significant number of Neur officers. The split accorded the government a perfect chink through which they insinuated their wedge, supporting the breakaway faction and heavily financing it. The Government of Sudan hoped that by using defectors from SPLM/A's rank and file, it would seriously weaken it. This was also a strategy the government used to deepen ethnic divisions among the Southerners so that the SPLM/A could remain perpetually weak.

Within months, internecine feuds within SPLM/A ensured that nearly 70 per cent of the Bor Dinka ethnic group in the Southern Upper Nile region had been displaced with thousands of civilians killed or wounded by SPLA-United. Garang's SPLM/A in turn raided villages occupied by the Nuer communities further escalating this intra-Southern fighting that went on throughout much of 1990s.

At one time, Riek Machar was reported by the British Broadcasting Corporation (BBC) as having overthrown John Garang. According to the BBC, Machar had overthrown Garang because he was not committed to peace. Two other top Commanders, Lam Akol and Gordon Kong, it was reported, had joined him. In an interview with the BBC, he is reported to have said, "John Garang has run the movement alone in a very dictatorial, authoritarian way. He has tried to manipulate even our own children to recruit them into the Army as child soldier.... he has turned this movement into warlordism and a reign of terror."

This was music to the ears of the government. A weak SPLM/A would be no match to the government army and a deliberate policy to encourage and fund the breakaway militia was adopted by Khartoum. Besides, if Machar could cross over to the government side, he would be an invaluable asset as his Nuer people controlled the areas around the oil-rich Adar-Yale field in Upper Nile. In fact, Machar was to sign a provisional peace treaty with Khartoum in April 1996 and pledged that his troops would fight alongside the government. In 1998, Bashir appointed a former SPLM/A guerrilla Commander Maj-Gen Kerubino Kwanyin Bol as Deputy President and Minister for Local Government and public security in Southern Sudan. The government was trying in every way to reap from the fallout in the SPLM/A.

Through the warlords and mercenaries now emerging, the government would fight a vicious war while at the same time evading war crimes by saying that the matter was a tribal issue. The government also hoped that the war would depopulate the South so as to eventually reduce it to an insignificant political entity.

One of the issues on which both Garang and Riek never agreed was the recruitment of child soldiers. Garang seemed in favour of it. Riek opposed it. But no one thought that this would be sufficient grounds for such a costly split.

In Nairobi, meanwhile, Garang's deputy held a press conference and asserted that Garang was in full control of SPLM/A. While Machar was even having trouble dealing with his lieutenants like Akol, Garang had managed to convince the high command that Machar and Akol were being supported by the National Islamic Front and Tiny Rowland, who by then had massive business interests in the country. He told the officers that the government had attempted to trick SPLM/A with a promise for the secession of the South after the fall of Mengistu and that he had rejected it. "So they turned to Riek and Akol." He continued to enumerate the reasons he had rejected the offer which included the fact that he did not trust the NIF to sustain the deal and that such a deal could only be validly made through a constitutional conference which would guarantee that the people in the Nuba Mountains, those in the Southern Blue Nile and the traditional Muslim political parties, which were then united with SPLM/A in opposition to NIF, would be treated fairly by the government. He doubted, he said, that the government would willingly give up the Southern riches.

As Garang managed to consolidate his power, the intra-Southern fighting escalated. Some of the worst hit areas were those shared by the Nuer and the Dinka in the Upper Nile, Pok Tap, Duk Faiwil, and Duk Fadiat. There were reports that Dinka commanders were killing Nuer officers in the areas under their control and Nuer officers started killing all those who supported Garang. But the fiercest of battles was fought at Bor, the home town of Garang.

Garang had managed to keep a Commander of the Nuer community, William Nyuon, in his top echelons. Nyuon attacked the Western Upper Nile and had his men occupy it for a week. But Riek Machar, Scroggins documents, rallied his people to his side and formed a formidable army of people who wore white ashes on their bodies and carried white spears. They called themselves the *jiech mabor* or "white army". It was a vicious ensemble which, when it attacked, drove Garang's men right into Bor. This is where the killing took its worst toll. Children were killed, the Dinka houses were burned, cattle was stolen and whatever could not be taken was shot. More than 100,000 Dinka fled the South before the Nuer advanced. But over 2,000 people died in the two weeks of fighting in what came to be known as the Bor Massacre. The Dinka cattle that was however, stolen, as fate would have it, turned out to be infected with rinderpest, and which in turn infected the Nuer and Shilluk herds, wiping out almost the entire flock and putting the entire livelihoods of the people at risk.

But if anything, the Bor Massacre served to illustrate that Riek's rebellion had turned tribal. Few people could understand why the massacre had to happen, why innocent people had to be killed just because Riek and Garang had disagreed. Many people saw Machar as just a tribal leader. But for both Riek and Akol, the beginning of the end had arrived brutally. Riek was not a leader of the South. He was a Nuer leader and any negotiations with him for peace would bear no fruits.

In 1994, Riek Machar changed his party's name from SPLA-United to Southern Sudan Independence Movement, but he was unable to secure weapons or finances from abroad and he increasingly turned to Khartoum for support, which was only too happy to keep both sides fighting. The war intensified. But in March 1995, the Sudanese Government bombed Uganda, prompting President Yoweri Museveni to break diplomatic ties with the Sudanese Government and increase support for the SPLM/A. Sudan also meddled with the internal affairs of Eritrea and Ethiopia which further pushed these countries into helping the rebels. The SPLM/A also enjoyed moral and political support from the US. In 1995, Garang visited the US where he was received warmly. The visit was a fillip to SPLM/A's war efforts, even though the US never offered any direct assistance.

Soon after, Machar and his Commanders were to be confronted with a stark choice: either join NIF or rejoin SPLM/A. Machar was under considerable pressure from his Commanders, some of whom felt that their faction had fully sold out to Khartoum. In fact, some were getting their arms from the Sudan Army headquarters. Machar was to suffer a further setback when he fell out with Lam Akol and the two parted ways. Machar christened his movement "South Sudan Independence Movement/Army (SSIM/A)" and Akol maintained the name SPLM/ United. Later, Akol rejoined Bashir in Government after finding that he had no military support for his faction. By aligning himself with NIF regime while all its oppressive laws and institutions that he purported to be fighting remained, Machar's commitment to the struggle was seriously impugned. In fact many thought that this gave lie to his earlier claim that he disagreed with Garang because he had become dictatorial and abusive of human rights. His collaboration with NIF was seen by even members of his community as a blatant betrayal of the cause of Southern Sudan. Many of these openly championed reunification of the movement and the cutting of links with NIF. As a result, Nuer members of SSIM/A met in Nairobi in 1995 and unanimously resolved that collaboration with the NIF was blatant treason. They demanded that those who were collaborating with the system be thrown out. Machar did not heed their pleas. However, later that year, both the SSIM/A and SPLM/A became conscious of the damage they had wrought to the cause of the Southern Sudan and the democracy of Sudan and sought to reunite. This led to the Lafon Declaration in which the two sides pledged to a ceasefire, reconciliation of all the peoples of the Sudan, reunification of the movement, integration of the armies and the restoration of peace in southern Sudan. The declaration was endorsed by the National Executive Council of SPLM/A. A few months later, Machar was overthrown by his Commanders who accused him of lack of vision and "unpatriotic stand against the unity of the Movement and the people of South Sudan." They also accused him of instigating tribal and factional fighting for his selfish interests.

A year after the Lafon Declaration, Commander Salva Kirr Mayardit, the number two man and Chief of General Staff at SPLM/A and John

Luk Jok, Commander-in-Chief of a breakaway SSIM/A, signed a treaty of unification in Nairobi. The treaty affirmed the reunification and the retention of the name SPLM/A for the movement and that John Garang would be its leader. The treaty also affirmed the integration of administrative and political structures of the two organisations and the merging of the armies.

At last, the South could speak in one voice and negotiate as a bloc. SPLM/A also recouped its credibility in the eyes of the world and this worried the government which was now bracing itself to face a united enemy.

Around that time, the government was also facing its own external problems. It was being isolated left right and centre. With Uganda, Ethiopia and Eritrea openly supporting the rebels, the government was something of a pariah. Eritrea gave base to the National Democratic Alliance, the Northern based party which was in alliance with SPLM/A after accusing Khartoum of supporting elements opposed to the Eritrean Government. After Sudan's support for Iraq during the Gulf War and its harbouring the terrorist, Osama Bin Laden, most of its allies tended to look away from it. Several North African countries broke ties with Khartoum for their support of insurgent groups.

In 1995, an attempt was made on the life of President Hosni Mubarak of Egypt in Ethiopia. This, many analysts believe, marked the turning point for Sudan. Ethiopia accused Khartoum of having been behind the attempt and effectively dampened the two country's relations which had been strong in the early 1990s. In 1996, The UN Security Council imposed non-economic sanctions on Sudan. The US continued to be more sympathetic to Garang with high ranking government officials led by the US Secretary of State, Madeleine Albright, meeting him twice during the Clinton Administration.

Despite its isolation, the Sudan Government, which in 1993 transformed itself from a military to a civilian government, still had some allies. Iran continued to provide military and economic support and Iraq also provided weapons and military aircraft. Thus, the war continued.

In 1995, SPLM/A mounted a series of attacks on the government and scored decisive victories, sending a clear message to Khartoum that even if they had been expelled from Ethiopia, they were still a force to reckon with. With little efforts being made to secure peace, it was not clear how long the war would go on. SPLM/A continued drawing support from allies abroad and the government continued with its hard line policy, shrugging off international pressure and believing somewhat that it could win the war. Efforts at moving towards peace and respect for human rights almost always turned defective. Like the revolution that brought Numeiri to power and promised clovers and perfume to the Sudanese, Bashir's government also made pretences at lurching the country to a peace settlement and political order but quickly withdrew it and relapsed into authoritarianism.

In late 1990s, a combination of military pressure and international isolation forced the government to institute some cosmetic political and human rights reforms. Many thought that at last, things would fundamentally change in Sudan. In May 1998, the government adopted a new constitution that promised basic liberties such as freedom of religion, freedom of association and self-determination for Southern Sudan. But the reforms were implemented by dribs and drabs, casting doubts that the government was really committed to change.

Less than a year later, the sceptics were proved right, for in December 1999, Bashir declared a new state of emergency, dismissed the Speaker of Parliament, Hassan Al Turabi, and dissolved Parliament only two days before it was to vote on a Bill designed to reduce presidential powers. The Bill had been crafted by Turabi. The era of repression was back in earnest. The National Security Act was amended to allow extra-judicial detention for indefinite periods without charge or trial. The government started drumming up support from Islamic allies on the claim that Islam was under assault and also amended the press law to introduce operational constraints and installing agents as editors in publishing houses.

Political parties were further restricted by an amended Political Associations Act which restricted competition and fundraising options for them. Public demonstrations were banned and even private meetings ran the risk of being termed subversive.

Bashir also extended his powers and made himself the sole appointing authority of all governors, state ministers and department heads. The country was in full flight into the days of darkness.

In the beginning of 2000, the expense of war and battle fatigue began to tell on the government and SPLM/A. The people wanted peace and the Inter-Governmental Authority on Development (IGAD) was willing to mediate. It was becoming clear that in spite of its oil wealth, Sudan would never reap its fruits so long as the war raged. The US Congress passed a legislation banning any company doing business in Sudan's oil industry from participation in US capital markets.

The war also started affecting the national budget. By 2001, the government was unable to pay its workers and pensioners and the cost of living was inexorably high. SPLM/A was also making serious assaults on the oilfields, making investments almost impossible.

For the country to progress, the war had to end. Several attempts had been made to end it. They had all failed. Though the IGAD Peace Process was still on, having been launched in 1993, it was glacial and there were doubts that at the rate it was moving, anything would be realised. In any case, Khartoum had walked out of the peace process at least once, virtually stalling the process.

Many other players had also jumped into the fray in an attempt to bring peace. There was the Egyptian-Libyan joint initiative which was launched in 1999, but which never went far. It set its objectives too low, with the main one being to reconcile the Northern parties and draw some of them back into government as a moderating influence on the National Islamic Front. Not surprisingly, the Southerners viewed this kind of arrangement with suspicion. Egypt was opposed to self-determination which was one of SPLM/A's key demands. The joint initiative centred on nine points, key of which were the preservation of the unity of Sudan, making citizenship the basis of rights, recognising Sudan's diversity, safeguarding democratic pluralism, guaranteeing basic freedoms, establishing a decentralised government, forming an interim government and cessation of hostilities. SPLM/A viewed that peace proposal as heavily tilted towards Khartoum and the government was opposed to a transition government. The failure of the joint initiative to address the three hot-buttons of the conflict religion, self-determination and resource sharing, effectively clamped its wheels.

Eritrea had also attempted to launch its own separate peace process, but also foundered in the coldness of Sudan's diplomatic reaction to its peace proposal. Nigeria had also had a try under the aegis of the Millennium Action Plan. The Plan was a cooperative effort among African leaders to promote Africa's development in the global economy. Nigerian President, Olusegun Obasanjo, was in charge of regional conflict issues for the Plan. In 2001, he attempted, but failed, to convene a Southern political forces conference in Abuja aimed at helping Southern Sudanese leaders – including representatives of the SPLM/A – reach a consensus on future peace negotiations.

On the main, both SPLM/A and the government had serious reservations about this effort. Indeed, a possible national conference, which had been touted as the next step towards attaining peace after the first attempt failed, was indefinitely postponed. According to ICG, the government most feared that Southerners would coalesce around a self-determination agenda while the Northerners would press for more democracy. The SPLM/A did not want to be placed at the same level with other Southern political forces and it wished to pursue and keep its options open on the issue of self-determination. Analysts believe that one of the drawbacks of the Nigerian initiative was that it viewed the war as a strictly North-South matter rather than as a national struggle also involving democracy and fundamental rights.

The US had also taken several unilateral efforts to support peace, including, as we shall see later, designating a special envoy, John Danforth, for a six-month mission to assess whether the US could play a role in the peace process. The US also unsuccessfully attempted to host an IGAD session in Washington. Its unilateral attempt failed because it was also viewed with suspicion especially on its ability to handle the critical issues of religion and self-determination.

This *pot-pourri* of failed attempts was enough to dampen the spirits of those who wanted peace to return to Africa's largest country. Yet, optimism and pessimism on this issue mixed liberally. The International Crisis Group observed in 2002:

> While there have been a number of peace talks aimed at ending the conflict in Sudan, none of these efforts have gained traction to date, and all have been lightly regarded by the warring parties. The majority of these peace efforts have been brokered by regional actors who have unfortunately not been able to put aside their more parochial interests in an effort to establish a more credible process. There appears little likelihood that either the government or the SPLM/A will approach the negotiating table in good faith given the flawed design of these current structures.

The scepticism that the world's longest civil war would be brought to an end that easily was given more credence by the fact that IGAD itself was having its own problems with some of its principles. Eritrea and Ethiopia were locked in a war. Eritrea had pulled out of the peace process and started its own effort arguing that IGAD could not work because of the Eritrea-Ethiopia conflict in which Sudan had taken sides. On the other hand, Uganda, a key member of IGAD, was at loggerheads with Sudan because of that country's support of the Lord's Resistance Army and Uganda's support for SPLM/A. Could such an outfit work?

When General Sumbeiywo then took that call from Moi and accepted to be the man to attempt to bring peace to this region, he knew only too well the kind of situation he was getting himself into. He knew the complexities involved, the past efforts to bring peace to the region, the fratricidal history of the Southerners, the intransigence of the government, the deep mistrust between Northerners and Southerners and the various vested interests that countries central to peace negotiations had. He was like Jeremiah being told by God to perform a task he feared he was ill-prepared to do.

"I am giving you this appointment because you are a Christian," Moi's words kept replaying on Sumbeiywo's mind. And onwards, Lt General Lazaro Kipkurui Sumbeiywo plunged, once again, into the lions' den.

****

The beginning of weeping, the Nigerians say, is the most difficult part. Afterwards, the tears cascade down effortless in a motion at once painful and pleasurable. The restarting of the peace process had this strange quality.

The first major assignment for Sumbeiywo was to attend an IGAD summit in Khartoum in January 2002. A joint communiqué signed by the Heads of States of Djibouti, Eritrea, Kenya, Uganda, Ethiopia and the Republic of Somalia called upon the Chairman of the IGAD Committee on Sudan to rejuvenate the IGAD Peace Process and invite other initiatives to coordinate the efforts. The Summit placed enormous pressure on Lt General Sumbeiywo. As the Army Commander, he had to balance between mediating in the peace process and doing his military work.

But it was not the military work that was daunting him. It was the fact that he had to literally start negotiations on the Sudan peace process anew, with belligerent foes as co-negotiators and a broke IGAD. (IGAD had no money at all and the donors were unwilling to commit new monies then because they did not have faith in its ability to achieve its goals.) The peace process had been laboriously slow and in some cases it appeared to stutter to a halt. Donors felt that they were throwing good money after bad and it was something of a Sisyphean feat convincing them that something could come out of it and would they please support it.

IGAD had a bill of KShs10 million. Even those few donors who were willing to commit money did not want it used retrospectively. Without first clearing the pending bill, IGAD could not hope to get anywhere.

President Moi realised this. His commitment to the peace process and his desire to see it completed before he left office at the end of the year was almost evangelical. He instructed the Treasury to clear the bill so that Sumbeiywo could start on a clean slate.

After that, donors were willing to come on board. The US had shown renewed interest in the IGAD Peace Process, which it had all along treated as a Kenyan affair. Under President Bush, the Administration had come under enormous pressure from the domestic front owing to the September 11 attacks in New York. The Sudan Peace Act had also come into force. It committed the US to pressuring Khartoum to end the war in South Sudan. Under pressure from a confederacy of two factions in Congress, the US found itself pushed into committing itself more meaningfully to the search for peace in Sudan. The anti-slavery lobby, which was led by the Congressional Black Caucus was fighting to stop the continuing practice of the enslavement of the Southerners and an evangelical Christian lobby sought to prevent the continued persecution of the Christians in Southern Sudan by the Islamist government. At the signing ceremony of the law, Bush was presented with a burnt Bible which had been found in the home of a Christian family in the South. "Pray for our persecuted brethren in Sudan," the activist who gave Bush the Bible asked.

"Thank you very much," Bush said, " I will do that."

The commitment of the US was now no longer in question. Afterwards, when Sumbeiywo travelled to the US with President Moi, the question Sumbeiywo was most frequently asked was, "How much money do you want?" his answer was always, "I do not know." In the United Kingdom, he met Allan Goulty who was later to become ambassador to Tunisia. He asked him the same question. He got the same answer.

By then, Sumbeiywo had not mapped out the enormity of his task. He wanted someone to capture his ideas and translate them into tangible issues for negotiations as well as formulating a budget for the process. The US promptly took the cue and offered the services of one of their personnel working in Rwanda by the name Dr Susan Page. Dr Page, a lawyer, was to become one of the most useful members of the negotiating team. She laid out the framework for the negotiations and initiated the first few steps that would later lead to a full motion of the peace process.

"When you start mediation, it is like starting a family," Sumbeiywo was to remark later, "Everyone knows everyone and everyone sympathises with everyone." Sumbeiywo was to realise this much more vividly when he met with the members of IGAD Partners Forum (IPF), a group of 17 countries initially called Friends of IGAD. IPF was co-chaired by Italy and Norway. These countries requested to have a few of them observe the negotiations to which Sumbeiywo had no objection. A troika was established that included the UK, US, Norway and Italy. But there was a problem. Some members wanted Italy to be left out of the troika, the fact that they co-chaired the IPF notwithstanding. Sumbeiywo had to resolve what looked like a family dispute. He aggressively fought for Italy to be included. His decision was to prove critical when the Italians assumed the presidency of the European Union and lent their full support to the Sudan Peace Process.

The first meeting with all the parties was held at the Kenya Commercial Bank's training centre in Karen, less than 10 kilometres from Nairobi city centre in May 2002. It is a quiet place, far removed from town and which resembles a fortress. Sumbeiywo liked this place. "It was peaceful," he says, "and it was serene." The two parties, including the antagonists, attended. But they were not feeling as easy as they used to at the premier Hotel Intercontinental in the heart of the city where the talks used to be conducted.

"They called the place an open prison or army garrison," he remembers almost with glee. But he knew that even if they wanted to leave, there was nowhere they could have gone. Karen is a bushy area and on the other side of the road is the Ngong Forest, notorious for criminal activities and a good population of animals.

The meeting observed that there were still some very contentious issues contained in the Declaration of Principles (DOP) which were yet to be resolved. It had taken over six years for the parties to agree on the implementation modalities of the Nairobi Declaration. Among the points to be ferreted out were an affirmation that a military solution could not bring lasting peace and stability to Sudan, that a peaceful and just political solution must be the common objective to the parties and an affirmation of self-determination for the people of Southern Sudan to determine their future status through a referendum. There were other issues: power sharing, wealth sharing, human rights and state and religion.

The Karen meeting was also supposed to discuss an agenda that included the judiciary and the rule of law, transitional period/ interim arrangements to be negotiated, comprehensive ceasefire and security arrangements as well as regional and international guarantees.

Everything looked clear-cut at first glance. But as Sumbeiywo was to realise, the issues dividing the SPLM/A and the Government of Sudan were so deep that when one side took a particular point of view, the other took the opposite. The Government of Sudan was fiercely opposed to the use of the words "interim period/arrangement to be negotiated." On their part, the SPLM/A did not like the phrase "transitional period."

He, at that time, also apparently did not understand that he would naturally run into a wall of mistrust in which anything he said, however innocuous, would be blown out of proportion and could even spell doom for the tenuous peace talks.

The government delegation was led by the State Minister in the Office of the Presidency, Idris Mohammed while the SPLM/A was led by Commander Elijah Malok Aleng, who is now the Deputy Governor of the Sudan Central Bank. He was later to be substituted by Nhial Deng Nhial who remained the chief negotiator while Salva Kirr remained leader of the delegation for the better part of the negotiations. Salva Kirr Mayardit also played a key role in SPLM/A as the chief of staff and the brains behind the military machinery of the movement.

The disagreement over these words led to a stalemate. The SPLM/A and Sumbeiywo signed the programme of work which outlined how the negotiations would be conducted. The Sudanese Government threw it in their faces and refused to sign it.

"You do not respect us," a member of the government delegation shouted at Sumbeiywo, "You will not get any respect from us." And the government delegation walked out. The meeting had to be called off.

SPLM/A had something to go back with. But the government did not. Later the government fired off an angry letter accusing Sumbeiywo of scuttling the talks by attempting to rush forward the meeting. They complained that they had "adopted a policy of constructive engagement and cooperation with the chair.... to assist the mediation at this very early stage and reaffirm the seriousness and commitment of the Government of the Sudan. However, that attitude seems not to be always well received."

In the letter signed by Idris Mohammed, the Government of Sudan lamented, "According to our assessment, the meeting was having every opportunity for success. Surprisingly, the spirit of rushing it towards certain conclusions, which suddenly prevailed, had aborted the meeting and ended it prematurely and inconclusively."

Idris accused the chair of issuing threats, warnings and accusations. "We strongly object in particular, to the disrespectful language used, especially the threat to report to the international community that 'the Government of the Sudan is a renegade'. Much of the prestige of the process could be eroded when the language used for mediation degenerates to this unprecedented level."

The Government of Sudan threatened to withdraw its support for Sumbeiywo charging that he was not capable of steering the peace process fruitfully. "The Special Envoy will not continue to enjoy the support of the Government of the Sudan unless he is strictly observing his mandate and working within his stipulated prerogative," Idris fumed.

SPLM/A did not react. No other party did. There was, however, a feeling that the government side had overreacted and Sumbeiywo had to wait for things to cool down. At this early stage, the negotiations had met their first serious hurdle. But at no time did it cross Sumbeiywo's mind that the negotiations would fail. A deeply religious man, he took a dip into the spiritual world of the Bible and remembered the words of Joshua Chapter One, verse 9, " Have courage for I am with you."
He knew that in mediation, tempers were likely to rise and that if one managed to keep one's cool, as the words of The Desiderata say, when everyone else is losing theirs, things would turn out fine. His motto was: You can shout all you want, but please do not shoot.

When he finally responded to Idris Mohammed's letter, it was to invite the parties to another meeting in a curiously toned-down communication which also indicated that the parties had had a "successful consultative meeting." For although no agreement was signed in Karen, the parties adopted the Modalities of the Task Force which was signed by both parties. The proposed meeting was to be held in June and Sumbeiywo called on both parties to prepare their delegations for it. Surprisingly, the Government of Sudan, probably fearful of being labelled a "renegade" or its commitment to peace questioned, acknowledged and agreed to the meeting. Machakos was chosen as the venue for this first set of talks.

11

Machakos

Machakos town is about 70 kilometres from the city of Nairobi. The small town lacks the vibrancy of Nairobi and Mombasa and it has little to write home about. But it is an ideal venue for serious meetings as it is well tucked away from town and has a hotel with excellent conference facilities. For the purposes of negotiations, it was far enough from the interference of embassies and near enough to allow briefings for those needing to be briefed. It was in this place that the delegates met on June 17, 2002, to get on with the tenuous business of negotiating for peace.

By now, Sumbeiywo had realised that mediation was also a political process. Having spent all his working life in the military, he was clearly sailing in uncharted waters. When his former boss, General Mulinge, whose home is not very far from Machakos town, met him at the venue of the negotiations, he was filled with both admiration and pity for the man. When they discussed what he was up to, General Mulinge, a politician himself at this time, realised that there was a great deal of politics involved.

"The man is not a politician," he told himself, "yet he is in a politician's den doing negotiations with politicians." But it also dawned on him that being an excellent military man, the issues at hand also had as much to do with fighting and the military as they had with politics. "When a man has the intelligence, he can handle any job," he said to himself. After all, politics is what one does every day. There is nothing one borrows. It is ingrained in one.

Sumbeiywo was also to realise that the negotiations had to be done in a situation where some parties, other than the two protagonists, were all suspicious of one another. There were envoys whose countries were not particularly at peace with the others. The Ugandans, for instance were at conflict with the Sudanese Government over the Lord's Resistance Army which was fighting the Ugandan Government from its base in

Sudan, and Eritrea and Ethiopia had just ended a border war with each other. There was then a quiet internal conflict within the mediation team. There was also the international community which wanted to hijack the negotiations, and there was the IGAD Secretariat to take care of. Sumbeiywo had to balance all that within what he was later to call "a spider's web."

The Sudanese Government delegation was, again, led by Minister Idris Mohammed. The SPLM/A changed its lead negotiator and brought in Nhial Deng Nhial. As the negotiations continued in Machakos, some members of the delegation became weary. They started falling off one by one. The only countries that were left in the negotiations were Uganda, Eritrea and Ethiopia. Even the Kenyan Foreign Affairs Ministry became a victim of weariness. The negotiations had become such a tedious affair that few had the strength or the will to sit through them.

However, Sumbeiywo was to get a great deal of encouragement and advice from former US President Jimmy Carter whom he met in Nairobi that month. He advised Sumbeiywo that unless he developed a single negotiating text, he would always run the risk of the negotiations getting bogged down by petty issues. He took those words very seriously. Initially, he had developed a single negotiating non-paper called "One country, two systems." But it was widely discredited by the parties.

In Machakos, the divisions that had plagued Sudan started bobbing up and down, like lifebuoys. The Sudanese Government still mistrusted Sumbeiywo, in fact it did battle with him in the same way it battled the SPLM/A, cavilling at every mistake he made and threatening to walk out whenever it felt that Sumbeiywo was getting too assertive.

The first hurdle the Machakos meeting was to face was in reaching an agreement on the single negotiating text. Since the aim of the following six weeks was to compile the key issues on the DOP into a Single Negotiating Text, the mediators and some observers decided to develop a draft that would provide the parties with a starting point. The draft they came up with covered the broad outlines on main issues that included the transition period, the pre-transition period, the need for a process of reconciliation and the equitable sharing of natural resources. It did not, however, specifically refer to the right to self-determination or secession. The SPLM/A was furious and the United States hit the roof. The US envoy to the process just walked out and the SPLM/A went red.

SPLM/A believed that the division of the country was imminent unless separation of state and religion was effected. "We are not Arabs," a member of the delegation stated, "We are separate people. Names of those in the South are not Islamic. They are Christian." But the government demanded of SPLM/A to have a national outlook.

"Choosing peace was a risky business," a member of the government delegation cautioned, "but we have taken it."

Sumbeiywo, a firm believer of the fact that in negotiations, one has to let all parties play it all out just listened and allowed them to argue. They argued over what it meant to be an Arab, over slavery, over what kind of the country they wanted to have.

Sumbeiywo found himself running a tight rope. The interests were shifting, the parties were getting more belligerent. Matters were not being helped by the fact that his relationship with the observers was getting trickier. The powerful backers of the process wanted him to defer to them. He had other ideas.

"It is all a circle," he says, "I was in the middle and the parties and observers formed a circle around me. Their interests constantly changed while mine did not." The interests of the parties was who gets the best deal, who succeeds in besting the other. Sumbeiywo defines his interest in the matter as peace in the Sudan.

The parties on the other hand were sceptical about whether Sumbeiywo understood the kind of Sudan he was propelling the parties towards. They could not agree on how to define peace in Sudan.

"I was not creating a new Sudan. Some observers wanted a New Sudan. My interest was peace between the North and the South. That was my mandate and I had to stick to it," he insists.

The issues were deep and divisive. Sumbeiywo was to get a lot of help in thrashing out these matters from two professional mediators, Nicholas Haysom, a South African constitutional lawyer who had worked closely for Nelson Mandela for many years, and Julian Hottinger from the Swiss Federal Department of Foreign Affairs and who was fluent in several languages. Between these two, they had an enormous range of mediation experience garnered from such countries as South Africa, Vietnam, Somalia, Burundi, Rwanda, Nepal, Sri Lanka and Nigeria. The two urged Sumbeiywo to adopt a technique where the parties vented their feelings and thrashed out the issues they had to negotiate before settling down collectively to debating them.

This was done through a series of workshops and plenary sessions. The negotiators responded to questions such as, 'What does it mean to be an African?' 'What does slavery mean to you?' or, 'What does self-determination mean to you?'

This usually degenerated into a farce. The government tried to justify slavery on the basis of tradition and some people said they had had to change their names into Moslem ones when they are in the Northern areas. Government officials also defended the existing rules on religious freedom, asserting that nothing stopped the Christians from building churches in the North. The Christians pointed out that one needed a permit to do so which were never granted.

Sumbeiywo allowed them to talk to each other and say everything they wanted. Later this method paid dividends and the line that was dividing the two sides started getting blurred. Though positions still continued to harden, there was at least a ray of light.

The government demanded that the unity of Sudan be given priority. Dr Ghazi Salahuddin Attabani, the advisor to the President of Sudan on Peace Affairs, isolated some principles on which the negotiations should be carried out: 1) unity of Sudan be given priority; 2) recognition of diversity; 3) choice of the Sudanese be respected; 4) creation of a constitutional arrangement.

Weighing heavily on both parties were what both were recognised as "bad history" in their country. They agreed to discard the memories of marginalisation and slavery and insisted that they were now a new generation of Sudanese. They also called for the Sudanese people to be proud of their culture whether one was a Muslim or a Christian and urged for compromise and accommodation. As a driver for negotiations, this did not sound bad. Out of what looked like a welcome compromise, a single negotiating text was developed. They called it a Negotiating Framework Document.

Though it was a rudimentary document, it captured some of the most contentious issues such as sharing of power and wealth. But it also had two contentious issues. The first was the separation of religion and state and the second was self-determination for the people of Southern Sudan. The issue of self-determination was to become particularly thorny. The envoys prepared a document stating that for the people of Southern Sudan, state and religion would be separated and that they would decide their destiny in a referendum. The government agreed to this but it insisted that the referendum could only be held in 10 years. The SPLM/A wanted a maximum of two years before the referendum.

Sumbeiywo watched in silence as both sides haggled over the years in which the referendum would be held. When no headway appeared to be found, he did what any mediator would do in the circumstances. He took the years the government proposed and added them to those of the SPLM/A and divided by two. The referendum would occur in six years. Both sides emphatically stated: No. The talks were deadlocked. The mediators held on to their position and gave both sides one hour to decide with two persons from each delegation. The government chose two people, Said Khatib and Yahya Babakir to negotiate with two from the other side, Nhial Deng Nhial and Deng Alor Kuol. With everyone out of the room, the four were left to talk. They were not to leave until they had an answer. After four hours, there still was no agreement. The men kept drinking tea and asking for more.

"Drink as much tea as you want," Sumbeiywo told them, "but please at the end of it, give us an agreed text." Khatib asked for more cigarettes and through billows of smoke, the negotiations proceeded. But instead of talking to each other, both sides were using their mobile phones to contact their superiors.

Finally, at 1.00 am, they called Sumbeiywo. "We have an answer," they said, "but we want you to modify the documents on the two issues," they requested. Sumbeiywo insisted only that if there were any changes, they had to be agreed upon by both parties.

On state and religion, the document stated, inter alia, "recognising that Sudan is a multi-cultural, multi-racial, multi-ethnic, multi-religious and multi-lingual country and confirming that religion shall not be used as a divisive factor, the parties hereby agree as follows: There shall be freedom of belief, worship and conscience for followers of all religious faiths or beliefs or customs and no one shall be discriminated against on such grounds." It also affirmed that eligibility for public office, including the presidency, public service and the enjoyment of all rights and duties shall be based on citizenship and not on religion, beliefs and customs. The national government, it was also agreed, shall take into account the religious and cultural diversity of the Sudanese people in all its laws. "A state may set aside the provisions of any law inconsistent with the customs or religions of the residents of that state." In effect, the parties believe that the Northern states would follow sharia law, and the Southern States would follow traditional customs and beliefs.

The document also addressed the issue of self-determination and stated that the people of Southern Sudan had a right to self-determination through a referendum to determine their future status. This would be done at the end of the six-year interim period agreed on by both parties. The referendum would be organised by SPLM/A jointly with GOS for the people of Southern Sudan to either adopt the system of government established under the Peace Agreement or vote for secession.

When both parties agreed to the un-amended document, Sumbeiywo said a prayer of thanks. It seemed that the biggest breakthrough had been achieved. For the first time since 1997, there would be a signed document between the two parties. He called State House, informed the President of the good news and it was agreed that the Machakos Protocol would be signed at State House. This was supposed to achieve two things: first, it would give the agreement a political angle, and second, it would give it an international outlook.

The road to the Machakos Protocol was, however, fraught with frustrations which Sumbeiywo had to fight off. First, the Americans had made up their minds on the issue of self-determination. They were not thrilled at the Machakos Protocol because they had initiated their own ceasefire in the Nuba Mountains, in fact, the US Special Envoy for Peace in Sudan, Senator John Danforth at one time told Sumbeiywo, "There is no problem in Sudan. Just divide the oil."

"But even if we divide the oil, there is still much more to it," retorted Sumbeiywo. The Americans apparently saw the problem in Sudan then as one brought about by inequitable distribution of wealth, not religion, not politics, not the subjugation of one set of people by another.

This view was, however, to be lent some ambivalence in Senator Danforth's "Report to the President of the United States on the Outlook for Peace in Sudan" on April 26, 2002. In it, he expressed caution about secession of Southern Sudan and proposed that self-determination should include the right of the people of Southern Sudan to live under a government that respects their religion and culture. In his Executive Brief to President Moi on Senator Danforth's document, Sumbeiywo noted that it had "predetermined in contradictory terms from the parties, an important and outstanding issue of self-determination, particularly in the light of the ongoing negotiations in the framework of the Declaration of Principles (DOP)."

Danforth proposed that self-determination could only work if the South agreed to live under a government that respected its religion and culture. In his view this did not mean the right for the Southerners to determine their future for themselves.

"The view that self-determination includes the guaranteed option of secession is contained in the IGAD DOP and is supported by many Sudanese. However, secession would be strongly resisted by the government of Sudan and would be exceedingly difficult to achieve," Danforth wrote in the report. "A more feasible, and, I think, preferable view of self-determination would ensure the right of the people of Southern Sudan to live under a government that respects their religion and culture. Such a system would require robust internal and external guarantees so that any promises made by the government in peace negotiations could not be ignored in practice."

This was a view not shared by the Southerners. The SPLM/A had all along insisted that the Southerners must be accorded a right to determine their future status in a referendum. But Danforth was trying to water down the meaning of self-determination as it related to the cause of Southern Sudan.

Senator Danforth was President Bush's personal friend and an ordained Anglican priest. His appointment was seen as an important signal to the US' commitment to peace in Sudan. The US did not commit substantial funds to the IGAD Peace Process, but it demanded a sizeable part of the process. However, the US Government role in the affairs of Sudan was not to be faulted. In fact, the US enacted the Sudan

Peace Act to handle the issues facing Sudan and to formulate policies on aid and how to bring a speedy end to the war. The Act authorised the President of the US to "provide increased assistance to the areas of Sudan that are not controlled by the Government of Sudan to prepare the population for peace and democratic governance, including support for civil administration, communications infrastructure, education, health and agriculture." The Act also recognised that a resolution "to the conflict in Sudan is best made through a peace process based on the Declaration of Principles reached in Nairobi, Kenya on July 20, 1994 and on the Machakos Protocol of July 2002." But as helpful as the Americans were, they were to be a major headache to Sumbeiywo and their palms were mainly empty when it came to funding the talks. In fact, the first draft that led to the Machakos Protocol, the single negotiating text, which was signed on June 20, 2002, was rejected out of hand by the Americans. Reason? Washington had not been contacted and involved in its preparation.

"Is Washington aware of this document?" an American observer inquired from Sumbeiywo. The Americans wanted to guide the negotiations, demanding that Washington be informed of everything that was happening.

But Sumbeiywo knew that to allow them to micro-manage the peace process would have an adverse effect on the process. He was the mediator and he would not cede this authority. He cocked a snook at the Americans and told them off.

"My friend," he told the inquiring observer, "I am not answerable to Washington." That message was relayed to Washington promptly. The Sudanese liked Sumbeiywo for standing up to the Americans; the British, Italians and the Norwegians wondered why the US wanted to interfere with the negotiations. They supported the stand taken by Sumbeiywo.

This was the beginning of problems between Sumbeiywo and the Americans. They distrusted the man and feared that he was far too independent-minded for them. They surreptitiously started spreading word that he was useless in the peace process. Nothing would be achieved with Sumbeiywo in the chair. Much later, when Special Envoy, former Senator Danforth visited the parties in Naivasha where they were concluding the talks, he stole up to Sumbeiywo and told him, "You have the patience of a saint." The delegates started calling Sumbeiywo, in a jocular manner, "The Saint." But there was also a "prophet" in their midst. The Envoy of Eritrea, Mohamed Ali Omaro, who was, as Sumbeiywo concedes, a very knowledgeable man on matters of Sudan, used to say, "I am the only internationally recognised black African prophet." When they argued over when they would get a peace deal, everyone used to say, "Ask the prophet."

Up to that time, the US had not given any funds to the peace process. They kept saying that there was 100,000 US dollars in Djibouti which had not arrived. In spite of this, they wanted to continue flexing their muscle, sometimes threatening to pull out, citing the slow progress of the talks.

Despite their rejection of the single negotiating text, Americans eventually supported it. The parties went ahead and adopted it, leading to the Machakos Protocol, a major breakthrough in the peace negotiations. The US Government was later to hail the Machakos Protocol in a document called "Memorandum of Justification Regarding Determination under the Sudan Peace Act (Public Law 107-245)." It also hailed the role played by Lt General Sumbeiywo and expressed confidence that things were moving on well. The document, prepared for the President of the US, read in part: "The accomplishments made by the sides towards peace so far suggest that the current process holds great promise to that end.... The Machakos protocol signed by the GOS and SPLM/A in July 2002 established a framework and over-aching blueprint for peace and change."

The document went on to commend Sumbeiywo: "The mediator, General Lazaro Sumbeiywo, has shown exceptional leadership in moving both sides past three hurdles. His dynamic approach has tested both parties' resolve to remain in the talks and has allowed observers to witness the results first-hand."

Earlier, Ambassador Michael Ranneberger, the US State Department's Head of the Sudan Program's Group, praised Sumbeiywo's role as facilitator in the peace process, "His (Sumbeiywo's) role and his involvement are really helping to create a dynamic process."

The Machakos Protocol was initialled in Machakos and the parties, mediators, observers and the Secretariat were feted at State House in a ceremony presided over by President Moi. Dr Ghazi Attabani and Salva Kiir Mayardit appended their signatures to this first Agreement in the rejuvenated peace process in July, 2002.

Everyone hailed it as a major breakthrough. But it was only Sumbeiywo and a few others who knew the enormity of the task ahead. "You should be smiling," Dr Sally Kosgey who then was the Head of the Civil Service, told Sumbeiywo at State House on the day the Machakos Protocol was signed. "You don't know what it has taken to do it and what is yet to come," he replied.

In a way, this was not even the beginning of the end. It was the beginning of another long journey with twists and turns, plenty of parking spaces, wiles, trickery, stubbornness and frustrations galore. But everyone recognised it as a watershed moment and even those who had no faith in Sumbeiywo began seeing him in another light. Many were falling over themselves in their haste to praise and warm up to the mediator.

Only a few people knew what he was going through. His Deputy Army Commander, General Kianga, lent him his full support and the senior army officers recognised that the man was swamped with work. He wanted to carry out his duties as Army Commander as best as he could, but he also wanted to steer the peace process as swiftly and successfully as he could.

"Sometimes I would go into his office and get the feeling that he was completely knackered," remembers Maj-Gen. Peter Ikenye, now retired, and a close friend and colleague of Sumbeiywo's in the Army. "At times I would see the frustration all over his face."

At one time, Major General Ikenye remembers getting into Sumbeiywo's office and finding a tired, frustrated and almost exhausted man. Sumbeiywo shared with him his frustrations.

"Remember that you are only remaining with two issues: wealth and power sharing. You are almost there," encouraged General Ikenye.

It was not as simple as that, but that helped put matters in their proper perspective. "He lit up," remembers Ikenye, "It was as though I had said something new."

Far from puffing him up, the success of the Machakos Protocol merely added pressure on Sumbeiywo. The ship that was widely reported as sinking was, after all, admirably afloat and the peace process was now in the limelight. All of a sudden, many more people wanted to come aboard. In the scramble for the cake of success, everyone wanted to be left holding at least a crumb. Letters began flying to the IGAD Secretariat and to the Government of Sudan. The Egyptians wanted to be on board, and so were the other Northern political parties too, which included the National Democratic Alliance, the Sudanese Women's Association in Nairobi, and the Sudan National Labour Party. They all wanted a seat at the negotiating table.

The Sudanese Women's Association in Nairobi wrote to Sumbeiywo thus: " We confirm our willingness and our ability to play a crucial and useful role in this process and believe that IGAD will support the effective participation of women in the peace process for the Sudan."

The French so badly wanted to join the process as observers that they sent an envoy with 100,000 US dollars to the Secretariat in exchange for a seat. As the chair of the African Union, South Africa wanted to come in, the Arab League and the United Nations too wanted to be in. Others wrote letters to President Moi asking to be incorporated into the team.

Faced with such a barrage of requests, Sumbeiywo had to be careful not to have the peace process hijacked by people who had, all along, stayed on the fence. Where had they all been and why had they never expressed interest before? Most had stayed on the sidelines and watched with a measure of disdain as the talks chugged along. Now that there was some light at the end of the tunnel, letters were flying all over asking for admission.

For Sumbeiywo, it was not going to be difficult to decide who would be involved. He invited the AU as an institution and also allowed the UN to join as observers. The rest were locked out.

****

The signing of the Machakos Protocol should have been a cause for joy for Sumbeiywo. But there was no time for self-congratulation. Buoyed by the signing of the critical document, negotiations resumed immediately.

On the morning they restarted in August 2002, Sumbeiywo was contemplating the new hurdles that had suddenly emerged on the road to a Comprehensive Peace Agreement. He had evidently underestimated the task at hand. Like a general who advances too fast and drops his guard, he had made a dash for the finish line, trying to reach the end of the negotiations within the deadline his boss had given him. He tried to discuss the issue of power sharing first.

Other members of the SPLM/A could have none of it. SPLM/A insisted that they could not continue with the negotiations without first tackling the three conflict areas, namely the Abyei area, the Nuba Mountains and the Blue Nile (also known as the Funj). These three areas had not been mentioned in the Machakos Protocol. Apparently, when the SPLM/A went back home, the leaders of these areas brought considerable pressure to bear on them and made it clear that it was an act of betrayal to sign a protocol that did not include the three conflict areas.

This was wholly unexpected. Although Sumbeiywo knew of the existence of the three areas and that the issue had been raised before, he did not expect it to become such a big matter as to threaten to derail the negotiations. He went into a consultative meeting with members of the SPLM/A to discuss the areas. As the meeting was going on, a delegate, Commander Malik Agar Eyrie, rose to speak. He was a tall hefty man who weighed not less than 250 pounds. He could scare anyone with his massive weight and his aggressive language. But he spoke good English. He was cool and collected. "General," the man said in a metallic, impersonal voice. The General turned to look at him.

"General, if you do not include the Funj people of Southern Blue Nile, we shall finish you."

At first, Sumbeiywo was taken aback. That was a threat. He did not know whether to take it lightly, but when he considered the voice of the man and his countenance, he began to understand how seriously some of the people felt about issues pertaining to their communities. But given his position, the hopes that all the negotiating parties had started cultivating in the peace process and understanding the enormous task bestowed on him, he knew that that was the time to be strong. Gen. Sumbeiywo later recalled, "in moments like these, you don't show emotions. You might even want to take on the person threatening you." But that person was not acting on his own behalf. He was acting and speaking for a community that had been oppressed for years and which had, all of a sudden, recognised a chance of redemption which was in danger of slipping away.

"Do not worry," Sumbeiywo assured Commander Malik, "your issue will be discussed. I give you my word."

"Let me remind you something," the man continued relentlessly, "It was not Yusuf Kuol who said in Addis Ababa that if the South border does remain as it was in 1956, we will continue fighting. You got it wrong. It was me."

Sumbeiywo caught the drift. In the negotiations, he had referred to Kuol's words in Addis Ababa during the negotiations that ended in disarray in August, 1998. Yusuf Kuol was the Commander of the Nuba Mountains then whose job was later taken by Abdel Aziz Al-Hilu, a quiet but very volatile man.

In negotiations such as this, the military man in Sumbeiywo told himself, one must either keep one's cool or hide behind a veil of diplomacy. Like his name, (the thorny shrub) Sumbeiywo climbed under a shrub of diplomacy and played the whole thing down.

"Sorry," Sumbeiywo replied. "I think I lost my memory. I thought it was Kuol because he was the leader of the Nuba Mountains then."

"It was me," Malik insisted.

This was a confrontation. The other members of the SPLM/A delegation watched in bemused silence. Since they had been accused of "selling out" on the cause of the three conflict areas, they were only too glad that the bitterness was coming out.

Sumbeiywo never took it seriously that the threat was directed at his person. But he thought it was a serious threat to the process. In fact, so confident was he that nothing untoward would happen to him that Sumbeiywo never had any security.

When Malik Agar Eyrie sat down, the members of the SPLM/A delegation knew the Commander had passed the message and he had received the reassurance he needed. Later, the leader of the delegation, Nhial Deng Nhial, came to see Sumbeiywo and implored him not to take seriously what Eyrie had said. "In these kind of negotiations," he told him, "people lose their tempers and say things they should never have said." Eyrie later became a very good friend of Sumbeiywo's but he was never to know what headache he had presented to the Special Envoy by his outburst.

Although SPLM/A did not formally boycott the talks at this point, their insistence that they could not go on until the three conflict areas were addressed posed a problem. What it meant was that the negotiations would have to go back instead of progressing in the manner laid out in the Machakos Protocol. This would, at any rate, be unacceptable to the Government of Sudan. As it turned out, the GOS did not need the insistence by the SPLM/A on discussing the conflict areas to walk out of the negotiations. The Government of Sudan had indicated to the mediators that the three areas were north of the 1956 boundary and did not fall within the IGAD mandate.

All this time, the fighting on the ground was still going on. Both sides still believed that a victory in war remained a viable alternative to a negotiated settlement. In fact, in signing the Machakos Protocol, Sumbeiywo had acquiesced in the SPLM/A seduction of negotiating without an agreed ceasefire. This presented no problem to Sumbeiywo whose military mind told him that war would, far from hindering the process, act as a deterrent and drive forward the peace process. He was wrong.

In September 2002, John Garang's army overran the town of Torit, killing a close friend of President Bashir and other high ranking GOS officers. The death of Mulla Ahmed Haj Nur who was a very close friend of Bashir's pained the President a lot. Nur had been instrumental in drafting the September 1983 Sharia laws under Numeiri. He was one of the clerics who had come to the South to fight a *jihad*. He fought in Juba, Nimule, Jabayei and later the Juba-Torit road. SPLM/A went on to occupy Torit for a while. Pained and humiliated, Bashir erupted. A few days later, the government fired off a letter to Sumbeiywo accusing him of giving in to the demands of SPLM/A far too easily. In the letter dated September 2, 2002, the government accused the SPLM/A of introducing other demands that were not in the Machakos Protocol, singling out power sharing, relations between state and religion, the structure of government and the boundaries of the South. The GOS was also unhappy with the SPLM/A's insistence that the three conflict areas be addressed and accused the IGAD Secretariat of accepting SPLM/A's demands with a view to pleasing them at the expense of the rules agreed to in May, 2002 in Karen. "A clear departure from the agenda is unmistakably present in the SPLM/A position, by introducing the complicated issue of the three areas, a departure that was not only met with the secretariat approval, but with active advocacy for including the issue...." GOS went further to accuse the Secretariat of accepting "this untenable position and (is) charging the Government's delegation with the absurd task of responding to it, without any comment on its flagrant defiance of the Machakos Protocol."

Just as the SPLM/A's demand to have the three conflict areas addressed caught Sumbeiywo by surprise, the Government reaction also caused serious ripples in the Secretariat. What, however, Sumbeiywo was not told by the GOS was that they were unhappy over the SPLM/A's capture of and brutal attack on Torit. "They did not have the guts to tell us that they were withdrawing because SPLM/A was fighting," he recalls.

This fact, however, came out in their protest letter which stated in part that, "The Government of Sudan has made it very clear that an immediate stoppage of the fighting is essential both for humanitarian reasons and for creating an atmosphere more conducive to a successful conclusion of the peace talks under the aegis of IGAD."

At that time, it became clear that Khartoum was divided on whether to continue with the talks or to walk away. President Bashir's camp wanted to continue but there was another camp, led by the First Vice-President, Ali Osman Mohammed Taha, whose representative at the talks was Nafie Ali Nafie, which was pressing to walk away.

Two tense days later, the GOS withdrew its delegation and released a statement explaining away their action. They stated that they were walking away because "the concerns of our negotiating team have not been adequately addressed and that the prevailing atmosphere is not conducive to constructive negotiations." The short letter also stated that, "Wide consultations and new formulations of certain positions were needed and also affirmed the GOS commitment to the Machakos Protocol and the IGAD peace process."

In spite of this, the Secretariat did not budge. Sumbeiywo and his people continued talking quietly with those who wished to go on. But the GOS position was that the entire delegation had to return to Khartoum.

At that time, many believed that the talks had collapsed. Sumbeiywo himself could have said, "Mission Impossible". As a military man, he knew that such setbacks were not uncommon on the road to either war or peace. He recognised the hiccup as just one of the many obstacles thrown on the path to peace this time by the government. Deep inside, however, Sumbeiywo felt that there remained a sliver of hope and he wanted to pursue it to the last house of its refuge.

The day the GOS delegation pulled out, he rushed to brief President Moi. Sumbeiywo convinced the President that he had to follow the Government side to Khartoum and talk them into returning to the negotiating table. At the same time, he convinced Garang to go and talk to President Moi on what he could expect for the negotiations to continue. Garang agreed to speak with President Moi on the condition that his movement's cause was not prejudiced. At State House, Nairobi, Moi asked Garang about Torit.

"How important is it to you?" President Moi asked him.

"It really is not important to us," Garang answered. But he continued to give a vivid account of how it was taken. He described, in a rather melodramatic way, the moves the SPLM/A made to overrun Torit, making sure that the SPLM/A's military might was not lost on the President. He had overrun the 10 square kilometre area using seven tanks and his soldiers had exhibited admirable panache, he affirmed. It was clear that Garang was elated at the capture of Torit.

It was not clear if President Moi was impressed. But using his ingenuity, Moi replied, "That was an important thing." Then he asked, "But was it important to do that?"

Garang paused. The man famed for his intelligence was at a loss for words. He appeared doubtful of the wisdom of what he had done. He admitted, however, that he wanted to make a statement; that the SPLM/A could still fight, that it was not a lesser partner in the negotiations and that the alternative to a negotiated settlement still remained blood and iron.

"Mzee," he told President Moi, "These people do not understand anything other than the barrel of a gun. I was showing them that it was not out of weakness that I was negotiating. If they want us to go back to war, we would ably do so."

President Moi listened as Garang talked. Garang always addressed Moi as Mzee, a Kiswahili term for a respected elder. He had a lot of respect for him. In turn, President Moi was a good listener and a charmer.

"No, we cannot do two things at the same time," President Moi retorted. "We cannot negotiate and fight. Let's go back to the negotiating table."

There was some silence. "I will work out a formula for returning to the negotiations." The President continued, " Will you accept it?"

"Yes, Mzee," Garang deferred to Moi, "I have always said that I will accept anything so long as it does not jeopardise the movement's position."

"And what is the movement's position?" Moi sought to know.

"The movement wants enduring peace." Garang said, leaving it as vague as that.

President Moi immediately detected a chink in the SPLM/A's robustness. They were still interested in negotiations and it was worth pulling all stops to ensure that the talks did not fail. It was by then becoming clear that the target of achieving any agreement that

President Moi had set was not going to be met. The year was ending and the grandstanding was still going on. The following year, Moi would be out of office. What, however, was more important to the old man was peace, at whatever cost and whatever duration of time.

Meanwhile, Sumbeiywo proceeded to Khartoum to convince the government to return its delegation to the talks. From the way the twig of negotiations was bent, he knew that First Vice-President Ali Osman Taha was a key figure in the talks. In fact, he had been given full authority by Bashir to steer them. His word was then law to the delegation. Sumbeiywo desperately wanted to meet Taha. He knew the man but every time he had attempted to see him, the man was not available. Genuinely, he was a busy man.

However, he managed to see the President later in 2002. But Bashir was still furious with what Garang had done in Torit. The fact that Garang's Army had humiliated the government by taking such a small town did not sting him as much as did the killing of his friend. In fact the war in Sudan had claimed so many people, including his own brother, Amir Isam Hassan Ahmed Al Bashir. Others were high ranking government officers. In 1998, for instance, the First Vice-President Zuberi Mohammed Saleh, while flying with a renegade SPLA officer, Arok Thon Arok who was formerly head of intelligence at SPLA and a man who was described as a very fine young officer, Shamsha el Din, were shot down in a helicopter around Nasir in Southern Sudan. This and the death of Mulla stung Bashir to no end. It continued to be a constant source of belligerence in him and the starkest reminder that he was up against a deadly enemy. In fact, Bashir later married the officer's widow in order to bring up his children. He insisted that he would not discuss anything with Garang unless there was total cessation of hostilities first. Bashir accused Garang of not being in charge of his troops. "They do whatever they want even when we are negotiating," he complained.

Sumbeiywo said he would talk to Garang and indicated that it was President Moi's desire that all hostilities ceased while negotiations went on. He asked President Bashir to send a small delegation to meet the SPLM/A to iron out the details of the cessation of hostilities and gave Bashir a draft Cessation of Hostilities Proposal Details to study.

After that, Bashir was calm. He even agreed to meet Sumbeiywo the following day. A few days later, the SPLM/A withdrew from Torit. But the damage had already been done. The harder task was now to bring the two sides to the negotiating table, again.

As luck would have it, Sumbeiywo had a friend who knew Garang well and who was influential, in a way, in his life. Abel Ariel, a Dinka, had been Second Vice-President in Numeiri's Government and President of the South after the Addis Ababa Agreement. He was also related to

Garang's wife, Rebecca. After discussions on how to restart the talks, Abel agreed to explore ways of how to go about it. After a week, they met in Nairobi and had a four hour lunch in which they plotted on how to restart the talks.

Eager to see the talks back on track, Kenya's Foreign Affairs Minister, Kalonzo Musyoka, called a subcommittee ministerial meeting to discuss the resumption. By that time, Sumbeiywo had drafted a document on cessation of hostilities. The Ministers discussed the document after which they invited the parties to a meeting. The meeting culminated in their signing an agreement called the Memorandum of Understanding on Cessation of Hostilities on 15th October, 2002 and the immediate resumption of the talks.

There evidently was a great deal of politics involved in the moving back and forth of the negotiations. For instance, on December 11, 2002, after the signing of the Machakos Protocol and the agreement on a few other contentious issues, the advisor to President Bashir, Ghazi Salahudin Atabani, wrote a tough and acerbic letter to Sumbeiywo decrying the Secretariat's biased stand on some issues and lamenting that SPLM/A was trying to deadlock the talks. He complained that SPLM/A had already announced the issue of bank notes in the South and displayed specimens. Attabani said that an SPLM/A spokesman Mr Samson Kwaje, had also indicated that SPLM/A was intent "upon establishing a Central Bank in Yei, Southern Sudan."

Attabani also complained that Garang had made an unprecedented visit to Kauda in Southern Kordofan. "He took part in a gathering there and made a statement that the case of Nuba Mountains is part and parcel of the conflict in Southern Sudan."

The advisor went on to caution, "the issue of bank notes and establishment of a Central Bank is(sic) viewed by the Government of Sudan as a provocative step that aims at pre-empting the current negotiations on wealth sharing in Machakos. In addition, such step would constitute a clear violation of the IGAD DOP, the Machakos Protocol, and the Memorandum of Understanding, all signed by the SPLM/A."

Attabani also fired a warning that, "The Government too has the interest and capacity to introduce new items on the agenda. If this is allowed, I shall instruct the government delegation to table some of these in the upcoming round on the 6th of January. Moreover, if there is any benefit in broaching such questions in the media as the ones raised by the SPLM/A leader, probably with the intention of educating the public about our differences, we could agree on such arrangement with the SPLM/A in the upcoming round."

This was no threat to the peace process, but it was a pointer to the thinking of the government and the suspicion that characterised the peace talks. The SPLM/A persisted in their insistence on discussion of the three conflict areas before moving on to power sharing and wealth sharing in detail. The government again refused saying that the areas were in the North. Again, negotiations within negotiations had to be held. Sumbeiywo asked the UK to mediate, but the SPLM/A rejected the British out of hand, saying that the UK would favour the government.

"Let us give it to the US then," Sumbeiywo suggested. The government said no. Eventually it was resolved that Kenya as a country be the mediator with negotiations led by General Sumbeiywo.

This was tricky. Sumbeiywo had to do it in such a way that it would not look like the other IGAD member states had been kicked out of the process. On the conflict areas, if he did it alone, Kenya would be accused of taking on the peace process alone. Cleverly, General Sumbeiywo "recruited" delegates from the other countries to be the resource persons and observers.

This was, however, towards the end of the year and the elections were now very near. As head of the Army, Sumbeiywo was badly needed at the headquarters. He was the one who was in charge of the handover and it was upon him and the senior Kenya government officials that a smooth transition depended.

Just before the elections, he travelled with Moi to the US in December 2002, where they met with President George W. Bush. Bush assured outgoing President Moi that the US would support Sumbeiywo in IGAD even after change of government. Present was Collin Powell, the Secretary of State, who also pledged his full support for Sumbeiywo. This greatly energised him. He had the support of the superpowers even though the political climate back in the country was uncertain. The US support was to prove invaluable a few months later.

By then, it was becoming pretty obvious that the ruling party, KANU, might lose the election to a motley of parties under the National Rainbow Coalition, NARC. As the head of the Army, Sumbeiywo had to be very careful. It would be difficult to balance his duties at IGAD with those of the military. So the talks were postponed until after the election.

After the election in December, KANU lost to the opposition and President Mwai Kibaki assumed the presidency. Sumbeiywo had the onerous task of organising the handing over ceremony, designing the Presidential stand of the new Head of State and organising the parade. He sold the whole plan to Moi who accepted it.

In conflict resolutions, things do not always go according to plan. The Cessation of Hostilities Agreement did not quite end the fighting on the ground and there was also the issue of the three conflict areas that hovered like a shadow over the talks. In fact, the talks were threatened by more than just one factor. Around this time, the government of Sudan was preparing to attack a place called Leer in Western Upper Nile. This is a very small area which is abundant with oil. Though General Sumbeiywo continued looking for modalities to get the negotiations back on track, the parties were not willing to continue. There was still a great deal of mistrust and bad faith. This was amply testified to by the open violation of the memorandum on cessation of hostilities. The government eventually did overrun Leer on January 28, 2003. SPLM/A refused to continue with the negotiations, insisting that the government stop the construction of the Bentiu-Adok road in Southern Sudan. The construction of the road through the oil-producing areas was a major cause of conflict between SPLM/A and the Government of Sudan with civilians caught up in the conflict as they were displaced in other areas. The government insisted that the road was necessary for "development" (oil exploration) and also sought to blame SPLM/A for the attack saying that it was the rebel group that had fired mortars at the government garrison at Leer the night before.

The SPLM/A denied those allegations and asserted that the government had regularly attacked and destroyed civilian villages along the path of the road construction to Leer. It also asserted, according to a report filed later by the Civilian Protection Monitoring Team, that the construction of the Bentiu-Adok road violated the Cessation of Hostilities Agreement.

This incident, coupled with the other ongoing violation of the MOU, presented one of the biggest threats to the negotiations. It was clear that the earlier MOU would be ineffective, having already been violated. It behoved Sumbeiywo to start negotiations within negotiations in order to strengthen the MOU on cessation of hostilities. He called Foreign Minister, Kalonzo Musyoka, who in turn called a Council of Ministers Meeting and who approved the plan for monitoring the cessation of hostilities.

In total, there were nine drafts on how to strengthen the MOU with a Monitoring Mechanism, but eventually the parties agreed upon a final document, an Addendum to the Memorandum of Understanding on Cessation of Hostilities. It was signed by both parties in Karen on February 4, 2003.

The document required the parties to inform the MOU Channel of Communications Committee in advance of all troop movements, including rotations and supply and re-supply of non-combat items. It also called on the parties to provide to the MOU Committee the identity and location of their own forces and all allied forces and affiliated militia.

Among other requirements, the MOU required both parties to allow a Verification and Monitoring Team (VMT), which may include personnel and aircraft from an expanded Civilian Protection Monitoring Team (CPMT), IGAD, AU, observer nations (Italy, Norway, UK and the US). Members of both parties would have the right to participate in verification and monitoring missions. The parties were also required to permit free access to the VMT to travel in and around areas where a complaint had been filed by any of the parties and that the team informs the MOU committee of its findings.

Both parties were also required to take immediate steps to ensure that any location taken over by any party in violation to the MOU since it came into effect on October 17th 2002, were immediately restored to the party that had control over them prior to the violation. In the addendum, the parties also resolved to suspend work on the Bentiu-Adok Road until the final, Comprehensive Peace Agreement was signed.

The US hailed this move and celebrated the return of the parties to the negotiating table. "Really on his own and without any prodding from us, General Sumbeiywo took a tremendously tough line," remarked Ambassador Ranneberger. Sumbeiywo's concerted pressure on the Sudanese Government led it to take a pretty extraordinary step and signed the addendum to the ceasefire.

12

New President, Retired General

Even as the signing of the Addendum to the MOU was being executed, things had greatly changed for Sumbeiywo. Moi, the man who had wholeheartedly supported the Sudan peace process, had finally retired. There was a new man at State House, Mwai Kibaki, whom Sumbeiywo was yet to know properly.

The advantage he had as a mediator was that he had full access to the President. He could walk into State House as many times as was necessary. He could lift up the phone and get the President on the line and he enjoyed the privilege of having known Moi very well and having worked with him in good and bad times.

When you share happy times and calamitous times with a man, a bond is effected that not even time is able to ravage. Sumbeiywo and Moi shared the vision of a peaceful, united Sudan and they had single-mindedly committed themselves to that cause. Though the new President was likely to continue with the process, it was not certain what level of access Sumbeiywo would enjoy and what kind of support would be extended to him.

Every President comes to power with his own men. Kibaki, of course, came to power with his own people. Even though he was careful not to shock the system of governance in the initial months of his presidency, there was heightened anticipation that radical changes would be carried out in government. There was a frisson of fear at Uhuru Park during the handover ceremony. For the first time in the history of Kenya, a regime had been democratically replaced by another. The death of the founding father of the nation, Jomo Kenyatta, had ushered in a peaceful transition. But this one was going to be different and difficult.

Under General Sumbeiywo, the Army organised what would be a smooth handover of power in a dispassionate and professional way. This was also a time when Sumbeiywo's professionalism as a soldier was put to the test. During the electioneering period, it was becoming clear that KANU was on its way out. But because KANU had been in government for so long, (in fact, it had been the ruling party since independence) it was almost unthinkable that it could lose. Not many people visualized Kenya without KANU at the helm. The civil service then was slow in accepting the eventuality of a change of government.

"No one wanted to anticipate a Kibaki win," recalls General A.S.K. Njoroge, "but Sumbeiywo was tough on it. He asked me to go on and do all that was necessary for a smooth handover."

As head of the Army, Sumbeiywo understood that the military had to be impartial. He therefore set about organising the inauguration ceremony of the new Head of State.

The favourite candidate was Mwai Kibaki who, only a month before the voting day had been involved in a bad accident that saw him hospitalised for three weeks, left him in a wheel chair and a neck brace. And if Kibaki became President, how would he inspect the guard of honour? How would he get up the dais? It was obvious to the Army bosses, led by Lt General A.S.K. Njoroge, who was then the Commander of the Eastern Division that was mounting the parade for the transition, that a ramp would have to be built. But government officials refused to see this. Rather than acknowledge that KANU, the feared ruling party, would lose, they sought to stay away. The Ministry of Public Works under which the construction of presidential daises is carried, refused to come on board for fear of being seen to have written the ruling party off. General Njoroge knew that if the Army did not do something, it would be caught unawares.

"You know anything can happen in this election. You must build a ramp. The military must not be caught unawares," Sumbeiywo instructed Lt Gen Njoroge. With minimal government support, Njoroge had to go and look for a private contractor to build the ramp.

As had been expected, Kibaki won the election and had to be sworn in his wheel chair and in a neck brace. Sumbeiywo's gamble had paid off and the Army was spared the embarrassment of being caught unawares. Despite the small hiccups experienced at Uhuru Park, the venue of the inauguration ceremony, the handover went on well and the Army saluted their new Commander-in-Chief and Head of State, in what would definitely be the beginning of major changes in the life of the country.

****

The changes began almost immediately. In February 2003, Sumbeiywo was unexpectedly called by the Chief of General Staff. He had just arrived from Sudan in another whirlwind mission of peace. He had been briefed that there would be a meeting of the Service Commanders and being one of them, he did not find anything unusual in the CGS wanting to meet him.

What he did not know was that the CGS had unpleasant news for him. "The government has made some changes in the Army and you have been retired," the CGS told him. This was a bit of a surprise for Sumbeiywo. His four year tenure had been cut by half and he was being retired after only two years at the helm of the Army. He listened as his boss spoke. Then Sumbeiywo calmly said, "This is OK. I am the one who has been kicking others out of the Army. This then should be my turn."

The CGS was relieved. He had been worried about how Sumbeiywo would take the retirement but he admired the calmness of the man and his positive outlook on life.

Sumbeiywo, however, made two requests: that the announcement should not go on air until he had informed his family, and two, that he hands over immediately so that he could go back to work on Sudan. Both requests were granted.

The two men then walked to the conference room where the Service Commanders' meeting was to be held. The announcement was made and Sumbeiywo's replacement was named as Lt General Jeremiah Mutinda Kianga, his former deputy.

The officers were shocked. They did not say much but it was clear that they could not quite comprehend what was going on. One of the Commanders looked at Sumbeiywo and asked him, "Do you understand what the CGS has just said?"

"Yes, I do," he responded, "but I am happy I am going where I am going. I request you to fully cooperate with my successor."

As the meeting broke, the Commanders all looked at Sumbeiywo and thought that the military was losing a dedicated reformer. But they accepted the changes as part of what happens when government changes hands. On his part, Sumbeiywo called all his senior officers and informed them of what had happened. He also ordered them to start handover preparations immediately.

His wife Lorna and the family were shocked. Lorna was having a cup of tea with a friend in Karen when Sumbeiywo called her. She remembers vividly her husband's voice and the words that almost changed her world and that of a family that had known their father as only a military man, "I have been called by the CGS," he told his wife, "and I was given a letter."

Lorna listened attentively as the voice on the other end completed what should have been bad news, "I have been retired. Call the children and tell them that." Lorna was dumbstruck but she knew that had to happen. Sumbeiywo's daughter, Flora Sumbeiywo, was very disappointed on receiving the news. She had to leave work early to be with the family. Rose, the other daughter could not disguise her shock too, "I had known Dad as a military man all my life," she remembers telling herself, "now he had been retired. We were all in shock but we were encouraged that he was taking it better than us."

In many ways, Sumbeiywo had expected some changes. But he did not expect to be retired so soon as he still had two more years to go. Nevertheless, there had been rumours that he would be retired and they had reached him in snippets. The retirement of an Army Commander after only two years had never happened in the history of the country. This is what made the likelihood of the rumours being true more remote. But as they say, rumours like rivers, have sources and the sources proved to be quite reliable.

Just to be sure that he was leaving the Army a clean man, Sumbeiywo later went to see the Head of the Civil Service, Ambassador Francis Muthaura about his early retirement. He wanted to know if he had been disloyal and if he was going to work as an Ambassador (to the peace process) in a government that did not trust him. He wanted reassurance that he still enjoyed the confidence of the government. Muthaura listened to him as he sought his answers and responded, "You had to go. You just had to go." There was no further elaboration.

Reminiscing on this incident, Sumbeiywo only remembers telling himself that it was time to commit his energies elsewhere, "I did not want to live in the past," he told himself, "I did not even feel hurt."

The senior officers understood the circumstances behind Sumbeiywo's departure quite well. "He had to go, not because of inefficiency, but because of politics," said General A.S.K. Njoroge, who was appointed the Deputy Army Commander in the changes.

"Everyone knew that the former President had a soft spot for him. Gen. Sumbeiywo was seen as too close to Moi. On the other hand, everyone knew that Sumbeiywo was a very strong and independent minded man as far as the military was concerned. This is not the sort of man many people in a new government might feel comfortable with," reminisced General Njoroge.

Two days after the announcement, the change of guard was clinically carried out. It was his wish to relinquish office as soon as possible. In an elaborate ceremony that would live in his mind for as long as he lives, the Army staged a colourful send off, covered by the local media and given extensive airtime on all TV stations in the country. This was the first time the media in Kenya had been allowed to cover a ceremony of the change of guard at the Army. Pictures of the General being ceremonially towed to the gates of the Army Headquarters to start life as a civilian entranced thousands of Kenyans.

After receiving his successor at the Army Headquarters, the two Generals in full uniform took the salute from the army band and a detachment of the Seventh Battalion of the Kenya Rifles. The two were invited to inspect a guard of honour in turns, starting with Sumbeiywo. After this, he handed over the Commander's flag to his successor.

Afterwards, the two boarded an open ceremonial Land Rover and were escorted to the main gate by officers and the army band. In a moment that would be indelibly etched on the minds of those who watched it, the Land Rover which was fitted with two thick ropes was pulled for about 300 metres from the Senior Officers' Mess to the gate by officers of the rank of Colonel and above. The event symbolised the old British tradition where a retiring General was escorted out of the military camp in a horse-drawn carriage. It symbolised that he had been sent off in dignity and honour and that he would always be welcomed as an ordinary citizen.

As he shook hands with the officers he had spent over 35 years with, General Sumbeiywo reflected on the three decades and a half that he had been at the military. And when the gates closed behind him, he was filled with a great sense of satisfaction. "I served in this profession with honour and dignity," he was later to say, "this should be the aspiration of every officer in uniform."

For Sumbeiywo, this was a sea change. All his adult life had been spent in the military. Now he had hung up his uniform, was out of the place he had known best and was re-entering a new world as a civilian with a huge task ahead of him. He had lived in the cocoon of the military, following orders, issuing some, wearing its uniform, guided by its rules and associating with its members since entering the cadet college. Now he was saying goodbye to all that. The silver lining on this cloud was that he was being released to perform his duties unhindered at IGAD, for President Kibaki made no changes to the Sudan peace process. He retained Sumbeiywo as the Special Envoy to the peace process and restated his commitment to seeing peace in the Sudan.

His former boss, General Mulinge, who had been the Chief of General Staff for 16 years, was also not shocked by the retirement. "Sumbeiywo was a gallant soldier and gallant soldiers move on to the next mission when one is over," he said. And so this gallant soldier moved on.

The peace process was proceeding on well and it was entering a new challenging phase. With lighter duties, he had no doubts that he would be able to steer the process even more firmly. But he was also to realise that every new administration presents considerable hiccups to the status quo. Even as he soldiered on, it became obvious to him that he would no longer enjoy unfettered access to the President. Though the new President had assured him that he was free to call him, bureaucracy and walls erected by the President's men ensured that no such thing happened often.

But what Sumbeiywo perhaps did not know was that even at the peace process, his position was threatened. Some people were convincing President Kibaki to drop him and appoint someone else. Owing probably to his tight ties with the earlier regime, they saw Sumbeiywo as a threat and did not want to have anything to do with him. In any case, this was in keeping with the new pattern where the people in the new government wanted nothing to do with those associated with the old, although many in NARC had at one time or another been part of the Kanu regime, including Kibaki, who served as Moi's Vice-President for nearly 10 years. Though the new President had retained most of the senior civil servants, there were those around him who felt mightily uncomfortable with officers associated with the Moi regime. Sumbeiywo was a marked man.

When Kalonzo Musyoka got wind of the news, he went straight to the President and convinced him that at that stage in the peace process, it would be suicidal to remove Sumbeiywo.

"Your Excellency," Kalonzo Musyoka remembers telling the President, "the negotiations are too advanced to be taken over by someone else. Besides, Sumbeiywo has done a perfect job." The President agreed with the Minister who had been re-appointed as Foreign Affairs Minister under Kibaki, and also asked him to deal directly with the General. At that time the President's health was a bit shaky and those around him did not want him to carry a huge burden upon his shoulders.

International pressure also ensured that the mediator was not changed. Eric Reeves, a professor of English at Smith College in Northampton, Massachusetts, USA and an expert on the Sudan expressed this concern: "There would be some temptation on the part of Kibaki and his coalition to engage in Governmental house cleaning. It would be extremely unfortunate if this were to extend to a reconsideration of General Sumbeiywo's role in the Machakos peace process." Reeves acknowledged that, "Sumbeiywo has become indispensable, both as a force for keeping the parties negotiating and as the only person who can render a fully authoritative account of responsibility should the talks fail in 2003 to yield a just peace."

The Americans made it clear that they were supporting Sumbeiywo. This view was given more buoyancy by the fact that Sumbeiywo had paid a courtesy call on Collin Powell in Washington in December 2002 and President Moi's meeting with Bush around the same time. This forced those who wanted him removed to soften. That hurdle overcome, Sumbeiywo now found himself dealing directly with the Minister for Foreign Affairs and later, the Minister for a newly created office of East Africa and Regional Affairs. Matters of protocol and access to the President or lack of it were to prove a little embarrassing to the negotiating parties and Heads of State who were keen on seeing the process completed and who continued visiting the negotiating parties in both Karen and Naivasha where the final phases were carried out.

But because Kalonzo was no stranger to Sumbeiywo, things went on well in the initial months of the Kibaki Presidency. They were nevertheless to change dramatically when Kalonzo was removed from the Foreign Affairs docket and a new Minister, Chirau Ali Mwakwere, brought in. The creation of the Ministry of East Africa and Regional Affairs headed by John Koech also complicated matters. No one seemed to be in charge of the peace process and this temporarily affected the pecking order of the process with regard to mediation and protocol.

Determination to see the Peace Process go on, however, ensured that no lapse occurred. When the two parties met in Karen to resume negotiations in 2003, things were to move at full throttle, interspersed by the twists and turns that had by now become a feature of the talks.

****

When the talks resumed in Karen in January 2003, Sumbeiywo was to find out that no business could be transacted without first tackling the issue of the three conflict areas. Like an apparition, the conflict areas kept reappearing and it was obvious that the negotiations would go nowhere if the matter was not immediately dispensed with. The negotiations on this particular problem took time to yield fruits. The three areas, as we have already seen, had similar problems that they wanted resolved, i.e. denial of political freedoms, political negligence by the centre, oppression, political marginalisation, political misrepresentation, lack of resources, oppression of women and a host of other social issues. There were also religious and cultural issues, for instance, in Southern Blue Nile, the people complained of the Government of Sudan Army's declaration of *jihad* against the Funj people, destruction of indigenous cultures and values, destruction of indigenous languages, forced Arabisation, forced Islamisation, religious persecution and discrimination and cultural assimilation.

In Abyei, there was a burning need to recognise and give expression to the Ngok Dinka connection to the Dinka in the South. The Dinka community in Abyei also wanted a say in the administration, equitable distribution of resources and a right to self-determination. They also felt that land disputes had to be resolved and a mechanism identified which would be competent or empowered to determine the questions of ownership, access to land resources and to determine the management of the resources. They also wanted the territory and relevant districts defined. It had to be determined from where Abyei would be governed during the Interim Period.

In Southern Kordofan, the absence of the promised regional autonomy had contributed to an unresponsive administration and lack of political influence. As part of the solution, the people wanted an agreement on the administrative systems and units. The population also was demanding an agreement on an education system acceptable to the people of the region and which took into account cultural aspects. All these issues had to be resolved before the peace talks could get back on an even keel. How were they resolved and what was the verdict?

Everything got underway soon after signing the Addendum to the Cessation of Hostilities. As the chairman of IGAD, Sumbeiywo's role in chairing talks within talks was onerous. With the support of observers and resource persons, he got the representatives in one room. But even this was not easy. The negotiations on the Abyei area would not start because SPLM/A insisted that the delegates were not from Abyei. There was no problem with the Southern Blue Nile delegation. They got on well to identifying the root cause of the problems, coming up with a method to solve them and finding a solution. But Nuba Mountains delegation insisted on self-determination. This, as we have already seen, was a thorny issue even in the main negotiations. SPLM/A and the Government of Sudan were finding it difficult to agree on it. How would the Nuba delegation hope to achieve it?

Sumbeiywo's frustration was immense. The talks proceeded glacially with the delegates moving back and forth. After two weeks, very little had been achieved. Sumbeiywo was left with no choice but to call off the talks on the conflict areas.

SPLM/A was happy that at last the conflict areas had come to the table of negotiations. Having already been accused of betrayal, they now had something to take back to the people even if it was not yet a definite settlement. But as part of looking for a long-lasting solution to the conflict areas, Sumbeiywo took to travelling in Sudan, visiting all the areas and hearing first-hand from the people what they really wanted.

13

Where is the Peace?

First, Sumbeiywo travelled to Khartoum and to most of the areas held by the SPLM/A in Southern Sudan. He went to Kurmuk in Blue Nile, Kauda in the Nuba Mountains and Agok where the Ngok Dinka from Abyei have settled. He met the elders, youth, religious leaders, and women groups and addressed public rallies everywhere he went. He also visited Rumbek, Yambio, Yei, Malaluakon and Ikotos. The stories he heard there from ordinary Sudanese people gave him the impetus to continue with his role as a mediator.

At Malalakuon, in Bahr-El-Ghazal, he met an old Dinka woman. She was wearing some fragments of garment made from animal skin. The haggard looking woman stopped the General and asked him, "Who is older, you or Garang?"

"It is Garang," Sumbeiywo humbly responded.

"I have heard that you are the man of peace. Why did you not bring peace?" the woman asked.

"We are still negotiating."

"Do not come back here until you have the peace," the woman said, looking Sumbeiywo straight in the eyes, "You see these tattered clothes I am wearing? I will not change them until you bring me peace."

Sumbeiywo was touched and challenged. He made a solemn promise to the woman, "I will do my best to see that peace comes to Southern Sudan and I shall come back to you once we achieve it."

"Do not come back without peace," the woman repeated and went away.

Much later when the peace deal was signed, Sumbeiywo inquired about the woman and learned her name and where she lived.

In almost all the places he went to under SPLM/A control, at stake was not the oil or the natural resources. The people did not mind dividing the oil or living under sharia law. This was not an immediate concern. All they wanted was to have their own Army.

"Stop the war," a group of people shouted, "Let's remain with our army, let the Arabs remain with their capital."

The people's understanding of the conflict had a profound effect on Sumbeiywo. He could at last see and touch the raw suffering of the people, he could listen to them, he saw their supplicatory eyes as they begged him to stop the war, he saw the immense faith they had in him. But he also saw a people who were determined to fight and die for their rights, he saw a people hardened by suffering and who did not mind doing a few more years of it so long as there was justification at the end.

After the visit to Damazin and Kadugli, he finally met First Vice-President Ali Osman Taha in Khartoum. Though they did not say a lot to each other, something told Sumbeiywo that that was the man calling the shots in Sudan.

"The body language told me he was in control," Sumbeiywo now recalls, "Taha was the power behind the throne."

The quiet, soft spoken and reflective man almost disarmed the General. The First Vice-President is a man who listens attentively and takes his time before speaking. These were qualities Sumbeiywo would use later to his advantage.

At the end of his trip, Sumbeiywo was requested to also visit areas in the South held by the government. The Sudanese Government used the First Vice President to make the request, to which Sumbeiywo had no objection. The first place he visited was Malakal, one of the state capitals and proceeded to the Heglig oil field in western Upper Nile. Here, Sumbeiywo was amazed to find Kenyans working furiously in the hospitality industry in the oil fields. He visited Rupkona, a military base before going on to Bentiu. Bentiu was a collection of grass-thatched houses. The place is inhabited by the Nuer community, an aggressive and warlike people. While he was addressing a public rally, the crowd surged towards him. He wondered what they were up to and because he knew they be could abrasive and easily irritated, he was, for a moment, fearful that something untoward would happen to him. The surging crowd surrounded him and, out of the blue, lifted him up to dance. He was later to learn that this was their way of showing appreciation. But they were still weary of him, principally because he was an outsider.

When Sumbeiywo met their leader, Major General Paulino Matip, both men hugged and the Nuer relaxed. What they did not know was that both men had earlier met in Khartoum. Matip, neither spoke English nor Arabic. Everything had to be translated into Nuer. The Nuer, a fiercely traditional people, were pro-government and they had bitter memories of their previous war with the Dinka. They were apprehensive that the Dinka would overrun them. They wanted reassurance from the General that that would not happen.

When he arrived at Wau, he found a huge crowd of people waiting. Wau is a big town and Sumbeiywo and his company decided to walk through the huge crowd. They walked one kilometre, mingling with the people, hearing their views and dropping some pellets of hope here and there. After walking for a kilometre, Sumbeiywo was persuaded to climb into an open Land Rover. He waved and the people cheered. It was like the President had arrived.

In Wau, Sumbeiywo decided to visit a camp for internally displaced people (IDP). What he saw cut his mind adrift. The people lived by a river in what was to all intents and purposes, dreadful squalor. "They tried to be happy when they saw us," he recalls, "but we could see they were hopeless."

Though Sumbeiywo tried to comfort them, the one question they heard in monotonous frequency was; "When do we go back to our homes?"

It was an answer the General did not have at the time but whose pursuit he felt he must hasten. The people were housed in shacks made of polythene bags. There were no latrines, no schools, no piped water and no basic amenities. The population numbered about one thousand and the eyes of malnourished children peered out of their sunken cheeks like weak fire flies. The limbs of emaciated adults flailed in the air, eternal symbols of the demoniacal nature of war.

In the suffering of these people, the entire evil of war was brutally telescoped for the General. Even as a military man he had never had to encounter this kind of suffering. He knew what the end result of war was but now that he was coming face to face with it, he was filled with an inescapable urgency to bring a speedy end to the conflict.

Sumbeiywo and his team of Mrs Keiru from the IGAD Secretariat, Dr Susan Page and Prof. Haysom spent the night in Wau. They were later to learn that the food they ate was brought all the way from Khartoum. The displaced people had nothing to eat. There was guilt and frustration, yet there was little they could do other than remain deeply committed to the search for an end to the conflict that had condemned these people to such horrifying misery.

In Juba, the people were agitated. At the public rally the General's team held, a chief rose to speak and started castigating the government. Every speaker castigated the government, asking for peace, self-determination and their own army. After this meeting, Sumbeiywo's team packed up and went back to Nairobi. They now had a better understanding of the situation.

****

There is a great deal of difference between a person who is forced to confront suffering in the raw and one who sees it via television. While the pictures of suffering conveyed via television deracinate the mind in their own peculiar ways, the medium's gaze, as Ignatieff noted, is "brief, intense and promiscuous and the shelf life of the moral cause it makes its own is brutally short. But a man who has confronted suffering in its epic horror never forgets that image, even when nothing of it is broadcast or televised." After his journey to Sudan and his talks with the ordinary citizens, who were the real sufferers in the conflict, Sumbeiywo was motivated. He was forced to interrogate himself and rise above the hurdles now threatening to slow down or derail the talks.

So when he returned to Nairobi, he begun writing a document called the *Framework on the Resolution of the Outstanding Issues Based on the Machakos Protocol*. The document sought to identify the critical remaining issues and try to resolve fairly what the Sudanese needed to resolve if peace was to be attained. He intended to present it to the negotiating parties as a draft on which the negotiations would be based. What he, however, could not have known at that time was that that document would stir the hornet's nest and almost become the bane of the talks.

Sumbeiywo and Foreign Affairs Minister, Kalonzo Musyoka, rallied the entire region to support the document. They went to see the Heads of States of Uganda, Eritrea and Ethiopia. They went to Algeria where they saw the President who advised them not to push the parties to the wall; they should leave the document to the last. This was almost prophetic. However, following briefings to both sides in Khartoum and New Site, a Southern Sudanese settlement, on the contents of the framework and receiving their go-ahead to pursue possible trade-offs within the text that the parties themselves could not present, Sumbeiywo convened a meeting in Nakuru in July 2003, attended by the parties and observers. At the same time, an African Union meeting was taking place in Maputo. Two important things happened. The government refused to negotiate on the document Sumbeiywo had prepared. And two, in Maputo, the Sudanese Foreign Minister presented a paper to the Council of Ministers praising the progress IGAD had made, but also requesting that the negotiations be now taken over by South Africa. The request was contained in a proposal the government gave to the Council of Ministers.

The talks in Nakuru became deadlocked. There was, according to Sumbeiywo, no hope of going forward. "These people have completely refused to negotiate," he sent his wife a text message on her mobile phone, "Let us pray that things work out well."

On the edge of his nerves, he had to call Kalonzo Musyoka in Maputo and brief him so that he would have something to report to the AU, whose meeting was underway. He got the Minister on the phone but even before he could fully explain, the Minister's hurried voice told him that all was not well.

"Wait", the Minister told the General who was now attempting to explain the deadlock, "We have a bigger problem here than you think." It was not until he faxed him the Sudanese Government proposal that Sumbeiywo knew that things were much more complicated than the Nakuru deadlock.

Earlier, Sumbeiywo had heard that the Sudanese Government, which by now had come to regard Kenya as too pushy on the question of peace, had approached South Africa with a proposal that they take over the negotiations. The South Africans had agreed. But Dr Attalla Bashir, the Executive Secretary at IGAD, Djibouti, had overheard the conversation and he quickly briefed Kalonzo in strict confidence on what the Sudanese Foreign Minister was attempting to do. Kalonzo immediately approached the South African Foreign Minister, Dr Zuma, who admitted that her country had indeed been approached with the proposal.

"Do you know at what stage the talks are?" Kalonzo asked her.

"No, we do not know that for sure."

Kalonzo explained to her why it was not in the interest of peace for Sudan for South Africa to take over the process. The talks were far too advanced for boats to be changed mid-stream. South Africa agreed to drop their acceptance of the proposal. "We are not touching it," Kalonzo remembers Zuma's words.

If South Africa were to take over the talks, all the gains made thus far would be reversed and talks would begin afresh with no reference to the IGAD-led peace process. Besides, there was no guarantee that the proposal to South Africa would be acceptable to SPLM/A, having come from the government. This then meant one thing: that the talks could collapse or the date for an agreement be pushed further indefinitely.

Having convinced South Africa about the "unworkability" of the proposal, Kalonzo had to go a step further and save the talks. In a move that was to prove crucial, he hurriedly convened an IGAD Ministerial meeting in Maputo to reject the proposal. The meeting also modified the proposal and asserted that IGAD must continue with the negotiations, but South Africa could take over the implementation process in terms of the reconstruction of Sudan after the Agreement.

So what was the whole idea about South Africa taking over the talks? Who was behind it? It was the view at the time that the Government of Sudan was trying to do everything to derail the talks. If they had already acknowledged that IGAD had made progress, why did they now want to change the mediator? The answer to the question lay in the fact that the Government had noticed that it was in a corner and now wanted to derail the talks. In Nakuru, the deadlock continued. Sumbeiywo's document was rejected *in toto* by the government. In it, he had proposed that there be a collegial decision making process between Khartoum and Garang. Arising from what the people had told him, he also proposed that there be two separate armies, one of which would be the Southerners'. The government rejected it and the SPLM/A would not make any concessions on the issue of the armies.

The Nakuru Document proposed among other things, that "until such times as elections are held, the current incumbent President (or his successor or nominee) shall be President and Commander-in-Chief of the Sudan People's Armed Forces (SPAF)".

The Vice-President shall be the current SPLM/A Chairman (or his successor or nominee) who shall at the same time hold the post of Chairman/Head of the Government of Southern Sudan and Commander-in-Chief of the Sudan's Peoples Liberation Armed Forces (SPLAF) the armed force previously referred to as Sudan People's Liberation Army (SPLA).

The first document also proposed that the President would take decisions with the consent of the Vice-President, such as declarations of states of emergency or states of national defence and their terminations, and, among others, summoning, adjourning, or proroguing the national legislature.

"Should the post of President fall vacant," the document proposed, "the office of the President shall be filled by a person elected by the National Assembly."

On Southern Sudan, the document proposed that until such time as elections are held, the current SPLM/A Chairman (or his successor or nominee) shall be Chairman/Head of Government of Southern Sudan (GOSS). He shall at the same time hold the post of Vice-President of the Sudan and Commander-in-Chief of the Sudan People's Liberation Armed Forces (SPLAF). The Vice-Chairman of the GOSS shall be appointed by the Chairman, it went on and the Southern Assembly would ratify such appointments by a simple majority vote. The document made extensive proposals on the seat of the national government, national legislature and distribution of civil service posts and targets. It also made proposals on the percentages with regard to representation at the national assembly, set rules on the creation of national ministries and the appointment of governors, wealth sharing, land and natural resources, division of government assets and accounting standards and procedures for fiscal accountability. Sumbeiywo and other envoys also made it crystal clear that the text was placed before the parties for the purpose of negotiating just as they had asked. Sumbeiywo explained that the document could be changed as long as both parties agreed to the changes and that it was not meant as a "take it or leave it text".

But when President Bashir received the document, he flew off the handle. "Whoever is the author of this document," he thundered, "should soak it, drink it and go to hell."

Later, President Bashir sent President Mwai Kibaki a letter through Dr Ghazi Atabani, in which he accused the IGAD Secretariat (meaning Sumbeiywo) of attempting to derail the peace talks by introducing a new draft document. "This is a particularly sensitive juncture in the negotiations," Bashir wrote, "the draft proposal presented by the IGAD Secretariat in the last round has complicated the situation at a time when we all believed that a peace deal was about to be concluded."

The Sudanese government accused Sumbeiywo of being amenable to the machinations of Garang, whom they also accused of doing everything to obstruct progress in the negotiations. And in a long critique to the Nakuru document, the government accused the secretariat, of among other things, setting unfair standards of governance, guaranteeing the SPLM/A full monopoly over the South (the document recognizes the SPLM/A as the organisation worthy of ruling the South almost exclusively, the government said in the critique) and revisiting the controversial issue of state and religion. It also claimed that the document was fostering instability by arousing fresh regionalistic and tribalistic tendencies. Finally, the government dismissed the document as renouncing all previously agreed texts.

There was no chance that the talks could continue. A government negotiator reportedly said, "We came to discuss the house with you but we find you entering even the kitchen and bathroom."

The government could not contemplate a sharia-free Sudan, especially in Khartoum. They argued that the Machakos Protocol had accepted that the North would be run under sharia law and argued that the mediators and the observers had sought to appease Garang by guaranteeing him a sharia-free Khartoum. One negotiator from the Government of Sudan retorted once, "Not an inch of Khartoum would be sharia free." He earned himself the name Mr One Inch, courtesy of the mediators.

Sumbeiywo insisted that the document had been fair. He was later to tell Voice of America on July 13, 2003, "They (Khartoum negotiators) have a right to suggest what they want. My proposal is fair and the international community agreed with me that it was fair. I am very impartial, and they have acknowledged so themselves on many occasions."

Despite the US insistence on certain aspects incorporated into the Nakuru Framework, particularly the clauses about the nature of the national capital, Senator Danforth also came near to disowning the document, declaring it as "only a draft" and hinted at the possibilities of further revision of the draft by the USA. His sentiments found echo in the Arab League whose Chief, Amre Moussa, and who was also a former Egyptian Foreign Minister, was quoted by Agence France-Presse on July 14, 2003, as urging mediators from IGAD to withdraw the draft peace accord. The Egyptian Government lent support to Khartoum with the Foreign Minister, Ahmed Maher being quoted by Deutsche Presse-Agentur as having "stressed to the US envoy the need for IGAD to display 'neutrality' as it goes about mediating a solution to the Sudanese conflict." This was clear that Egypt regarded the IGAD mediators and Sumbeiywo in particular as lacking in neutrality.

The Nakuru Document spurred a lot of speculations about the future of the talks. Now that Khartoum had rejected Sumbeiywo's draft, on what basis would negotiations proceed if they were to proceed at all? Who would draft another document to guide the negotiations? Further, it was argued that because Sumbeiywo had made it clear that he regarded the Nakuru draft as "fair" and "balanced" and that the "international community had agreed that it was fair", he could not retain his authority and integrity if he now abandoned a document he had characterised in those terms.

Some people even hinted at Sumbeiywo's resignation. The Sudan Emancipation and Preservation Network asked on its website, SEPNet.org, "If Sumbeiywo resigns, who can possibly replace him at this juncture? Who would assume the lead role in the negotiating process? Who can bring to bear, at the critical moment, the experience of leading the process for the last year and more? Who can bring this experience to bear at the moment of truth for Machakos (Protocol)?"

At that time, questions were being asked as to whether Danforth and the US had any idea about what the collapse of the talks in Nakuru portended. Danforth was accused of downplaying the diplomatic difficulties contained in the negotiations and the eventuality of their collapse. He had earlier been quoted in Nairobi by Reuters as saying, "The remaining issues, while they are certainly significant issues, are not as difficult and not as contentious as the two that have already been resolved. Wealth-sharing, power-sharing, security and the state of the capital are in my opinion very solvable."

Unfortunately, Danforth did not seem to recognise that the issues he had termed as solvable were the ones that had proved a hard nut to crack despite intense negotiations. There had not been any substantial progress on any of those issues since the signing of the Machakos Protocol a full year down the line.

This suggested that the US was growing impatient with the process and that Khartoum's strategy of derailing the talks just when they seemed to be progressing well was bringing much fatigue to some of the key players. Danforth spread blame across both sides. On July 18, 2003, he was quoted by South Africa's News 24 as saying, "That has always been the question – whether the two sides really want peace."

Danforth chose to ignore the fact that it was Khartoum that had walked out of the talks and that the SPLM/A had accepted the Nakuru Document as a basis for negotiations. There was thus no grounds for implying that both parties were equally culpable in their response to the draft of a final peace agreement and the rejection of the Nakuru Document. Analysts thought that by failing to recognize that the GOS had overreacted to the Nakuru draft and that the SPLM/A did not seem to have a problem with it, the US was being too accommodating of Khartoum's temper tantrums and that it was trying to push the SPLM/A to accept the terms of peace as laid out by Khartoum.

Danforth also hinted that the US was becoming impatient with the process. "An agreement has to be found soon," he told the UN Integrated Regional Information Networks on July 18, 2003, "or else the current high levels of international interest will wane."

This "waning" or abandoning of the search for peace was what Khartoum was playing at. The resignation of Sumbeiywo was also apparently key to their plans. Unfortunately for them, Sumbeiywo did not resign and never showed any signs of being disappointed at the rejection of his draft. Doggedly, Sumbeiywo called for the next meeting in Nanyuki. He was unwilling to change the document unilaterally, but there was willingness on the part of the parties to find a way around it. The meeting was slated for August 10, 2003.

On the very first day of the talks, an SPLM/A delegate rose on a point of order. "We want to have the rules of procedures for the negotiations," he demanded. Naively, Sumbeiywo accepted and proposed that they adopt the earlier methodology they had used before which was to deal with the parties separately. SPLM/A said No. They wanted direct talks. As the rules were being made, the government rejected SPLM/A's proposal and insisted on having proximity talks or indirect talks which means that the mediators had to deal with each party separately. The twists and turns started all over again. It was clear that there was a huge spanner in the works. But who had thrown it in? It was to be slowly revealed to the General. Later that day, as he took a walk, he overhead a minister talking on the phone in Arabic. He was saying "yes sir" repeatedly in a deferential tone. He knew it was either the First Vice-President or the President he was talking to. He edged closer to determine who it was that the person was talking to. He really wanted to know who it was who was calling the shots at the talks. His answer came slowly, revealed by one of the negotiators. He had no doubts that the man was talking to the First Vice-President, Ali Osman Taha.

By now, everything was falling apart. The talks were deadlocked again. For the first time since the talks began, Sumbeiywo was assailed by doubts and a grim foreboding of what lay before him. On his own, he could not get the talks to move any further. He needed higher authorities to do this and an intervention of either Bashir or Garang. He quickly telephoned Kalonzo again. He was in Cairo, delivering a letter from President Kibaki to President Hosni Mubarak. Sumbeiywo requested Musyoka to fly to Khartoum to ask President Bashir to allow Taha to meet with Dr Garang in Nairobi. Dr Garang, Sumbeiywo told him, had indicated his willingness to speak to Taha on the talks and the way forward.

Convincing Bashir to send over Taha was not going to be an easy task. On two occasions, Dr Garang had declined an offer to meet with Taha, once in Nairobi and another time in Abuja, Nigeria. President Bashir was unwilling to send Taha again to be humiliated once more by a rebel leader.

Kalonzo called Sumbeiywo; "He told me what the President had said and sought an assurance from me that Dr Garang would indeed be available to meet Taha," he remembers.

He confirmed that he would indeed produce Dr Garang on September 1, 2003.

But when Kalonzo sought Garang to confirm the appointment, Garang was mad at him. Apparently, when in Cairo addressing a joint press conference with the Egyptian Foreign Minister, Ahmed Maher, on the issue of Sudan, the Egyptian had said something in Arabic that was abusive of Garang. Garang had immediately picked it up through his extensive network. He was livid and did not want to hear anything to do with Arabs.

"The Arabs have abused me," he raved at Kalonzo when he suggested a meeting with Taha.

"I do not understand Arabic so I do not know what they said. But would you be ready to meet Taha?" he asked.

"I do not mind meeting anybody even if that person is the devil himself." he answered.

Garang had given the same assurance to Sumbeiywo when the General called him while he was at the Jomo Kenyatta International Airport in Nairobi. Garang assured him that he would turn up to meet Taha on September 1. The meeting was set. On August 23, Sumbeiywo called off the Nanyuki meeting. The General convinced Kalonzo further that the meeting would indeed take place. Kalonzo immediately drafted a letter of invitation to Taha and Garang. With that, the stage was set for the biggest meeting of all. Sumbeiywo had taken a mighty chance that he would almost regret later.

****

The Great Rift Valley Lodge is a magnificent resort nestling in the scenic valleys of Naivasha. Only about 100 kilometres from Nairobi, it is a place where those who love to relax go to unwind and is popular with many Kenyans and tourists. General Sumbeiywo had booked the lodge for four days in anticipation of the epic first ever meeting between Dr John Garang and Ali Osman Taha. It would be the first time the two leaders were meeting and it was expected that their encounter would either achieve a breakthrough in the negotiations or set them back.

But because both had agreed to meet, Sumbeiywo was optimistic that all would go well. He had given his word to President Bashir that Garang would attend and he had also assured Taha that the date would be kept.

Ali Osman Taha arrived promptly on September 2. Around that time, Kenyans were mourning the death of their Vice-President Michael Kijana Wamalwa, who had died in London after a short illness. Taha was patient enough to wait for Garang. He proceeded to the late Vice President's residence to give condolences, joining a multitude of leaders and dignitaries pouring in to mourn the fallen leader.

This was a key and tactical move by Sumbeiywo and his team. For when Garang failed to arrive in the morning, there was a niggling fear that he might not keep the appointment. He had failed to keep it twice before and, who knew, he could fail again. If he did, the media would become nosy and question why Taha was in the country and they would definitely get wind of the planned meeting. This would be a major embarrassment to the Government of Sudan and for IGAD too, and Sumbeiywo would have an incredible mess in his hands.

Realising this, the General initiated a subtle damage control process, should the cookie crumble. He organised everything in such a way that if Garang eventually failed to turn up, the word that would be given out to the media was that Taha had come to Kenya to attend and represent his government at the state burial of the Vice-President. After giving his condolences, Taha returned to the Lodge. There still was no sign of Garang.

The First Vice-President is a cool, patient man. Those who know him well are amazed at the man's patience. He is also famed to have a razor sharp intellect. "He is a man who carefully weighs his words," a Sudanese who has served with him in the government says. "He takes his time before responding to you."

He did not show any signs of impatience. But Sumbeiywo was becoming nervous. Ever an optimistic man, he had to pose until the really unthinkable thoughts, the ones he had all along avoided, started forming on his mind. What if Garang failed to turn up? What if this turned out to be the one event that would deal the peace process the irredeemable blow? Had he taken too risky a gamble by arranging for this meeting? Several calls to the SPLM/A command only elicited responses that, "the Chairman is on the way."

On the second day, there still was no sign of Garang. Sumbeiywo was now frantic. He called Minister Kalonzo Musyoka: "I have the Vice-President here, but I cannot see John." He complained. Musyoka abandoned all he was doing and rushed to Naivasha to reassure Taha.

"Mr Vice-President," he pleaded with him, "I have word that the Chairman is on the way. Taha held his cool. He too could sense there was something wrong. The appointment was late by two days now.

The Minister stayed with the Vice-President the whole day. On the third day there still was no sign of Garang. Word, however, seeped through that Garang was somewhere in Rumbek, stranded. Sumbeiywo was now getting worked up. The climate was feverish in the secretariat and he was frantically trying to tell the SPLM/A command in Nairobi to bring the Chairman in at whatever cost. At about midday, the command called to say that the chairman's people in Rumbek had switched off their radios and phones. There was no further communication.

Sumbeiywo was now completely in a panic mode. He thought of chartering a plane and flying to wherever Garang was said to be. But there was no knowing where exactly he was. Did the Chairman have any intentions of keeping that appointment? Should he tell the Vice-President to go home, with all the dreadful consequences this would have on the peace talks? Should he declare the entire process hopelessly deadlocked?

The following morning, Sumbeiywo avoided seeing the Vice-President. What was he to tell him? How would he explain the fact that he had assured the President and Taha himself about Garang's availability for the meeting?

That morning, he learned that actually Garang had been informally held hostage by his own soldiers who had learnt of the intended meeting in Naivasha. They knew Taha was in town but they were insisting that the Chairman should not meet with the Vice-President. President Bashir had to be there. They were preventing him from going.

But his representatives in Nairobi were embarrassed and fearful of what would happen if their chairman precipitated another major embarrassment such as he was now threatening to do. Sumbeiywo told them to do whatever they had to do to bring the Chairman to Naivasha and made it clear that if he failed to keep the appointment, he would no longer receive the kind of warm hospitality he had received in Kenya throughout the years. He particularly called the Nairobi representative of SPLM/A, Dr Justin Yac Arop, and told him in no uncertain terms, "If we do not have Garang here today, we will kick you out of the country."

The SPLM Nairobi office quickly relayed a message to the Chairman. One commander later confided in the General what kind of message was relayed; "If you do not come," the message read, "You won't find us here and the Kenya Government won't allow you in." Coming from some of his very senior Commanders, he had to take it seriously.

Thus, on the fourth day, there was word that the Chairman was airborne and would arrive at 4.00 o'clock. Taha had already indicated that after waiting for Garang for four days, he would not wait any longer. He would be leaving on the fifth day, but not before attending Wamalwa's burial which was set for that Saturday and making it look like that that was why he had been in the country in the first place.

At 6.00 p.m. in the evening, Garang arrived. Sumbeiywo received him at the airstrip and they did not exchange any pleasantries. "We are meeting in 15 minutes," he told him,

"OK," Garang curtly replied, well aware of the inconvenience he had caused everyone.

At 6.30, the Minister and the General took the two men into a room and sat them opposite each other. Since it was the first time they were meeting, their security people were suspicious. They wanted to be in the room, but Sumbeiywo insisted that the two would have Kenyan security guards. Their men stayed out.

The introductions being done, each man remarked, "Yes, I have seen him on TV."

****

The long wait was finally over. What, however, the General did not know at the time, was that Garang had written a letter to Minister Musyoka explaining to him that he would not make it for the meeting. The letter read in part, "Your letter .... was received by Dr Justin Yac Arop of our Nairobi office on 29/8/2003 and transmitted to me by radio the same day. I received it on Saturday 30/8/2003 and instructed Dr Justin to inform you that the date of September 2nd suggested in your letter for a meeting between me and the First Vice-President of Sudan, Mr Ali Osman Mohammed Taha, was not practical for several reasons. However, I understand that Your Excellency could not get this message until today, Monday 1st September, because of the intervening weekend."

The letter expressed Garang's wish to meet with the Vice-President pursuant to the promise he had given General Sumbeiywo "at Nairobi

JKIA as I was leaving for the Sudan on Wednesday 20th August." But he expressed fears that there was confusion in Khartoum and that there was conflicting information and signals concerning the meeting. "I believe it is in the interest of peace that this confusion be sorted out first before the meeting takes place so that we do not inadvertently contribute to it (the confusion)."

The letter went on to state: "We shall verify in our own ways as much as I am sure that you and others will do the same. If indeed Mr Ali Osman Mohammed Taha is the person the GOS wants me to meet, I would absolutely have no hesitation and an appropriate date suitable to the two sides can then be coordinated through your good office. In the meantime, I will take advantage of the time it will take to sort out the confusion in Khartoum and for you to make the necessary scheduling arrangements for me to have more time with my officers at the SPLM/A Senior Officers' Conference, which is currently underway." But the letter was intercepted by senior SPLM/A Commanders and was never handed to either Sumbeiywo or to the Minister. His people thought that it was unreasonable for Garang not to come, having already given an undertaking that he would meet the First Vice-President.

But now that he was here, things were looking slightly up. Although everyone was upset at the delay, Kalonzo did not want to pursue the matter.

"Mr Chairman," he told Garang as the two settled down, "It would be prudent for you to apologise to your colleague for keeping him here."

Dr Garang looked at the Vice-President and said, "I apologise. You know, our country has been at war for many years. I am a rebel and I do not have resources. The government has all the resources that is why I could not get here in time."

Taha light-heartedly took the apology and requested that they be left alone. Between them, they had one bottle of water and two glasses. What the Sudanese might never know to this day is that the fate of peace in their country hung on this bottle of water whetting the two men's tongues.

The two men settled into a light banter. Surreptitiously, each eyed the bottle of water waiting for the other to open. Taha was the more superstitious of the two. He reckoned that if he was the first to open the bottle, the meeting would not be successful. If the bottle was not opened at all, the talks won't bear fruits.

Garang bid his time. The two men talked about their days at Khartoum University where both taught, but never met each other.

But there was apprehension. The two sized each other in the manner of a cat and mouse. But uppermost on their minds must have been the question of the bottle. Would it ever be opened? Who would be the first to open it? The more they talked, the more Garang relaxed and looked like he had no need for water. And Taha did not even want to think of opening it.

Then all of a sudden, almost in a reflexive manner, Garang opened the bottle, took Taha's glass and poured in some of the water. He then poured some for himself. There was a palpable sigh of relief from Taha. The two protagonists raised their glasses and silently drunk to the peace of their nation. The atmosphere changed, tension subsided and the two men relaxed. The talks, Taha now believed, would be successful. He also believed he was going to go back home in two days after this ground-breaking meeting. How mistaken he was.

The following day, the entire delegation had to move from the Great Rift Valley Lodge. They had overstayed their welcome and there was a golf tournament booked for the venue. Sumbeiywo had to urgently look for alternative accommodation. They landed at Lake Naivasha Simba Lodge, the only place in Naivasha that could accommodate a large delegation. But the hotel management did not trust them. They wanted advance payment. There was no cash at the time and they had to plead with the manager of the Great Rift Valley Lodge to vouch for them. This was to be the home of the Sudan Peace Process for over a year. The First Vice-President who had anticipated leaving after four days also found himself stuck in Kenya for three months, shuttling between Naivasha and Khartoum.

But those three months turned out to be fruitful. After intense negotiations, the two parties signed an Agreement on Security Arrangements. On September 25th, 2003, the parties agreed to an internationally monitored ceasefire to come into effect from the date of signature of a Comprehensive Peace Agreement. This was a key breakthrough. Sumbeiywo thought it a good time to adjourn the meeting to prepare the delegates for what was ahead. "I always insisted: accept what you can live with not what you always want," he said.

By now the delegates had increased and IGAD needed the international community more than ever. Money was running out and Sumbeiywo could not tell the parties to pay. Besides, one of the parties did not have money, a fact that he voiced loudly. One of the delegates asked, "Why don't you say which that party is?"

"I think they understand," responded Sumbeiywo. Evidently, the party in question was the SPLM/A. Though the money started coming in bits and pieces, the budget that IGAD had set aside was upset by the increasing number of delegates and the continuous negotiations beyond the originally estimated time.

Norway and Denmark came in strongly and Italy, being the Chair of the European Union, also galvanised other countries to rally around the peace process. Many people continued to visit the delegates at Simba Lodge in Naivasha. Key among them was the Norwegian Minister for International Development Cooperation, Hilde Johnson, and the US Secretary of State, Colin Powell. During his visit, Powell, upon noticing the steely patience exhibited by Sumbeiywo and that at last the talks were headed somewhere, took Sumbeiywo aside and told him, "General, you make us Generals proud."

Powell promised to invite the parties to the State of the Union address the following year and also petition Congress to remove long-standing sanctions on the Sudan. But the Americans were also itching to see a conclusion to the talks. Their representative, Jeff Millington started prodding Sumbeiywo on to have key agreements signed. There were suspicions that the Americans wanted to hijack the peace process, once again or push the parties to hastily concluded settlements. But Sumbeiywo would have none of it. Though he was known for his humility, there were times the soldier in him came out so powerfully that he almost intimidated those around him

"Sometimes, he would speak in such a commanding voice that everyone was left with no doubt who was in charge," observes Kalonzo, "The soldier in him stood him in good stead many of the times."

Sumbeiywo has a fiery temper. At various stages of the talks, a number of people were to come face to face with the man's frankness and ballistic temper. Jeff Millington will perhaps never forget the day he rubbed the General the wrong way and the consequences for that. Millington was peeved at Sumbeiywo's patience and the fact that he was allowing all the parties to extensively and windingly deliberate on issues before a conclusion could be arrived at.

"You are not serious," Millington at one time told Sumbeiywo, "You are allowing them to go on and on. This thing has to come to a closure."

"You may be a superpower," Sumbeiywo lost his cool, "but you do not understand this very well. It is the Sudanese to decide on how to progress and how they want the peace deal clinched, not the Americans."

Millington was not one to take things lying down. He attacked, "You have something against Americans?"

"No," General Sumbeiywo responded, clearly biting the bullet, "I have something against you."

Sumbeiywo threatened to shoot Millington and then threw him out of his office. This left the observers in shock. But they also knew that Sumbeiywo was right though they dared not talk. Privately, however, they expressed their pleasure at the way Sumbeiywo had handled the matter. From then henceforth, they coined the phrase: "Don't play with General Sumbeiywo, he will Millington you."

Much later, Sumbeiywo would have no regrets about this. "As a military man, I had to be tough. I had to deal with each party firmly. If they erred, I told them so. I did not mince my words." In many ways, his temper helped him push forward the talks. He commanded both fear and respect from the parties. But it also helped them get to know the real feelings of the man.

"Sometimes you got to see the real General in action. He would command, as in an army, he would thunder, he would growl," remembers Kalonzo.

But this also created a certain transparency around the man. The loss of temper as some people in the negotiating team were to admit later was seen as pointer to his emotional transparency, his outspokenness, his fairness and his commanding authority. It did not matter who the person he lost temper with was. It could be an ambassador, a minister or one of the parties. At one time, a woman working with the Chinese Government in Kenya as Political Counsellor, by the name Ms Guan Ruoxun, called him and requested to come to Naivasha. She came to the hotel and requested to see Sumbeiywo. But meanwhile she had sneaked the Chinese ambassador into the venue who was busy interacting with the mediators and was attempting to reach the parties.

"I sensed there was something wrong," he says, "I asked her to leave immediately." She did not leave. In fact on January 7, 2004, the day the Wealth Sharing Agreement was being signed, which was also the most taxing day for the mediator, Ruoxun stole up to Sumbeiywo and asked him, "Why isn't this thing signed?" The General lost his temper.

"By the time I turn, I do not want to see you here. You must leave and leave now and I do not want ever to see you again."

The woman ran to the Permanent Secretary in the Ministry of Foreign Affairs, Mr Peter Nkuraiya. "I have been abused by the General," she complained. After listening to her, Nkuraiya pleaded with Sumbeiywo to cool down but he was adamant.

"Please, let me handle this," he told the PS who was a good friend of his, "she has to leave." Ruoxun went to the Foreign Affairs Minister who pleaded with Sumbeiywo to apologise to her because failure to do so would bring diplomatic trouble.

"Just do a diplomatic move and apologise to her," Kalonzo told him. Sumbeiywo was adamant.

"I told her to go to hell or do whatever she wants to do," he says. He never apologised and Guan Ruoxun was thrown out.

Sumbeiywo does not make anything big out of this incident or the Millington one, "I have thrown many, many diplomats out of my office. I do not fear any diplomatic repercussions. I fear only God."

In a way, this rough behaviour helped in the final days of the talks. It became apparent that if visitors continued streaming in at the rate they were doing, negotiations would suffer and might even be compromised. Sumbeiywo called the two leaders of the delegation and sought their views on how to proceed. They too were becoming concerned at the profusion of visitors and the increasing number of delegates. They resolved to leave the matter to Sumbeiywo and made it known that all visitors who approached the parties should be referred to the chairman.

The Americans used to come to the venue in droves. Sumbeiywo knew that sooner rather than later, he would run up against them. He did not have to wait for long. Concerned at the fact that the Chief Mediator was limiting the number of the visitors, the US Ambassador to Kenya, William Bellamy, made his feelings known about the matter.

"Whether you like it or not," he told Sumbeiywo, "My government wants to know what is happening. I will come." And Bellamy came. He wanted to see the negotiating parties but they were reluctant to meet him. Finally they agreed to meet him together, but Bellamy wanted to meet each side separately. Bellamy had a message for them: they would sign the peace agreement in Naivasha but exchange the document at the White House.

The suspicions that Sumbeiywo had from the start that the Americans wanted to hog the success of the talks poured out into the open. There was a prevalent view that having waited for the talks to collapse without success, some Americans now wanted to hijack the process at this crucial stage and claim victory.

"There was silent hostility from the Americans," Sumbeiywo remembers, "they promised funds that never came and they kept questioning every move the parties made. Sometimes though they gave us critical backing they wanted to throw their weight around too." When a proposal was made, an American delegate would ask, "Is Washington aware of this?"

But the mediator was not answerable to Washington and he made it known that he was not happy with the constant reference to Washington. This suspicion seeped into the parties which were henceforth wary of what "so-called" Washington was up to. When Ambassador Bellamy then came up with his proposal that the final agreement be exchanged in Washington DC, both parties understood the American chicanery in the proposal and merely said, "Let's first sign the agreement. The rest will follow."

The negotiations speeded down the bumpy road of power sharing and wealth sharing through the better part of December 2003. Sumbeiywo had to rush away to attend his daughter Flora's wedding which was held on December 20. But he only managed to get away on

December 19 to find all the preparations for the wedding had been made without him. At that time, the parties were negotiating the tricky issue of wealth sharing. Before they could arrive at an agreement, Sumbeiywo came down with acute food poisoning, staying in bed for four days on a drip, during which time he refused to go to hospital. Meanwhile, the parties were stuck on the percentages on the issue of wealth sharing. At issue was not only the percentages of oil revenues to go to both the North and South but also how to share the wealth perceived as indigenous to the South and which was in the non-oil category. One of this was Gum Arabica of which Sudan is the biggest producer in the world.

Garang did not want to share this. After much negotiations, he accepted to share it 70:30. Eventually a 50:50 percent arrangement was agreed on. This, however, took them 90 days to resolve. The Wealth Sharing Agreement was signed on January 7, 2004. The parties continued negotiating on other topics until the talks adjourned later that month.

The adjournment of the talks created further speculation as to their future. Ostensibly, the talks were adjourned to allow some of the Moslem negotiators including Ali Osman Taha to attend the Hajj. In his closing remarks, Sumbeiywo wished all those attending Hajj a safe and peaceful time. But the international community was not convinced that the talks had adjourned for this purpose.

Some people suggested that the Khartoum negotiators wanted direct contact with their government as things were not going their way and they wanted to skip or delay negotiations on the three conflict areas. This was given more weight by the fact that long before negotiations, rumours had started flying that Taha, who was Khartoum's lead negotiator, would be going for Hajj. Reuters quoted Ahmed Dirdeiry, then Sudan's Deputy Ambassador in Nairobi, as saying that Taha had indicated his willingness to take the break. Because Taha had been on the Hajj twice before (The Koran requires a Moslem to go on Hajj at least once in a lifetime, funds and health permitting) questions were asked as to why he needed to go at that time. Taha's going on Hajj, it was widely felt, meant that he was not "serious" and that he was part of the camp in Khartoum that did not want peace.

Again, fears started sprouting that the talks were breaking up. US Congressman, Frank Wolf, wrote to President Bush declaring that, "I am extremely concerned that the peace process is at risk of collapsing," and expressed fears that Khartoum was not engaged in "good faith" in the peace negotiations. Wolf was the powerful Chair of the House Appropriations Subcommittee on Commerce, Justice, and State, the Judiciary, and Related Agencies and his letter was bound to have a profound impact in the way the US viewed Khartoum's commitment to the peace negotiations. The talks did adjourn, but a clear date was set for their resumption, February 17th 2004.

Upon resumption, first on the agenda were the three conflict areas. They were, as expected, to prove a major hot potato for the negotiations. There had been suggestions, though not put on paper, that the contested areas could be abandoned if they proved to be an obstacle to peace in the South. But the people of those areas looked to the South to support them in their quest for freedom and justice. "We fought side by side in the trenches for 20 years, they can't just abandon us now," was a saying often heard during the peace negotiations.

The negotiators were also concerned about what would happen if the three conflict areas were abandoned by the South. They feared that a potential military alliance between Darfur, the Beja, the Nuba, the Ingessena and the people of Abyei would prove terrible for both North and South. One Funj Commander ominously put it, "I know every tree in the South." Sadiq Al Mahdi and Hassan al Turabi warned against a bilateral peace agreement that did not address the grievances of Sudan's marginalised northern populations.

"If the peace process is a bilateral process, it will be a very temporary peace that will unravel very soon," Mahdi was quoted as saying. The negotiations on the three conflict areas then had to form a part of the warp and woof of the final peace agreement. In May 2004, the issue of the three conflict areas was resolved, and two separate agreements were signed to that effect on the 26th May, 2004.

The trickiest part of the negotiations was the bit on power sharing and the issue of Abyei's boundaries (whether they should remain as they were and whether to hold a referendum or not). Eventually, it was resolved that upon the signing of the peace agreement, the residents of Abyei would be citizens of both western Kordofan and Bahr el Ghazal with representation in the legislatures of both states. It was also resolved that after the Interim Period, Abyei would also cast a separate ballot simultaneously with the referendum for Southern Sudan. This would be done through a Referendum Commission established by the Presidency. It was also agreed that the national government would provide Abyei with assistance to improve the lives of the peoples of Abyei, including urbanisation and development projects.

In Southern Kordofan and Blue Nile states, the parties agreed, among other concessions, that human rights and fundamental freedoms shall be guaranteed to all individuals in the state as prescribed in the Interim National Constitution and that the diverse cultural heritage and local languages of the population of the state shall be developed and protected. Agreements were reached on the state executive, structure of the state government, the state legislature, the state share in the national wealth, the state land commission and security arrangements.

On Security Arrangements, the redeployment of forces and the funding of the SPLM/A as a force also proved hard to navigate. The government argued that it could not fund a rebel movement that had been fighting against it. SPLM/A on the other hand, insisted that there should be equal treatment of the forces in line with the Agreement on Security Arrangements, and thus, both armies should be paid from the national budget. Finally, it was agreed that SPLM/A could source to pay its army, particularly as the SPLM/A refused to detail the strength of its forces. After the agreement on power and wealth sharing the two parties asked for a few days break.

"Probably, there will be claims and counterclaims of victory and of defeat," Sumbeiywo was to tell the parties later after the signing of these important protocols, "It would be false to claim that one set of people of the Sudan have lost to the other. What will be true is to declare that it is the people of the Sudan who have won."

14

The Nairobi Declaration and After

As the parties broke off, Sumbeiywo started organising for them to sign a declaration summarising what had already been agreed up on during the process (i.e. the Six Protocols, MOU and Addendum signed up to that time). The Secretariat wanted to give the signing a high profile so it organized for it to be signed at State House, Nairobi. The parties also were happy with this arrangement as they wanted to use the document to appeal to the international community to support them. The mediators prepared a document, henceforth known as the Nairobi Declaration and set up June 5, 2004, as the date of the signing. When the Sudanese heard that the agreement would be signed at State House, they turned up in large numbers at the gates of the Kenyan President's official residence. However, many were disappointed as they were denied clearance. The ceremony was dogged by a few hiccups, however. Way before the date of the signing, the General had given the Ministry of Foreign Affairs a draft speech for the President. But when he arrived at State House, he was asked for the draft, again. Someone had not forwarded it to State House. He had to give another copy to the Director of Political Affairs in the Ministry of Foreign Affairs who immediately started drafting a speech for the President only hours before the official signing ceremony.

When Minister Kalonzo arrived, he too needed a speech from the secretariat. Sumbeiywo did not have any so he offered him his. But Kalonzo did not consider it suitable and had to work on his own speech.

At State House Garden, the podium where the agreement was to be signed had a table set for three people, Vice-President Taha and John Garang who were to append their signatures and Kalonzo who would be the witness. But when the Head of the Civil Service, Ambassador Muthaura, came to inspect the arrangement, he insisted that another chair be added.

"Who is it for?" the General asked.

"It is for the President."

The General was surprised. His idea was that the President would remain in his seat at the podium and only come forward at the precise moment when the documents were to be exchanged. He tried to explain this to Muthaura who insisted, "It has been decided that that is the way things are going to be." That was final. The agreement was signed in pomp and ceremony and ushered the negotiations into the homestretch.

The final phase of the negotiations in Naivasha was to prove much more daunting. Like sprinters rushing to the finish line, both sides wanted to exact major concessions in as short a time as possible. The parties were to realise that the gains they had made so far had awakened their people back home, who were now following the negotiations much more keenly. General Sumbeiywo noticed that every time a step was taken forwards, two were taken backwards.

"Whenever the parties made a step," he was later to observe, "there was a quick reaction from the people at home. It was a see-saw."

The General understood very well that even though the parties had signed the Nairobi Declaration, the real problem was on what to implement, who to do it and how to do it. When he introduced this to the parties, they did not seem to understand it. "They had not prepared their minds that it would be implemented and therefore the implementation was nowhere in their minds."

In fact, most of the delegates sat back, listened to what their people were saying and just waited for the final signing ceremony. When the General tried to impress upon them the need for a proper programme of implementation many of them simply argued, "But we already have an agreement on this. What are further deliberations for?" The euphoria that had come about with the signing of the last protocols and the Nairobi Declaration had somehow overshadowed the importance of this final phase and made the parties believe that they had achieved all that there was to be achieved.

They were backed by the US and the UK, who thought that Sumbeiywo was getting into details that were not necessary and thus delaying the date of the Comprehensive Peace Agreement (CPA). The Americans wanted Sumbeiywo to take only 10 points in the Agreement that were considered particularly critical and leave the rest for the pre-Interim Period, the time immediately after the signing of the CPA. Their insistence on this created a dilemma among the parties as to whether to follow the international community or the mediators. At one point the Americans accused Sumbeiywo of delaying the Comprehensive Peace Agreement because, as they said, he would not have a job after it was signed. This did not go down very well with him. "You can sign this thing tomorrow or the day after," he snapped "and I will be fine. This is not particularly an enjoyable job and I want to be over with it as soon as possible."

The General could not understand why the parties were in such a rush as to fail to see that that phase was critical in stipulating how and when the mechanisms, as defined in the Peace Agreement, would be set into effect. The Norwegians, however, could see the importance of the final phase and supported Sumbeiywo, urging him to go for a programme of implementation. Sumbeiywo stuck on with his determination to put out an agreeable negotiating formula. "There was nothing too small or too big," he argued, "everything has to be taken care of." It is a vital lesson he had learned in the military. He also understood very well, and tried to make the parties understand that the six and a half years of pre-Interim and Interim period was a long time and the working out of details of implementation and monitoring was critical. This was what was lacking in the 1972 Addis Ababa Agreement and therefore was not to be overlooked. He, therefore, came up with a document called *Proposal on Method of Work for Conducting the Negotiation Session on Implementation Modalities, Including Regional and International Guarantees.*

In the proposal, each party was to have 12 delegates, which meant 10 delegates plus two members of the respective secretariat. The reason for this was to allow a minimum of two delegates per party and per cluster and one representative of the secretariat. The work was to be done in clusters. The first cluster would deal with the issues arising from the Machakos Protocol and the Power Sharing Protocol, the second cluster would deal with Wealth Sharing Protocol, a third cluster was to deal with the Three Conflict Areas and finally a fourth one would deal with the Security Arrangements.

Working in clusters had several advantages. First, the parties could work on the protocols in parallel. At the same time, and through such a layout, there was a possibility of establishing the sequencing of events as the information arrived. But for the clusters to work well, it was necessary for one of the delegates from each of the parties to have a good and in-depth knowledge of the protocol he/she was working on. It was extremely important, Sumbeiywo stressed, to have one delegate from each party in each cluster who took part in the negotiations. It was also necessary that the Secretariat obtained the necessary resource persons so as to help the cluster.

In the resource group, there were four main categories. The first group was to be composed of the resource persons who had taken part in the negotiations during the last few years and had a good knowledge of the protocols. The second resource group was to be made up of those specialists who had been brought in, in the past, to negotiate a precise protocol or a precise issue. The fourth group would be composed of experts from organisations which would be taking part in the implementation of the agreement itself, like the United Nations.

Sumbeiywo also set out the method of work. He reminded the parties that when it comes to dealing with the establishment of the modalities of implementing the Peace Agreement, it was often quite hard to talk of past experiences and of other processes. "Each case is strongly conditioned by the method of negotiations and by the results obtained," he told them. Nevertheless, there were some basic techniques which could be used. One of the easiest ways of working on the implementation modalities was to establish a list of what had to be done (i.e. what committees, commissions, or other obligations had been established in the protocols). Once the list was there, he exhorted them to ask a set of questions: When do committees have to be created? What would be their precise functions? What would be their composition? How long was needed to fulfil the task and how should the committees fulfil the task?

Once all the committees or commissions had been properly identified, the second step was to introduce them into an agenda to enable them fulfil their tasks at the required time. Sumbeiywo outlined the dangers involved in the setting up of the committees and the delineation of duties. "One party could feel that the establishment of a committee X or Y is the result of its demand and they would want to obtain a maximum gain from the work of the committee while the other party could envision this as a concession they had to make." When establishing the sequences of what had to be done, therefore, it was important to make sure that the sacrifices and benefits were evenly distributed since "the parties would tend to obtain the benefits and drop the sacrifices."

The third step was the calculating of the expenses and funding of the implementation. This was particularly important because of the pre-interim period which would begin on the day after the signing of the final Comprehensive Peace Agreement and well before the donors' pledging conference in Oslo took place. It was, therefore, critical to identify as early as possible the commissions, committees and work groups that had to be established in the pre-interim period so as to calculate the amount of funds needed. Once this had been done and some work already started before the session on implementation and monitoring, the parties would then be able to look at a second category of commissions, committees and working groups that had to be set up during the first three years of the interim period. This would then pave way for the establishment of the last group of committees, commissions and working groups for the second part of the six-year interim period.

The proposal outlined that in principle, and if the parties got the layout correct, the most intensive part of the interim period when it comes to the monitoring and implementation would be between the first one to three years. Between the third and sixth year, there would be a gradual de-phasing before an intensive sixth year with the referendum for the people of Southern Sudan. The fourth one was to outline how clusters work and what advantages there are.

This methodology required the parties working on the implementation and monitoring of the agreement to read and interpret what they had agreed upon differently. The best technique, Sumbeiywo emphasised, was to start the implementation and monitoring on a very technical and detailed structure, leaving what was eventually problematic and subject to some form of political decision aside. During the last week of the implementation, the political leaders could be called to sort out the non-agreed issues because quite often the technical delegates did not have the political authority to do so. Sumbeiywo, however, acknowledged that this could complicate the process somewhat as towards the end of the implementation and monitoring session there would be a small drafting committee which would be going through the protocols and drafting the final Comprehensive Peace Agreement.

However, what Sumbeiywo thought would be merely a session to work out how the agreement would be implemented turned out to be full negotiations once again over everything. For instance, the SPLM/A was really captivated by the idea of the referendum, but the government wanted to start with the security agreement. The parties were haggling over everything once again, each taking the opposite of the other's preference and dragging down the sessions. All this, however, changed when Garang and Taha came back to the negotiations and started directing their parties over how to go about things and the final phase was on in full throttle.

Dignitaries visited the venue in droves, but all were convinced that the end was nigh. On July 8th 2004, the United Nations Secretary General Kofi Annan came to Nairobi. He had a burning desire to see General Sumbeiywo. But Sumbeiywo was confused. For at that time there had been a reshuffle in government that saw Kalonzo Musyoka being transferred from the Foreign Affairs docket to the Environment Ministry. Moreover, there was now a Minister for East Africa and Regional Affairs, John Koech.

The new Foreign Affairs Minister, Hon. Ali Chirau Mwakwere, was at sea about the peace process. Besides, he argued that IGAD was not his docket, it was the responsibility of the Minister for East Africa and Regional Affairs. On his part, John Koech had no clue as to what was happening.

To receive such a high profile guest as Annan required full adherence to protocol. But no one seemed in charge and the Secretary General did not know with whom to discuss the issue of peace in Sudan. Frustrated, he jumped protocol and asked to see General Sumbeiywo.

They met at Windsor Golf Club, ten kilometres from the city. Annan wanted to know how far away the peace process was to an agreement. Sumbeiywo highlighted the importance of the final phase, emphasising that it was the most critical part of the negotiations. This was said for the benefit of the British and Americans who wanted a short cut to the final peace agreement. The General also explained to the Secretary General the predicament he was in due to the change of the Ministers. The Secretary General agreed to discuss with President Kibaki. Kalonzo Musyoka was retained in the process, but not for long before Koech took over.

"In my military training," the General observed, "there is nothing too small not to be considered. There is no room for short cuts." Sumbeiywo urged Annan, as the boss of the UN which was the lead agency, to clearly define their role in the peace monitoring and particularly on how soon they could make their entry into the Sudan. He also asked the UN to work out how the transition should be handled.

He had one Parthian shot for the Government of Sudan in relation to the Darfur region. "Doubts have been raised particularly on the seriousness of a government that is seeking peace on one hand and fighting its citizens somewhere else," he said. "It is the mediator's view that, if the GOS is serious in resolving the conflict in the South, there should be sufficient provision in the same agreement to address the conflict in Darfur and the other marginalised areas."

On hearing this, Annan became particularly alert. He, however, only promised to look into the issue. But what was clear was that the Secretary General had heard and understood what Sumbeiywo meant. His support on the issue of Darfur led to the UN Security Council's holding of their meeting in Gigiri, Nairobi, from the 18th to 19th November, 2004. This was only the fourth time ever that the Security Council was holding its meeting outside of New York.

Deftly, the Chief Mediator guided the talks through this final phase. But once again, somewhere in November, the talks were stuck. The bone of contention this time was on when the final agreement would be signed. At that time, the US was holding the Chairmanship of the UN Security Council and Senator Danforth, now US Ambassador to the UN, was the Chairman. The man who at first was sceptical about Sumbeiywo's ability to steer the peace process would turn out to be one of the biggest assets to the process. The Security Council was concerned more about Darfur in Sudan where there was fighting and where thousands had been turned into refugees. Sumbeiywo saw this as a grand chance to enlist the Council's help in resolving the deadlock on the signing date. He called Danforth and explained to him the situation.

"Would it be helpful if I brought the UN Security Council to Nairobi?" Danforth asked him, perhaps expressing Kofi Annan's wish to have the meeting in Nairobi in order to give both the peace talks and the issue of Darfur, as discussed earlier with Sumbeiywo, the much needed fillip.

This was perhaps the most decent proposal Sumbeiywo had heard in a long time. He wanted to shout, "Of course, of course." But there was a problem. The Chinese, Pakistanis, Algerians and Russians were opposed to the idea of the Council coming to Africa. Yet, the import of the Council members in Nairobi was such that it would give the talks the sorely needed impetus. A way had to be found to bring it around without arousing unnecessary suspicions. So Danforth organised it in such a way that everyone would think that the Council had made a detour to Nairobi from the Great Lakes region and was merely passing by Nairobi to encourage the Sudanese in the negotiations. In fact, the Council flew directly from New York to Nairobi. This subterfuge worked perfectly. When they arrived, there was a dramatic change in the spirit of the negotiations. The US and the UK had proposed 31st December as the final day of negotiations and January 7 as the signing day. They had rallied the Council to this cause. Garang and Taha met the Council and confirmed that those were the dates when things would happen. Later, Sumbeiywo had a meeting with them and had them sign a document detailing the conclusion of the talks as 31st December. This was a surprise. He did not expect the change of heart to work so smoothly in people who had all along been suspicious of one another. They asked him to book Naivasha for the signing ceremony and he immediately booked Simba Lodge, the place they all knew only too well.

On November 19th 2004, the Security Council meeting in Gigiri, a few kilometres from Nairobi city centre, endorsed the parties' consensus to conclude negotiations. At last the end had arrived.

On December 31 2004, President Al Bashir flew to Nairobi to witness the signing. He had President Thabo Mbeki of South Africa with him. The two Chief Negotiators, John Garang and Ali Osman Taha, were there too. The two Presidents arrived in Nairobi to find that President Kibaki was in Mombasa and could not receive them. Because Sumbeiywo did not have direct access to President Kibaki, the President was not properly briefed about the visit. However, some high ranking Foreign Affairs Ministry officials were told of the impending visit and asked to relay the message to the President. They did not. Instead, some government officials were later to accuse Sumbeiywo of inviting Heads of State into the country without following protocol.

This was, however, too historic an occasion to be allowed to be bogged down by a diplomatic snafu. The Presidents had come to witness the signing of what was to mark the official end of the 21-year-old civil war in Sudan. Realising the importance of the day (New Year's Eve, 2004) the Vice-President, Moody Awori, was sent to represent the President and Kalonzo Musyoka was sent to accompany President Bashir. They all stayed on until 7.00 p.m. in the night when the Agreement's cover seals were finally signed. The Presidents then took off in the dark in two helicopters to Nairobi and then flew to Khartoum. Sumbeiywo was accused of allowing Heads of State to fly off in the night, but he had no control over the affairs of other Heads of State. Besides, the bigger war was almost won and he had a long night ahead of him.

That night, all the parties stayed up late, signing every single page of the Comprehensive Peace Agreement. They did not notice the old year slide into the new. At about midnight, someone popped open a bottle of champagne. Its pop went largely unnoticed by the parties. Some were busy translating the Agreement into Arabic, because the parties had insisted that the agreement would not be complete without an Arabic translation. But as the New Year came upon the country, Sumbeiywo and the negotiating parties also knew that a new era, more significant than the New Year, had dawned upon their country. But even amid the excitement, Sumbeiywo stole some time to send a text message to his family: "Happy New Year all of you. It is done," the message read.

When his wife received the message, she knelt in prayer. Later when daughters Flora and Rose heard about it, they exclaimed, "Yes! We knew he would make it." In the tradition of their father, they also said a quiet prayer.

General Mohammed was in North Eastern Province when he heard that Lt General Sumbeiywo had pulled off what many others before him had failed to do. He was overjoyed. It was such a great honour to hear that he had accomplished it. "Here was my kid who had achieved so much. Now I was seeing what I knew all along the man was capable of doing."

His colleagues in the army heard the news and exploded in jubilation. "It was joy for all of us," remembers Lt. General A.S.K. Njoroge. "It was an honour for all of us. This man was not a diplomat. He was a soldier and he had done it."

****

The days that followed the signing of the Comprehensive Peace Agreement (CPA) were extremely busy for Sumbeiywo. He was busy organising for the signing ceremony and determining how the event would be financed. He wanted a ministerial subcommittee to deal with this. But it was New Year festivities and few government officials were around. Foreign dignitaries had to be invited and the President was still holed up in Mombasa.

Sumbeiywo and his team spent many hours in the office in Nairobi and at the Government Printer. They even broke the rules by inviting foreigners into the printing premises to help them in translation as no one else could read Arabic.

But if Sumbeiywo thought that the peace talks had been a headache, he was to encounter a bigger one. The government officials from whom he sought help did not appear to know how to go about the event. And neither did the importance of the occasion appear to sink into them. Sumbeiywo wanted the Regional Affairs Minister, Koech, to call for a Ministers' meeting and the Head of the Civil Service, Ambassador Muthaura, to call up all those who would be involved in the signing ceremony. This was when, as Sumbeiywo was to remember later, he realised that the senior people in government did not know what he had been doing all along. They took everything casually, moving at their usual lackadaisical pace and probably hoping that things would sort themselves out.

"I tried to tell them about my personal experience on such events but nobody wanted to listen to me," Sumbeiywo reminisces. Even as the days hurtled down to the grand finale, which was the 9th of January, the government was still taking its sweet time. Sumbeiywo had to prepare a list of those who would come. But some nations did not want to divulge who would represent them. It became difficult to come up with a comprehensive list of guests in good time.

Eventually, with only two days to go, Sumbeiywo managed to see the President. Present were Mwakwere and Koech who had, all of a sudden, awakened to the fact that there was a big ceremony about to take place. When going through the draft, Mwakwere interjected, "I will be the Master of Ceremonies." As if he had been pinched, Koech shot up and said, "This is my Ministry. It is me who will be the Master of Ceremonies."

The two Ministers started quarrelling over who would be in charge, in a fashion that ruefully reminded Sumbeiywo of the warring parties that had just mended their differences. Koech argued that the talks fell under his docket. Mwakwere insisted that since he was the Foreign Affairs Minister, he was the man to be in charge.

But a petulant Koech would have none of it. He accused Mwakwere of impinging upon his authority and encroaching upon his Ministry. He was in charge of regional affairs, he made it clear, and Mwakwere had nothing to do with it. Mwakwere insisted that his docket went beyond regions. This was an international affair and it involved foreign dignitaries and so he had to be the one to oversee it.

Sumbeiywo watched in acute embarrassment. "This was the most degrading thing to happen in front of my Commander-in-Chief," he was later to tell his family. All the while, President Kibaki just looked at the two and listened as they quarrelled. He did not want to take sides. Sumbeiywo realised that the argument was getting nowhere and if he had succeeded in mediating for peace between two implacable foes, he might as well do the same here. So he calmly pointed out that all state ceremonies are usually under the Office of the President. But Mwakwere went ballistic, "It has to be under my Ministry. It has to be me."

Realising that none of the Ministers would give way, Sumbeiywo jumped into the fray too. Though he did not want to be in the limelight, he suggested, "Your Excellency, I think I should be the Master of Ceremonies. After all, I am the one who mediated." As if struck by a sudden revelation, the President said emphatically, "Yes, you should be." Everyone kept quiet. But Mwakwere would not leave without a piece of the cake, "But I will introduce the dignitaries," he insisted.

The matter had been resolved and they could now get on to the other matters pertaining to the ceremony.

The next headache was the venue. The Sudanese wanted the documents signed and exchanged at the Moi International Sports Complex, Kasarani, on the outskirts of the capital city. Others suggested the Nyayo National Stadium at the heart of the capital. The Permanent Secretary in the Office of the President, Dave Mwangi, suggested Bomas of Kenya, seven kilometres from the capital and which is usually used for cultural events and conferences. It can sit 2,000 people. But it was pointed out to him that the venue he was suggesting was too small.

"We will get closed-circuit TVs," was all he said. Garang knew that there would be more than 2,000 people at the signing ceremony. He wondered why the government officials could not see that. As the haggling over the venue continued, Garang became frustrated. He called President Kibaki to tell him that he would be having 27 buses full of people coming to the signing ceremony and could he, therefore, direct that a bigger venue be selected for the ceremony? The President agreed with Garang and directed that the ceremony be held at Nyayo National Stadium. Everyone in government thought Sumbeiywo had gone behind their backs in having the venue fixed.

****

The hour before dawn is the darkest. For Sumbeiywo, the night before the signing ceremony was his longest. Frustrated by lack of coordination and unable to do much because he did not have a clear mandate, he kept darting from one place to the other to check if everything was all right. He visited the venue at midnight, to check that everything was going well and then he was at the Government Printer at 2.00 am. There, he found that there was a mix-up in the signatories and some pages had to be redone. Just before dawn, he went home to change, having not slept a wink, and went back to the venue.

The seating arrangement was totally chaotic. The Government of Sudan officials had arrived early and taken up all the seats including those reserved for Heads of State. To add insult to injury, some Kenya Government Ministers had also taken up seats not reserved for them. Sumbeiywo had to ask them to move to give space to other dignitaries. The Head of Civil Service was not amused. He reprimanded Sumbeiywo for showing disrespect to Ministers.

Americans had taken 10 seats including the front ones reserved for Heads of State and Ministers, while the Norwegians, who were signatories as witnesses, did not have any. Sumbeiywo had to take one seat by force. This enraged one of the American security men who tried to be tough on him. He told him to go to hell, whereupon he was enraged to a point of engaging Sumbeiywo. But one of the Americans who knew Sumbeiywo told the security man to leave him alone.

Eventually, Sumbeiywo had some luck with the Kenyan Ministers. They all moved except Raila Odinga, then Minister for Roads and Public Works, and William Ole Ntimama of the Office of the President, both of whom remained in seats reserved for Heads of State.

Sumbeiywo himself, the man whose efforts had made this ceremony possible, had no place to sit. He fetched two seats, one for himself and the other for his wife, to go and sit in the sun. The most enduring picture of the event was of General Sumbeiywo carrying a seat on his shoulder and looking for somewhere to settle. The Members of the Secretariat sat with Sumbeiywo in the sun, the Comprehensive Peace Agreement baking along with them. He also had a white friend from the UK, Mike Donnelley, whom he dragged to go and sit with him in the sun. His skin peeled off prodigiously.

In total, the arrangements were chaotic. The Chief of Protocol had a hard time trying to make things work. At one time, President Museveni was nearly run over by a security car right at the venue.

From where he sat in the sun, Sumbeiywo watched silently as the First Vice-President, Ali Osman Taha, and Dr John Garang signed the Peace Agreement. He saw many years of hard work, disillusionment, cajoling, persuading and literally begging the two sides to see sense slowly pass in front of him. He had stayed with the parties for so long that he knew them by name. They were like a family and he knew then that at the end of the ceremony, they were all going to leave.

"It was like my family was signing itself away," he remembers. But when Garang and Taha held hands, emotions almost overwhelmed him. He breathed a deep sigh and silently said, "It is done."

That evening, he rang all officers who had worked with him to say 'Thank you.' Then drifted into the sleep of the just. It was the first night he slept early in years.

15

Epilogue

On January 11, 2005, a few days after the signing of the Comprehensive Peace Agreement, Lt General Sumbeiywo told BBC's Network Africa Programme, "I feel humbled that God really chose to use me in these negotiations, I feel very humbled. It has been very difficult and it has been very frustrating, at times, very trying."

Though he could not admit it then, in retrospect, he saw the negotiations as having been a monumental task, and as he told the BBC, "Mission Impossible." Yet, he never allowed this thought to cross his mind during the negotiations. There were times, as his wife has admitted in this book, when he was very down, when he felt that probably he could not go on. But he kept chugging along. He likes attributing this to his religious faith. In fact, prayer, he admitted, was an integral part of his *modus operandi*.

"To understand the man," observed Kalonzo Musyoka, "You have to understand that he is a deeply religious person who believes in the ability of faith to move mountains." For him, the mountain of war was moved by prayer and tenacity. When you are negotiating, various hurdles are thrown in your way meant to make you give up and leave. But as Sumbeiywo says, "I never ever had the thought of leaving it. Especially when you have travelled in the Sudan, you will never leave it."

He had to contend with situations where, after a deadlock, one side would pack their bags and send them down to the hotel lobby, intending to leave. Then they would come back to the table. There were, however, moments when there were serious threats of a walkout, particularly by the government side.

When he attended the installation of the Presidency on July 9, 2005, in Khartoum, six months after the signing of the Peace Agreement, he reflected on all that went on in those three years of intense negotiations. There were many sleepless nights, especially when both parties dug in their heels and refused to compromise. When the Nakuru Document was thrown in his face and all looked lost, he sought refuge in prayer. He understood only too well that that document could be the negotiations' Waterloo. He had praised it as fair and balanced and even made it clear that it had the support of the international community. When it was rejected, a lesser spirit could have thrown in the towel. Analysts even predicted his imminent resignation and some in Khartoum opposed to peace started dancing on the grave of the peace process. But it is the mark of this mediator that he chose to eat the humble pie, amend the document, and if need be, throw it out altogether for the sake of peace.

Never mind the fact that the final document was not significantly dissimilar to the Nakuru Document. All the protocols signed were a vindication of the document which the Sudan Government had obstinately rejected. The security arrangements and the wealth-sharing protocols were, for instance, much closer to Sumbeiywo's position than the Sudan Government's. But rather than stick to his position or beat his chest later in an "I-told-you" posture, the mediator chose the path of compromise.

Throughout the negotiations, he found himself having to deal with many peripheral threats to the peace process. Apart from the brinkmanship of Khartoum and the intransigence of some of the SPLM/A negotiators, he had to face up to US pressure. He was accused of not being neutral, of not deferring to Washington, of not respecting Khartoum. Letters were written to the President in an attempt to pressurise him to drop Sumbeiywo, attempts were made to hijack the peace process and hand it over to the South Africans. But he faced those pressures with amazing fortitude. Much later, the negotiating parties were to admit that though the man occasionally rubbed them the wrong way, he was an invaluable asset to the whole process. When the talks speeded down on the homestretch, he kept on the sidelines, allowing himself to be overshadowed by Ali Osman Taha and John Garang. It was the mark of the man that he did not want to appropriate the glory of the success of the talks. "All I wanted was peace." Many mediators would not have been happy to do this. But he also recognised that his role was only to guide and facilitate the process and that no one could resolve the problem better than the Sudanese themselves.

Even after the parties initially so mistrusted Sumbeiywo, they came round to liking and trusting him. They came to understand that his toughness was borne out of an innate desire to see peace come to Sudan. Even as the government criticised him and almost had him removed as the Chief Mediator after the Nakuru Draft, he never took any offence.

The government and SPLM/A saw his duels with the international community as an act in protection. "He protected us from the international community. He catered more for our interests and he did not want interference," one Sudanese admitted. He was acclaimed as a hero for holding at bay the mighty America, for protecting the parties and holding the process together.

But he was also a fair man. In spite of his frequent misunderstandings with the US Government, he still believes that the talks would have gone nowhere without the US and British support and certainly without the personal involvement of Senator Danforth.

Sumbeiywo is a study in conflict resolution. He went boldly into a task that many had written off as impossible. What can one soldier do in a conflict that had gone on for 20 years? How could he possibly succeed where the US, Nigeria, Libya and the Arab nations had failed? And, even when a change of government in Kenya threatened to undermine his authority in the peace process, he was unfazed. In the end, his maxim that "you may shout all you want, but for God's sake, do not shoot," acquired a new, fresh shade of meaning.

He was also to realise one cardinal truth that guided him through the negotiations; there were no major differences between Sudan's Northerners and Southerners. "They are very soft-hearted people. They are very homely people and they hate being pushed around."

But as he admits, all this would not have been possible without God. Sumbeiywo is a staunch Christian and he believes single-mindedly in the power of prayer. "I fear no one but God," he keeps saying. This is a quality that was to prove a bit of a problem for the observers who knew how seriously Sumbeiywo took it. They knew that however mighty their nations could be, they could not hold sway over Sumbeiywo. You do not fight with a man whose shield is the Lord. An elder in the Africa Inland Church in Nairobi, he always briefed the congregation every Sunday on the progress of the talks. Sometimes, when the process was stuck, he asked for prayers through text messages. At times he told the pastors and elders of the agenda of the negotiations so that they could pray for specific protocols to be achieved. When a breakthrough was made, his first act was to pray.

"All honour and glory is to the Lord," he demurely says, "It is not to me."

Thanks to his tenacity and the support of the international community, the Kenya Government and the people of Sudan who so desperately wanted peace, there is a new government in Sudan, the sound of gunfire has been silenced and the people of Southern Sudan can now sit back and say with Sumbeiywo, "It is done."

Unfortunately for the country, just as everything was settling down, something that might perhaps change the entire course of the country's history happened. It was late July and John Garang, who had already been sworn in as the country's First Vice-President, was in Rwakitura, Uganda to meet with his long-time ally, President Yoweri Museveni of Uganda. He was treated to a sumptuous meal of roast goat at the president's private residence. On his way back to Southern Sudan aboard the Ugandan presidential Mi-72 helicopter, he crashed. Initially, Sudanese state television reported that Garang's craft had landed safely in Sudan. But Abdel Basset Sabdarat, the country's Information Minister, went on TV hours later to deny the report. His wife, Rebeccah, tried to reach him on his cellular phone but there was no answer. Garang's helicopter could not be traced.

Later, in a statement released by the Office of President, Bashir confirmed that a Ugandan presidential helicopter crashed into "a mountain range in Southern Sudan because of poor visibility and this resulted in the death of Dr John Garang de Mabior, six of his colleagues and seven Ugandan crew members." There was disbelief in Sudan and, indeed, all over the world.

His death immediately sparked riots in Khartoum and Juba, lasting three days. Over 200 people died and the cities were placed under a curfew. There were immediate fears that the death of a man who was considered so instrumental to the fate of Sudan would spell doom to the peace process. Though President Bashir and Garang's deputy, Salva Kiir Mayardit, tried to reassure the people that the CPA would be honoured, there was scepticism all around.

Garang's body was flown to New Site, a Southern Sudanese settlement near the scene of the crash, and his body interred in Juba on August 3, 2005. The man who had spent 21 years fighting in order to achieve peace had spent only 21 days in office.

Soon after, Mayardit was appointed as the head of SPLM/A and the country's First Vice-President to replace Garang. On the day after Garang's burial in Juba, Sumbeiywo prayed with the deceased's family, Rebecca and her children. They prayed that the peace that had been so painstakingly searched would prevail. But he could not stop thinking about the fate of Sudan after Garang. Shortly after the burial, he held talks with Mayardit, a man with whom he had worked in the early negotiations for a peace deal and who led the Southern team to Machakos where one of the key protocols leading to CPA was signed in 2002.

Mayardit's ascension to the highest position in Southern Sudan aroused some scepticism. While many expected him to be the natural successor to Garang, many doubted that he had the stature of the fallen leader. He was a good soldier, many said, but would he be a good politician?

A member of the Dinka tribe, Mayardit joined the separatist Anyanya movement as a teen in the 1960s. When that rebellion ended with a peace deal in 1972, he joined the Sudanese Army and rose to the rank of Captain. But in 1983, he joined Garang in deserting the army and forming the SPLM/A.

Mayardit had more military experience than Garang who had also been in Anya-nya but who took time out for studies in the United States and was, therefore, a key figure in SPLM/A. Many of the biggest successes in battle were attributed to his leadership. In 1999, he was made the SPLA Chief of Staff. He is known for having a cool head and being able to resolve disputes. The US representative to Sudan, Roger Winter, was quoted by Al Jazeera TV saying, "The man is no slouch intellectually, and he is a leader." Dr Ghazi Sala al-Din Atabani, the presidential advisor in the peace talks was quoted as saying that despite his political inexperience, Mayardit's calm temperament would help him greatly.

"Those dealing with him are always at ease, more than they used to be in the presence of Garang. He is more capable of handling a political action with wisdom and would be able to unify the Southerners."

He is a well liked man and has a broad following. In spite of the fact that he is a military man, Mayardit is said to be different from Garang in some respects. He is said to be more collegial in the way he does business as opposed to Garang's tendency of 'one-man-show-ship'. Though he is said to favour separatism over unity, he might yet find this ideology one of the things that will endear himself more to the Southern Sudanese. A USAID survey conducted recently showed that 96 per cent of Southerners want to secede. But he has said that he will do everything to ensure that the Comprehensive Peace Agreement is adhered to. With Garang gone, and the peace found, the onerous task of ensuring implementation of the CPA now rests on President Bashir and Salva Kiir Mayardit.

Appendix 1

Declaration of Principles

We, representatives of the Government of the Republic of the Sudan (hereinafter referred to as the GOS), the Sudan People's Liberation Movement/Sudan Peoples' Liberation Army and the Sudan Peoples' Liberation Movement/Sudan People's Liberation Army – United (hereafter referred to as the SPLM/SPLA and SPLM/SPLA – United, respectively);

Recalling the previous peace talks between the Government of the Sudan on the one hand, the SPLM/SPLA and SPLM/SPLA-United on the other, namely; Addis Ababa in August, 1989, Nairobi in December 1989, Abuja in May/July 1992, Abuja in April/May 1993, Nairobi in May 1993, and Frankfurt in January 1992;

Cognisant of the importance of the unique opportunity afforded by the IGAD peace initiative to reach a negotiated peaceful solution to the conflict in the Sudan;

Concerned by the continued human suffering and misery in the war affected areas;

Taking note of the agreement of 17th May, 1994, on Operation Lifeline Sudan (OLS) corridors for relief supplies and humanitarian assistance to war affected areas;

Hereby agree in the following Declaration of Principles (DOP) that would constitute the basis for resolving the conflict in the Sudan:-

1. Any comprehensive resolution of the Sudan conflict requires that all parties to the conflict fully accept and commit themselves to the position that:-
    1.1 The history and nature of the Sudan conflict demonstrate that a military solution cannot bring lasting peace and stability to the country.
    1.2 A peaceful and just political solution must be the common objective of the parties to the conflict.
2. The rights of self-determination of the people of South Sudan to determine their future status through a referendum must be affirmed; and
3. Maintaining unity of the Sudan must be given priority by all the parties provided that the following principles are established in the political, legal, economic and social framework of the country;

- 3.1 Sudan is a multi-racial, multi-ethnic, multi-religious and multi-cultural society. Full recognition and accommodation of these diversities must be affirmed.
- 3.2 Complete political and social equalities of all peoples in the Sudan must be guaranteed by law.
- 3.3 Extensive rights of self-administration on the basis of federation, autonomy, etc., to the various peoples of the Sudan must be affirmed.
- 3.4 A secular and democratic state must be established in the Sudan. Freedom of belief and worship and religious practice shall be guaranteed in full to all Sudanese citizens. State and religion shall be separated. The basis of personal and family laws can be religion and customs.
- 3.5 Appropriate and fair sharing of wealth among the various peoples of the Sudan must be realised.
- 3.6 Human rights as internationally recognised shall form part and parcel of this arrangement and shall be embodied in the Constitution.
- 3.7 The independence of the judiciary shall be enshrined in the Constitution and laws of the Sudan.
4. In the absence of agreement on the above principles referred to in 3.1 to 3.7, the respective people will have the option to determine their future including independence, through a referendum.
5. An interim arrangement shall be agreed upon, the duration and the tasks of which should be negotiated by the parties.
6. The Parties shall negotiate a ceasefire agreement to enter into force as part of the overall settlement of the conflict in the Sudan.

Appendix 2

Abridged Provisions of the Comprehensive Peace Agreement (CPA)

Chapter 1: THE MACHAKOS PROTOCOL (signed at Machakos, Kenya, on 20th July, 2002)

The Preamble, Principles, and the Transition Process

WHEREAS the Government of the Republic of the Sudan (GOSS) and the Sudan People's Liberation Movement/Sudan People's Liberation Army (SPLM/A) herein after referred to as the Parties, having met in Machakos, Kenya, from 18th June, 2002, through 20th July, 2002; and
WHEREAS the Parties are desirous of resolving the Sudan Conflict in a just and sustainable manner by addressing the root causes of the conflict and by establishing a framework for governance through which power and wealth shall be equitably shared and human rights guaranteed; and
MINDFUL that the conflict in the Sudan is the longest running conflict in Africa, that it has caused horrendous loss of life and destroyed the infrastructure of the country, wasted economic resources, and has caused untold suffering, particularly with regard to the people of South Sudan; and
SENSITIVE to historical injustices and inequalities in development between the different regions of the Sudan that need to be redressed; and
RECOGNISING that the present moment offers a window of opportunity to reach a just peace agreement to end the war; and
CONVINCED that the rejuvenated IGAD peace process under the chairmanship of the Kenyan President, H.E. Daniel T. arap Moi, provides the means to resolve the conflict and reach a just and sustainable peace; and
COMMITTED to a negotiated, peaceful, comprehensive resolution to the conflict based on the Declaration of Principles (DOP) for the benefit of all the people of the Sudan;
NOW THEREFORE, the Parties hereby agree as follows:

Part A: Agreed principles

1.1 That the unity of the Sudan is and shall be the priority of the Parties and that it is possible to redress the grievances of the people of South Sudan and to meet their aspirations within such a framework.

1.2 That the people of South Sudan have the right to control and govern affairs in their region and participate equitably in the National Government.

1.3 That the people of South Sudan have the right to self-determination, *inter alia*, through a referendum to determine their future status.

1.4 That religion, customs and traditions are a source of moral strength and inspiration for the Sudanese people.

1.5 That the people of the Sudan share a common heritage and aspirations and accordingly agree to work together to:

1.5.1 establish a democratic system of governance taking account the cultural, ethnic, racial, religious and linguistic diversity and gender equality.

1.5.2 find a comprehensive solution that addresses the economic and social deterioration of the Sudan and replace with social, political and economic justice that respects the fundamental human and political rights of all the Sudanese people.

1.5.3 negotiate and implement a comprehensive ceasefire to end the suffering and killing of the Sudanese people.

1.5.4 formulate a repatriation, resettlement, rehabilitation, reconstruction and development plan to address the needs of those areas affected by the war and redress the historical imbalances of development and resource allocation.

1.5.5 design and implement the Peace Agreement so as to make the unity of the Sudan an attractive option especially to the people of South Sudan.

1.5.6 undertake the challenge by finding a framework by which these common objectives can be best realised and expressed for the benefit of all the Sudanese.

Part B: The transition process

2.0 There shall be a Pre-Interim Period, the duration of which shall be six (6) months.

2.1 During the Pre-Interim Period:
   a) The institutions and mechanisms provided for in the Peace Agreement shall be established;
   b) If not already in force, there shall be a cessation of hostilities with appropriate monitoring mechanisms established;
   c) Mechanisms to implement and monitor the Peace Agreement shall be created;
   d) Preparations shall be made for the implementation of a comprehensive ceasefire as soon as possible;
   e) International assistance shall be sought; and

f) A Constitutional Framework for the Peace Agreement and the institutions referred to in 2.1 (a) shall be established.
2.2 The Interim Period will commence at the end of the Pre-Interim Period and shall last for six (6) years.
2.3 Throughout the Interim Period:
   a) The institutions and mechanisms established during the Pre-Interim Period shall be operating in accordance with the arrangements and principles set out in the Peace Agreement.
   b) If not already accomplished, the negotiated comprehensive ceasefire will be implemented and international monitoring mechanisms shall be established and operationalised.
2.4.1 The composition of the Assessment and Evaluation Commission shall consist of equal representation from the GOSS and the SPLM/A and not more than two (2) representatives respectively, from each of the following categories: member states of the IGAD SubCommittee on Sudan (Djibouti, Eritrea, Ethiopia, Kenya and Uganda); Observer States (Italy, Norway, UK and US); and any other countries or regional or international bodies to be agreed upon by the Parties.
2.4.2 The Parties shall work with the Commission during the Interim Period with a view to improving the institutions and arrangements created under the Agreement and making the unity of Sudan attractive to the people of South Sudan.
2.5 At the end of the six (6) year Interim Period there shall be an internationally monitored referendum, organised jointly by the GOSS and the SPLM/A, for the people of South Sudan to: confirm the unity of the Sudan by voting to adopt the system of government established under the Peace Agreement; or to vote for secession.
2.6 The Parties shall refrain from any form of unilateral revocation or abrogation of the Peace Agreement.

State and Religion

6.1 Religions, customs and beliefs are a source of moral strength and inspiration for the Sudanese people.
6.2 There shall be freedom of belief, worship and conscience for followers of all religions or beliefs or customs and no one shall be discriminated against on such grounds.
6.3 Eligibility for public office, including the presidency, public service and the enjoyment of all rights and duties shall be based on citizenship and not on religion, beliefs or customs.
6.4 All personal and family matters including marriage, divorce, inheritance, succession and affiliation may be governed by the personal laws (including Sharia or other religious laws, customs or traditions) of those concerned.
6.5 The Parties agree to respect the following Rights:
6.5.1 to worship or assemble in connection with a religion or belief and to establish and maintain places for these purposes;
6.5.2 to establish and maintain appropriate charitable or humanitarian institutions;

6.5.3 to make, acquire and use the necessary articles and materials related to the rites or customs of a religion or belief;

6.5.4 to write, issue and disseminate relevant publications in these areas;

6.5.5 to teach religion or belief in places suitable for these purposes;

6.5.6 to solicit and receive voluntary financial and other contributions from individuals and institutions;

6.5.7 to train, appoint, elect or designate by succession appropriate leaders called for by the requirements and standards of any religion or belief;

6.5.8 to observe days of rest and to celebrate holidays and ceremonies in accordance with the precepts of one's religious beliefs;

6.5.9 to establish and maintain communications with individuals and communities in matters of religion and belief and at the national and international levels;

6.5.10 for avoidance of doubt, no one shall be subject to discrimination by the National Government, state, institutions, group of persons or person on grounds of religion or other beliefs.

6.6 The Principles enumerated in Section 6.1 through 6.5 shall be reflected in the Constitution.

Part C: Structures of Government

3.1 Supreme Law

3.1.1 The National Constitution of the Sudan shall be the Supreme Law of the land.

3.1.2 A representative National Constitutional Review Commission (NCRC) shall be established during the Pre-Transition Period which shall have as its first task the drafting of a Legal and Constitutional Framework to govern the Interim Period and which incorporates the Peace Agreement.

3.1.3 The Framework mentioned above shall be adopted as shall be agreed upon by the Parties.

3.1.4 During the Interim Period an inclusive Constitutional Review Process shall be undertaken.

3.1.5 The Constitution shall not be amended or repealed except by way of special procedures and qualified majorities in order that the provisions of the Peace Agreement are protected.

3.2 National Government

3.2.1 There shall be a National Government which shall exercise such functions and pass such laws as must necessarily be exercised by a sovereign state at national level. The National Government in all its laws shall take into account the religious and cultural diversity of the Sudanese people.

3.2.2 Nationally enacted legislation having effect only in respect of the states outside Southern Sudan shall have, as its source of legislation, Sharia and the consensus of the people.

3.2.3 Nationally enacted legislation applicable to the Southern States and/or the Southern Region shall have, as its source of legislation, popular consensus, the values and the customs of the people of Sudan (including traditions and religious beliefs, having regard to Sudan's diversity).

3.2.4 Where national legislation is currently in operation or is enacted, and its source is religious or customary law, then a state or region, the majority of whose residents do not practise such religions or customs may:
- (i) Either introduce legislation so as to allow or provide for institutions or practises in that region consistent with their religion or customs, or
- (ii) Refer the law to the Council of States for it to approve, by two-thirds ($^2/_3$) majority or initiate national legislation, which will provide for such necessary alternative institutions as is appropriate.

The Right to Self-determination for the People of South Sudan

3.3 That the people of South Sudan have the right to self-determination, inter alia, through a referendum to determine their future status.

3.4 An independent Assessment and Evaluation Commission shall be established during the Pre-Transition Period to monitor the implementation of the Peace Agreement during the Interim Period. This Commission shall conduct a mid-term evaluation of the unity arrangements established under the Peace Agreement.

3.5 At the end of the six (6) year Interim Period, there shall be an internationally monitored referendum, organised jointly by the GOSS and the SPLM/A, for the people of South Sudan to confirm the unity of the Sudan by voting to adopt the system of government established under the Peace Agreement or to vote for secession.

3.6 The Parties shall refrain from any form of unilateral revocation or abrogation of the Peace Agreement.

CHAPTER II: Power Sharing

(Signed at Naivasha, Kenya, on 26th May, 2004)

Part 1: General Principles

1.1 In accordance with the Machakos Protocol, the following Protocol on power sharing forms an integral part of the overall Peace Agreement.

1.2 The Parties reaffirm their acceptance of the Agreed Principles (of Governance). The modalities of implementation of these principles are the object of the present Protocol on power sharing.

1.3 In accordance with the Machakos Protocol, the structures of governments in the Sudan shall be as follows during the Interim Period:

   1.3.1 The National level of Government, which shall exercise authority so as to protect and promote the national sovereignty of Sudan and the welfare of its people;

   1.3.2 The Southern Sudan level of Government, which shall exercise authority in respect of, the people, and States in the South;

   1.3.3 The States throughout Sudan which shall exercise authority at the state level and render public services through the level of government close to the people; and 1.3.4 The level of local government throughout the Sudan.

1.4 The Parties agree that the following principles shall guide the distribution of power and the establishment of structures:

   1.4.1 Recognition of both the sovereignty of the nation as vested in its people as well as the need for autonomy of the GOSS and States throughout the Sudan;

   1.4.2 Affirmation of the need for both national as well as state and Southern Sudan norms and standards so as to reflect the unity of the country and the diversity of the Sudanese people;

   1.4.3 Acknowledgement of the need to promote the welfare of the people and protect their human rights and fundamental freedoms;

   1.4.4 Recognition of the need for the involvement and participation of the people of South Sudan at all levels of government and national institutions as an expression of the national unity of the country;

   1.4.5 Pursuit of good governance, accountability, transparency, democracy, and the rule of law at all levels of government to achieve lasting peace;

   1.4.6 Recognising the need to legitimise the arrangements agreed to herein, fair electoral laws shall be adopted, including the free establishment of political parties. Elections at all levels of government shall be held by universal adult suffrage.

1.5 Principles of Administration and Inter-Governmental Linkages

   1.5.1 In the administration of the Government of National Unity, the following provisions shall be respected:

1.5.1.1. There shall be a decentralised system of government with significant devolution of powers, having regard to the National, Southern Sudan, State, and Local levels of government;

1.5.1.2. The Interim National Constitution shall be the Supreme Law of the land and the Southern Sudan Constitution, state constitutions, and the laws of all levels of government must comply with it;

1.5.1.3. The linkage between the National Government and the states in the Southern Sudan shall be through the GOSS, subject to paragraph 1.5.1.4 below, and as provided for in the Interim National Constitution and the Southern Sudan Constitution;

1.5.1.4. In their relationships with each other or with other government organs, all levels of government and particularly National, Southern Sudan, and State Governments shall:
(a) Respect each other's autonomy;
(b) Collaborate rather than compete in the task of governing and assisting each other in fulfilling each other's constitutional obligations;
(c) Perform their functions and exercise their powers in accordance with the provisions of this Agreement.
(d) Allow the harmonious and collaborative interaction of the different levels of government within the context of national unity and for the achievement of a better quality of life for all.

1.6 Human Rights and Fundamental Freedoms

1.6.1 The Republic of the Sudan, including all levels of Government throughout the country, shall comply fully with its obligations under the international human rights treaties to which it is or becomes a party. These include the International Covenant on Civil and Political Rights, the International Covenant on Economic, Social and Cultural Rights, the International Convention on the Elimination of All Forms of Racial Discrimination, the Convention on the Rights of the Child, the Slavery Convention of 1926, as amended, and the related Supplementary Convention, the International Convention on the Suppression and punishment of the Crime of Apartheid, the International Convention Against Apartheid in Sports, the Convention Relating to the Status of Refugees and the Related Protocol, and the African Charter on Human and People's Rights. The Republic of the Sudan should endeavour to ratify other human rights treaties that it has signed.

1.6.2. The rights and freedoms to be enjoyed under Sudanese law, in accordance with the provisions of the treaties referred to above, include in particular the following:

1.6.2.1 *Life*: Every human being has the inherent right to life.

1.6.2.2 *Personal Liberty*: Everyone has the right to liberty and security of person.

1.6.2.3 *Slavery*: No one shall be held in slavery.

1.6.2.4 *Torture*: No one shall be subjected to torture.

1.6.2.5 *Fair Trial*: Anyone who is arrested shall be informed promptly of the reasons for his/her arrest; everyone shall be entitled to a fair and public hearing; everyone shall be presumed innocent until proved guilty; no one shall be held guilty of any criminal offence which did not constitute an offence at the time when it was committed; and everyone shall be entitled to be tried without undue delay, in his/her presence and to defend himself/herself.

1.6.2.6 *Privacy*: No one shall be subjected to arbitrary or unlawful interference with his/her privacy.

1.6.2.7 *Freedom of Thought, Conscience and Religion*: Everyone shall have the right to freedom of thought, conscience and religion.

1.6.2.8 *Freedom of Expression*: Everyone shall have the right to freedom of expression.

1.6.2.9 *Freedom of Assembly and Association*: The right of peaceful assembly shall be recognised.

1.6.2.10 *Family and marriage*: The right of men and women of marriageable age to marry and to found a family shall be recognised.

1.6.2.11 *Right to Vote:* Every citizen shall have the right and the opportunity to vote and to be elected at genuine periodic elections.

1.6.2.12 *Equality Before the Law*: All persons are equal before the law.

1.6.2.13 *Freedom from Discrimination*: The law shall prohibit any discrimination – race, colour, sex, language, religion, political or other opinion, national or social origin, property, birth or other status.

1.6.2.14 *Freedom or Movement*: Everyone has the right to liberty of movement and freedom to choose his/her residence.

1.6.2.15 *The Rights or Children*: Every child shall have the right to such measures of protection as are required by his/her status as a minor.

1.6.2.16 *Equal Rights of Men and Women*: The equal right of men and women to the enjoyment of all civil and political rights shall be ensured.

1.7 Reconciliation

1.7.1 The Parties agree to initiate a comprehensive process of national reconciliation and healing throughout the country as part of the peace building process. Its mechanisms and forms shall be worked out by the Government of National Unity.

1.8 Population Census, Elections and Representation:

1.8.1 Population census throughout the Sudan shall be conducted and completed by the end of the second year of the Interim Period.

1.8.2 The preparation, planning and organisation for the census shall commence as soon as the Peace Agreement is signed.

1.8.3 General Elections at all levels of government shall be completed by the end of the third year of the Interim Period.

1.8.4 Six months before the end of the periods referred to in sub-paragraphs 1.8.1 and 1.8.3 the Parties shall meet and review the feasibility of the dates set out in the above-mentioned sub-paragraphs.

1.8.5 Certain considerations should be taken into account with respect to the timing of the elections (including, inter alia, resettlement, rehabilitation, reconstruction, repatriation, building of structures and institutions, and consolidation of the Peace Agreement).

1.8.6 Whoever runs in any election must respect, abide by, and enforce the Peace Agreement.

1.8.7 International observers shall participate in the elections.

1.8.8 Representation of the north and the south at the National level shall be based on population ratio.

1.8.9 The percentages agreed herein are temporary and shall either be confirmed or adjusted on the basis of the census results.

PART II: Institutions at the National Level

2.1 During the Interim Period, the institutions at the National level shall consist of:
    2.1.1 The Legislature;
    2.1.2 The Executive;
    2.1.4 The Judiciary; and The Institutions and Commissions specified in this Agreement and the Interim National Constitution.

2.2 **The National Legislature**
    2.2.1 There shall be a bicameral National Legislature (NL) comprising a National Assembly; and a Council of States.
    2.2.2 In the establishment of the National Legislature, the following principles shall apply: equitable representation of the people of Southern Sudan in both legislative chambers; and relevant considerations shall be taken into account in determining what constitutes equitable representation.
    2.2.3 The National Legislature shall be structured as follows: the National Assembly, which shall be elected in accordance with the procedures set forth by an impartial and representative Electoral Commission; and the Council of States comprising two representatives from each state.
    2.2.4 Pending the elections referred to above, the National Assembly shall consist of such members representing the Parties to the Agreement in such proportions to be determined by the Parties prior to the conclusion of the Peace Agreement.
    2.2.5 Prior to the Parliamentary elections, the seats of the National Assembly shall be allocated as follows:
        (a) The National Congress Party (NCP) - 52%;
        (b) Sudan People's Liberation Movement (SPLM) - 28%;

(c) Other Northern political forces -14%;
(d) Other Southern political forces - 6%;

- 2.2.6 Both Chambers of the NL shall approve the allocation of resources and revenues, as well as the annual National budget.
- 2.2.7 Amendments to the National Constitution shall require approval of three-quarters (75%) of all the members of each chamber. The draft amendment must be introduced at least two (2) months prior to debate.
- 2.2.8 Any bill duly approved by the NL shall be signed into law by the President within thirty (30) days, failure to which it shall be deemed to have been so signed. Where the bill is re-introduced to the NL it shall become law if it passes by a two-thirds majority of all the members of the respective house or houses in which the assent of the President shall not be required.
- 2.2.9. The exclusive legislative powers of the NL shall be in respect of the matters set forth in Schedule A, annexed hereto.
- 2.2.10 The concurrent legislative powers of the NL shall be those matters as set forth in Schedule D, read together with Schedule F, annexed hereto.
- 2.2.11 The residual legislative powers shall be exercised in accordance with Schedule E annexed hereto.
- 2.2.12 Both chambers of the NL shall elect their respective Speakers, Deputy Speakers and other officers at their first sitting. The two Parties shall be adequately represented in these offices.
- 2.2.13 Both Chambers of the NL shall respectively determine their own rules, procedures, committees, and other matters of a similar nature.

2.3. **The National Executive**
- 2.3.1 The National Executive shall consist of the Presidency and a Council of Ministers.
- 2.3.2 There shall be established the institution of the Presidency consisting of the President and two Vice-Presidents.
- 2.3.3 The functions of the two Vice-Presidents shall be clearly defined by the parties to this Agreement.
- 2.3.4 There shall be a partnership and collegial decision-making process within the institution of the Presidency in order to safeguard the Peace Agreement.
- 2.3.5 Until such time as elections are held, the current incumbent President (or his successor) shall be the President and Commander-in-Chief of the Sudan Armed Forces (SAF). The current SPLM Chairman (or his successor) shall be the First Vice-President and shall at the same time hold the posts of President of the GOSS and Commander-in-Chief of the SPLA.
- 2.3.6 In respect of the following matters, the President shall take decisions with the consent of the First Vice-President, namely: the declaration and termination of a state of emergency; declaration of war; appointments that the President is required

to make according to the Peace Agreement (to be specified); and summoning, adjourning, or proroguing the National Legislature.

2.3.7 The President shall be elected in national elections, the timing of which shall be subject to the agreement of the two parties. The President elect shall appoint two Vice-Presidents, one from the South and the other from the North. If the President elect is from the North, the position of the First Vice-President shall be filled by the person who has been elected to the post of President of the GOSS, as the President's appointee to the said position. In the event that a person from the South wins the Presidential elections, the President elect shall appoint the First Vice-President from the North. All the other provisions in this Agreement relating to the presidency shall continue to apply.

2.3.8 Should the post of the President fall vacant, the functions of the President shall be assumed by a Presidential Council comprising of the Speaker of the National Assembly, the First Vice-President and the Vice-President. The Speaker of the National Assembly shall be Chairperson of the Council in the period prior to elections, after elections the First Vice-President shall be the chairperson of the Council.

2.3.9 Should the post of the President fall vacant in the period prior to elections, the Office of the President shall be filled by the nominee of the NCP within two weeks.

2.3.10 Should the post of the President fall vacant in the period after the elections, the post shall be filled through presidential elections which shall be held within sixty (60) days.

2.3.11 Should the post of the First Vice-President fall vacant prior to elections, the office shall be filled by the nominee of the SPLM within two(2) weeks. After the elections, the President shall appoint a First Vice-President in accordance with the Interim National Constitution and the provisions of this Peace Agreement.

2.3.12 The President shall, within thirty (30) days of the entry into force of the Peace Agreement, and in consultation with the First Vice-President, establish a Council of Ministers, having due regard to the need for inclusiveness and diversity in a Government of National Unity.

2.3.13 The President, the First Vice-President and the Vice-President shall be members of the Council of Ministers.

2.3.14 The National Legislature shall be required to approve declarations of war or state of emergency, but in either event, there shall be no derogation from the provisions of the Peace Agreement, except as may be provided herein.

2.3.15 Any Executive Orders or other legal acts by the President of the Republic shall be discussed with, and adopted by the Council of Ministers.

2.4 **National capital**

2.4.1 Khartoum shall be the Capital of the Republic of the Sudan.

2.4.2 The Administration of the National Capital shall be representative; and during the Interim Period the two Parties shall be adequately represented in the administration of the National Capital.

2.4.3 Human rights and fundamental freedoms as specified in the Machakos Protocol, and in the Agreement herein shall be guaranteed and enforced in the National Capital.

2.4.4 Law enforcement agencies of the Capital shall be representative of the population of Sudan.

2.4.5 Without prejudice to the competence of any National Institution to promulgate laws, judges and law enforcement agents shall be guided by the following: tolerance and behaviour that is based on cultural practices and traditions which do not disturb public order and personal privacy.

2.4.6 A special commission shall be appointed by the Presidency to ensure that the rights of non-Muslims are protected in accordance with the above guidelines.

2.4.7 Additionally, a system of mechanisms of guarantees shall be established to operationalise the above points, which includes judicial circulars and specialised Attorney General circuits.

2.5. **The Government of National Unity (GNU)**

2.5.1 During the Interim Period, there shall be a Government of National Unity reflecting the need for inclusiveness, the promotion of national unity, and the defence of national sovereignty, and the respect and implementation of Peace Agreement.

2.5.2 The Presidency and Council of Ministers shall exercise the Executive powers and competencies.

2.5.3 Cabinet posts and portfolios in all clusters, including the National Sovereignty Ministries, shall be shared equitably and qualitatively by the two Parties.

2.5.4 Representation of the SPLM and other political forces from the South in each of the clusters shall be determined by the parties signatory to agreement prior to the conclusion of the Peace agreement.

2.5.5 Prior to elections, the seats of the National Executive shall be allocated as set out in section 2.2.5.

2.5.6 The GNU shall be responsible for the administration and functioning of the State and the formulation and implementation of nation policies in accordance with the Interim National Constitution.

2.5.6 The GNU shall be responsible for establishing recruitment systems and admission policies to national universities, national institutes, and other institutions of higher education based on fair competition, giving equal opportunity to all citizens.

2.5.8 The GNU shall make decisions related to the ongoing or future activities of the organisations of the United Nations, bilateral, national, or international governmental and non-governmental organisations (NGOs).

2.5.9. The GNU shall implement an information campaign throughout Sudan in all national languages in Sudan to popularise the Peace Agreement, and to foster national unity, reconciliation and mutual understanding.

2.6 **Civil Service**

2.6.1 The GNU shall also ensure that the National Civil Service, notably at the senior and middle-levels, is representative of the people of Sudan.

2.6.2 In order to create a sense of national belonging and address imbalances in the National Civil Service, a National Civil Service Commission shall be established.

2.7 **National Security**

2.7.1 There shall be a National Security Council the composition and functions of which shall be determined by the law and which shall define the new national security strategy based on the analysis of the new security threats.

2.7.2 There shall be one National Security Service whose details of establishment shall be worked out under the implementation modalities.

2.8 **Language**

2.8.1 All the indigenous languages are national languages, shall be respected, developed and promoted.

2.8.2 Arabic language is the wide spoken national language in the Sudan.

2.8.3 Arabic, as a major language at the national level, and English, shall be official working languages of the National Government business and language of instruction for higher education.

2.8.4 In addition to Arabic and English, the legislature of any sub-national level government may adopt any other national language(s) as additional official working language(s).

2.8.5 The use of either language at any level of government or education shall not be discriminated against.

2.9. **Foreign Policy**

2.9.1 During the Interim Period, Sudan's Foreign Policy shall serve the national interests, which include: promotion of international cooperation, enhancement of South-South and international cooperation, striving to achieve African and Arab integration, non-interference in the affairs of other states, promotion of good neighbourliness, and combating international and transnational organised crimes and terrorism.

2.10 **Other Independent and/or National Institutions to be Established in Accordance with the Peace Agreement**

    2.10.1 The National Constitutional Review Commission shall detail the mandate and provide for the appointment and other mechanisms to ensure the independence of the following institution: the National Electoral Commission; Human Rights Commission; National Judicial Service Commission; National Civil Service Commission; and, an *ad-hoc* Commission to monitor and ensure accuracy, legitimacy, and transparency of the Referendum as mentioned in the Machakos Protocol on Self-Determination for the People of South Sudan; Fiscal and Financial Allocation and Monitoring Commission; and, any other independent commission/institution set forth in the Peace Agreement or as agreed upon by the Parties.

2.11 **The National Judiciary**

    2.11.1 The powers of the Judiciary shall be exercised by courts and other tribunals. The Judiciary shall be independent of the Legislature and the Executive. Its independence shall be guaranteed in the Interim National Constitution.

    2.11.2 There shall be established at the National Level: a Constitutional Court; a National Supreme Court; National Courts of Appeal; and, any other National Courts or tribunals as deemed necessary to be established by law.

    2.11.3 The Constitutional Court shall be established in accordance with the provisions of this Peace Agreement and the Interim National Constitution. The decisions of the Court shall be final and binding.

    2.11.4. The National Supreme Court shall be a court of review and cassation in respect of any criminal or civil matter arising out of or under national laws and may establish panels for the purposes of considering and deciding appeals on matters requiring special expertise.

2.12 **Constitutional Review Process**

    2.12.1 The Peace Agreement shall be signed by the leaders of the two Parties.

    2.12.2 Upon signature, the Parties shall be bound by the Agreement and shall assume the obligations arising therefrom, more especially the obligations to implement the Agreement and to give legal and constitutional effect to the arrangements agreed therein.

    2.12.3 Upon signature, the Parties commit themselves to ensure that all the organs, committees and structures under their control, including their members, shall observe the terms of the Agreement.

    2.12.4 After the Agreement has been signed, the text thereof shall be forwarded to the National Assembly and the SPLM National Liberation Council for approval.

2.12.5 The National Constitutional Review Commission shall have as its first task the preparation of a Legal and Constitutional Framework text in the constitutionally appropriate form, based on the Peace Agreement and the current Sudan Constitution, for adoption by the National Assembly. The same text shall be presented to the SPLM National Liberation Council for adoption. In the event of a contradiction, the terms of the Peace Agreement shall prevail in so far as that contradiction exists.

2.12.6 Without prejudice to the provisions of 2.12.5 above, the National Constitutional Review Commission shall draw upon relevant experiences and documents as may be presented by the Parties.

2.12.7 Upon adoption by the National Assembly and the SPLM National Liberation Council, the Constitutional Text shall become the Interim National Constitution for the Sudan during the Interim Period.

2.12.8 Pending the adoption of the Constitutional Text, the Parties agree that the legal status quo in their respective areas shall remain in force.

2.12.9 The National Constitutional Review Commission shall also be required to prepare such other legal instruments as is required to give effect to the Peace Agreement.

2.12.10 Without prejudice to the provisions of the Peace Agreement, the National Constitutional Review Commission shall be responsible for organising an inclusive Constitutional Review Process.

2.12.11 Without prejudice to the functions of the State Legislatures, the National Constitutional Review Commission shall prepare model Constitutions for the States, subject to compliance with the National Constitution, and the Constitution of Southern Sudan.

PART III: Government of Southern Sudan

3.1 In respect of the Southern Sudan, there shall be a Government of Southern Sudan (GOSS), as per the borders of 1/1/56, which shall consist of the Legislature of Southern Sudan; the Executive of Southern Sudan; and the Judiciary of Southern Sudan.

3.2 The GOSS shall function in accordance with a Southern Sudan Constitution, which shall be drafted by an inclusive Southern Sudan Constitutional Drafting Committee and adopted by the Transitional Assembly of Southern Sudan by a two-thirds majority of all members. It shall conform to the Interim National Constitution.

3.3 The powers of the GOSS shall be as set forth in Schedules B and D, read together with Schedules E and F, the Interim National Constitution, Southern Sudan Constitution, and the Peace Agreement.

3.4 A primary responsibility of the GOSS will be to act as an authority in respect of the States of Southern Sudan, to act as a link with the National Government and to ensure that the rights and interests of the people of Southern Sudan are safeguarded during the Interim Period.

3.5 **Legislature of Southern Sudan**

3.5.1 Pending the elections, the First Southern Sudan Assembly shall be an inclusive, constituent legislature comprised of the SPLM, which shall be represented by 70 per cent, the NCP 15 per cent, and the other Southern political forces, 15 per cent.

3.5.2 The Southern Sudan Assembly shall provide for the election of its Speaker and other office holders.

3.5.3 When enacting the Constitution of Southern Sudan, the Assembly of Southern Sudan shall be empowered to assign such powers as set forth in Schedules B and D, read together with Schedules E and F, to the GOSS.

3.5.4 The Southern Sudan Constitution shall make provisions for the Assembly of Southern Sudan, re-constituted through elections in accordance with the provisions herein related to the timing of general elections. The Constitution of the Southern Sudan shall also make provisions for the election of the President and appointment of the Vice-President of the GOSS.

3.5.5 The Assembly of Southern Sudan may amend the Constitution of the Southern Sudan by a two-thirds (2/3) majority vote of all members.

3.5.6 Apart from applicable national legislation, legislative authority in Southern Sudan shall be vested in the Assembly of Southern Sudan. It shall establish its own offices, committees and rules of procedure.

3.6 **The Southern Sudan Executive**

3.6.1 An Executive Council of Ministers appointed by the President of the GOSS, in consultation with his/her Vice-President and approved by the Assembly of Southern Sudan, shall be established in accordance with the Southern Sudan Constitution. The Executive Council of Ministers shall be accountable to the President of the GOSS and the Southern Sudan Assembly in the performance of their functions and may be removed by a motion supported by two-thirds (2/3) of all the members of the Southern Sudan Assembly.

3.6.2 The Executive Authority of Southern Sudan shall establish such independent institutions as the Peace Agreement, the Interim National Constitution and the Southern Sudan Constitution contemplate. It shall be empowered to establish such further commissions and institutions compatible with its powers as it deems necessary to promote the welfare of its people, good governance and justice.

3.6.3 The GOSS shall be established with due regard to the need for inclusiveness.

3.6.4   Prior to elections, the GOSS shall be allocated as follows: SPLM, 70 per cent; NCP, 15 per cent; and other Southern political forces, 15 per cent.

3.6.5   The GOSS shall discharge its obligations and exercise such rights and powers in regard to administration, security, financial, and development issues as is set forth in the Southern Sudan Constitution, the Interim National Constitution, the Peace Agreement and any other agreement relating to the reconstruction and development of the Southern Sudan.

3.6.6   (a) Should the post of the President of the GOSS fall vacant, and pending the nomination and swearing in of the new President, the functions of the President shall be assumed by the Vice-President of the GOSS;

(b) Should the post of the President of the GOSS fall vacant in the period prior to elections, the Office of the President of the GOSS shall be filled by a nominee of the SPLM within two (2) weeks;

(c) Should the post of the President fall vacant in the period after the elections, the post shall be filled through elections which shall be held within sixty (60) days.

3.7 **The Judiciary of Southern Sudan**

3.7.1   There shall be at the Southern Sudan Level: a Supreme Court of Southern Sudan; Courts of Appeal; and any such other courts or tribunals as deemed necessary.

3.7.2   The Constitution of Southern Sudan shall provide for a Supreme Court, which shall be the highest court in the South.

3.7.3   The Southern Sudan Supreme Court shall: be the court of final judicial instance in respect of any litigation or prosecution under Southern State; have original jurisdiction to decide on disputes; adjudicate on the constitutionality of laws; be a court of review and cassation; and have criminal jurisdiction over the President and Vice-President of the Government of Southern Sudan and the Speaker of Southern Sudan, and such other jurisdictions as determined by Southern Sudan Constitution, the Peace Agreement and the Law.

3.7.4   Judges of the Courts of Southern Sudan shall perform their functions without political interference, shall be independent, and shall administer the law without fear or favour.

3.7.5   Without prejudice, the Legislature of Southern Sudan shall provide for appointments, terms of service and dismissal of appointed Judges.

Part IV: Institutions at the State Level

4.1 The Institutions at the State level shall consist of:
    4.1.1   The State Legislature;
    4.1.2   The State Executive; and
    4.1.3   The State Judiciary.

4.2 There shall be legislative, executive, and judicial institutions at state level, which shall function in accordance with this Agreement, the Interim National Constitution and, in respect of the states of Southern Sudan, also with the Constitution of Southern Sudan.

4.3 Local Government is an important level of Government and its election, organisation and proper functioning shall be the responsibility of the States, in accordance with the relevant state constitution.

4.4 **The State Legislature**
  4.4.1 There shall be a State Legislature comprised of members elected in accordance with the electoral provisions.
  4.4.2 Pending the elections, the composition of the state legislatures shall be comprised as follows: NCP, 70 per cent in the Northern states and the SPLM, 70 per cent in the Southern states; the remaining 30 per cent in the Northern and the Southern states to be allocated as 10 per cent in the Southern states to be filled by the NCP and Northern states to be filled by the SPLM respectively, and 20 per cent in the Northern and Southern states, to be filled by representatives of other Northern and Southern political forces respectively.
  4.4.3 Elections (referred to in sub-article 4.4.1) shall take place on the same date as the elections for the National Assembly.
  4.4.4 The state legislatures shall prepare and adopt state constitutions provided that they are in conformity with the National Constitution, the Peace Agreement, and for Southern States, the Constitution of Southern Sudan.
  4.4.5. The State Legislature shall have law-making competence in respect of the functional areas.
  4.4.6. Members of the State Legislature and the State Council of Ministers, including the Governor, shall have such immunities as are provided by law.
  4.4.7. The State Legislature shall decide its own rules, procedures, and committees, and elect its Speaker and other officers.

4.5 **The State Executive**
  4.5.1 Prior to elections, the state executives shall be allocated as follows: NCP, 70% in the Northern states and the SPLM 70% in the Southern states; and the remaining 30% in the Northern and the Southern states shall be allocated as 10% in the Southern and Northern states, to be filled by the NCP and SPLM respectively, and 20% to be filled by representatives of other Northern and Southern political forces, respectively.
  4.5.2 As part of the 10% share of the NCP in Southern states, the Governor of one Southern State shall be a nominee of the NCP; one Deputy Governor in a different Southern State shall be a nominee of the NCP; and one Deputy Governor in a different Southern State shall be a nominee of the NCP.

4.5.3 The States' Council of Ministers shall be appointed by the Governor in accordance with the State Constitution, having regard to the need for inclusiveness.

4.5.4 The Governor shall, together with the States' Council of Ministers appointed by him/her, exercise the executive powers of the state.

4.5.5 State Governors must sign any law duly approved by the State Legislature, failure to which, after thirty (30) days, it shall be deemed to have been signed into law by the State Governor.

4.6 **State Judicial Institutions**

4.6.1 The State Constitutions shall provide for the establishment of such state courts by the State Judiciary as necessary.

4.6.2 State legislation must provide for: the appointment and dismissal of State-appointed judges (lay magistrates), and guarantees of the independence and impartiality of the judiciary.

4.6.3 State Courts shall have civil and criminal jurisdiction in respect of State, Southern Sudan, and National Laws, save that a right of appeal shall lie as provided in this Agreement.

4.6.4 Notwithstanding sub-paragraph 4.6.3, the National Legislature shall determine the civil and criminal procedures to be followed in respect of litigation or prosecution under National laws in accordance with the Interim National Constitution.

4.6.5 The structures and powers of the Courts of the States of Southern Sudan shall be subject to the provisions of this Agreement and the Constitution of Southern Sudan.

PART V: Schedules (see the complete version)

Schedule A: National Powers
Schedule B: Powers of the Government of Southern Sudan
Schedule C: Powers of States
Schedule D: Concurrent Powers
Schedule E: Residue Powers
Schedule F: Resolution of Conflicts in Respect of Concurrent Powers.

Chapter III: Wealth Sharing (signed at Naivasha, Kenya, on 7th January, 2004)

1.0 **Guiding Principles in Respect of an Equitable Sharing of Common Wealth**

    1.1   The Parties agree that the guiding principles and provisions below shall be the basis for the comprehensive text on wealth sharing.

    1.2   The wealth of Sudan shall be shared equitably so as to enable each level of government to discharge its legal and constitutional responsibilities and duties.

    1.3   The National Government shall also fulfil its obligation to provide transfers to the GOSS.

    1.4   The sharing and allocation of wealth emanating from the resources of the Sudan shall ensure that the quality of life, dignity and living conditions of all the citizens are promoted without discrimination on grounds of gender, race, religion, political affiliation, ethnicity, language, or region. The sharing and allocation of this wealth shall be based on the premise that all parts of Sudan are entitled to development.

    1.5   The Parties agree that Southern Sudan faces serious needs to: (i) be able to perform basic government functions, (ii) build up the civil administration, and (iii) rehabilitate and reconstruct/construct the social and physical infrastructure in a post-conflict Sudan.

    1.6   The Parties agree that Nuba Mountains, Southern Blue Nile, Abyei and other war-affected areas face serious needs as 1.5 above.

    1.7   That Southern Sudan and those areas in need of construction/reconstruction, shall be brought up to the same average level of socio-economic and public services standard as the Northern states.

    1.8   That revenue sharing should reflect a commitment to devolution of power and decentralisation of decision-making in regard to development, service delivery and governance.

    1.9   The development of infrastructure, human resources, sustainable economic development and the capacity to meet human needs shall be conducted within a framework of transparent and accountable government.

    1.10   That the best known practices in the sustainable utilisation and control of natural resources shall be followed.

    1.11   This Agreement sets out the respective types of income, revenue, taxes and other sources of wealth to which the various levels of government are entitled.

    1.12   The Parties recognise that the National Government, during the Interim Period, needs to mobilise additional national resources.

    1.13   There is a limit on how much additional national resources can be mobilised part of the national needs in a post-conflict Sudan will have to be met by assistance.

1.14 The National Government shall not withhold an allocation due to a state or the GOSS. Any level of Government may initiate proceedings in the Constitutional Court should any other organ or level withholds monies due to it. The National Government shall make transfers to the GOSS based on the principles established.

1.15 In agreeing to these wealth-sharing arrangements, the Parties signal to the international community that it will have to play a strong and constructive role in providing post-conflict construction/reconstruction assistance especially to Southern Sudan and other war affected and least developed areas.

1.16 The National Government shall assist the GOSS during the Pre-Interim Period, in cooperation with international organisations to develop and implement a programme for capacity enhancement in the South.

2.0 Ownership of Land and Natural Resources

2.1 Without prejudice to the position of the Parties with respect to ownership and subterranean natural resources, this Agreement is not intended to address the ownership of those resources. The Parties agree to establish a process to resolve this issue.

2.2 The Parties agree that the regulation, management and the process sharing of wealth from subterranean natural resources are addressed below.

2.3 The Parties record that the regulation of land tenure, usage and exercise of rights in land is to be a concurrent competency exercised at the appropriate levels of government.

2.4 Rights in land owned by the Government of Sudan shall be exercised through appropriate or designated levels of Government.

2.5. The Parties agree that a process be instituted to progressively develop and amend the relevant laws to incorporate customary laws and practises, local heritage and international trends and practises.

2.6 Without prejudice to the jurisdiction of courts, there shall be established a National Land Commission that shall have the following functions:

2.6.1 Arbitrate between willing contending Parties on claims over land, and sort out such claims.

2.6.2 The party or group making claims in respect of land may make a claim against the relevant government and/or other Parties interested in the land.

2.6.3 The National Land Commission may at its discretion entertain such claims.

2.6.4 The Parties to the arbitration shall be bound by the decision of the National Land Commission on mutual consent and upon registration of the award in a court of law.

2.6.5 The National Land Commission shall apply the law applicable in the locality where the land is situated or such other law as the Parties to the arbitration agree, including principles of equity.

2.6.6 Accept references on request from the relevant government, or in the process of resolving claims, and make recommendations to the appropriate levels of government concerning land reform policies and recognition of customary land rights and/or law.

2.6.7 Assess appropriate land compensation, which need not be limited to monetary compensation.

2.6.8 Advise different levels of government on how to coordinate policies on national projects.

2.6.9 Study and record land use practices in areas where natural resource exploitation occurs.

2.6.10 The National Land Commission shall be representative and independent. Its Chairperson shall be appointed by the Presidency.

2.6.11 The National Land Commission may conduct hearings and formulate its own rules of procedure.

2.6.12 The National Land Commission will have its budget approved by the Presidency and will be accountable to the Presidency for the due performance of its functions.

2.7 In accordance with this Agreement and without prejudice to the jurisdiction courts, there shall be established a Southern Sudan Land Commission which have the following functions:

2.7.1 Arbitrate between willing contending Parties on claims over land and sort out such claims.

2.7.2 The party or group making claims in respect of land may make a claim against the relevant government and/or other Parties interested in the land.

2.7.3 The Southern Sudan Land Commission may entertain such claims at its discretion.

2.7.4 The Parties to the arbitration shall be bound by the Southern Sudan Land Commission's decision on mutual consent and upon registration the award in a court of law.

2.7.5 The Southern Sudan Land Commission shall apply the law applicable in the locality where the land is situated or such other the Parties to the arbitration agree, including principles of equity.

2.7.6 Accept references on request from the relevant government, or in the process of resolving claims, and make recommendations to appropriate levels of government concerning land reform policies and recognition of customary land rights and/or law.

2.7.7 Assess appropriate land compensation, which need not be limited to monetary compensation.

2.7.8 Advise different levels of government on how to coordinate policies on the GOSS projects.

2.7.9 Study and record land use practises in areas where natural resource exploitation occurs.

2.7.10 Be representative and independent. The Chairperson shall be appointed by the President of the GOSS.

2.7.11 The Southern Sudan Land Commission may conduct hearings and formulate its own rules of procedure.

2.7.12 The Southern Sudan Land Commission shall have its budget approved by the GOSS and shall be accountable to the President of the GOSS for the performance of its functions.

2.8 The National Land Commission and the Southern Sudan Land Commission shall cooperate and coordinate their activities so as to use their resources efficiently. Without limiting the matters of coordination, the National Land Commission and the Southern Sudan Land Commission may agree:

a) To exchange information and decisions of each Commission;

b) That certain functions of the National Land Commission may be carried out through the Southern Sudan Land Commission;

c) On the way in which any conflict between the findings or recommendations of each Commission may be resolved.

2.9 In the case of conflict between the findings or recommendations of the National Land Commission and the Southern Sudan Land Commission that cannot be resolved by agreement, the matter shall be referred to the Constitutional Court.

3.0 **Oil Resources**

A. Guiding Principles for the management and development of the petroleum sector

3.1 The Parties agree that the basis for an agreed and definitive framework for the management of the development of the petroleum sector during the Interim Period shall include the following:

3.1.1 Sustainable utilisation of oil as a non-renewable natural resource consistent with:
 (a) the national interest and the public good;
 (b) the interest of the affected States/Regions;
 (c) the interests of the local population in affected areas; and,
 (d) national environmental policies, biodiversity conservation guidelines, and cultural heritage protection principles.

3.1.2 Empowerment of the appropriate levels of government to develop and manage the various stages of oil production during the Interim Period.

3.1.3 Give due attention to enabling policy environment for the flow of foreign direct investment.

3.1.4 A stable macroeconomic environment that emphasizes stability of the petroleum sector.

3.1.5 Persons enjoying rights in land shall be consulted in respect of decisions to develop subterranean natural resources and shall share in the benefits of that development.

3.1.6 Persons enjoying rights in land are entitled to compensation on just terms arising from acquisition or development of land.

3.1.7 The communities in whose areas development of subterranean natural resources occurs have the right to participate in the negotiation of contracts for the development of those resources.

3.1.8 Regardless of the contention over the ownership of land and associated natural resources, the Parties agree on a framework for the regulation and management of petroleum development in Sudan during the Interim Period.

B. National Petroleum Commission (NPC)

3.2 The Parties agree that an independent National Petroleum Commission (NPC) shall be established during the Pre-Interim Period and its decisions shall be by consensus.

3.3 Taking into account the provisions elsewhere in this Agreement, the NPC shall be constituted as follows: (a) The President of the Republic and President of the GOSS as Co-chairs and permanent members; (b) four (4) permanent members representing the National Government; (c) four (4) permanent members representing the GOSS; and (d) not more than three (3) representatives of an oil producing State/Region in which petroleum development is being considered, as non-permanent members.

3.4 The NPC shall have the following functions:
  3.4.1 Formulate public policies and guidelines in relation to the development and management of the petroleum sector consistent with paragraph 3.1.1.
  3.4.2 Monitor and assess the implementation of those policies to ensure that they work in the best interests of the people of Sudan.
  3.4.3 Develop strategies and programmes for the petroleum sector.
  3.4.5 Negotiate and approve all oil contracts for exploration and development and ensure they are consistent with the NPC's principles, policies and guidelines.
  3.4.5 Develop its internal regulations and procedures.

3.5 In performing the functions referred to in paragraph 3.4 above, the NPC shall take into account relevant considerations, including the following:
  3.5.1 The extent to which the contract provides benefits to local communities affected by the development.
  3.5.2 The extent to which the views of the State/Region and the affected groups are incorporated in the proposed contracts.
  3.5.3 If the NPC decides to approve the contract, persons holding rights in land who are aggrieved by the decision shall seek relief through arbitration or in a court of law.
  3.5.4 If the non-permanent members of the NPC representing the oil producing State/Region collectively disagree with the decision of the NPC to approve the contract, the National Minister of Petroleum shall not sign the contract and shall refer the matter to the Council of States/Regions. If the Council of States/Regions rejects the objection by two-thirds ($^2/_3$) majority, the Minister shall sign the contract. The arbitration decision on respect shall be binding.

3.5.5 If the NPC approves the contract the National Minister of Petroleum shall sign the contract on behalf of the Government of the Sudan.

3.5.6 In performing functions 3.4.1, 3.4.2, 3.4.3, and 3.4.5 of paragraph 3.4, the NPC shall include only its permanent members.

3.5.7 In performing function 3.4.4 of paragraph 3.4, the NPC shall include its permanent members and representatives of oil producing States/Regions.

4.0 Existing Oil Contracts

4.1 The SPLM shall appoint a limited number of representatives to have access to all existing oil contracts. The representatives shall have the right to engage technical experts. All those who have access to the contracts will sign confidentiality agreements.

4.2 Contracts shall not be subject to re-negotiation.

4.3 If contracts are deemed to have fundamental social and environmental problems, the Government of Sudan will implement necessary remedial measures.

4.4 The Parties agree that 'existing oil contracts' means contracts signed before the date of signature of the Comprehensive Peace Agreement.

4.5 Persons whose rights have been violated by the oil contracts are entitled to compensation.

5.0 Guiding Principles for Sharing Oil Revenue

5.1 The Parties agree that the basis for an agreed and definitive framework for the sharing of the wealth emanating from oil resources of Southern Sudan shall include the following:

5.1.1 The framework for sharing wealth from the extraction of natural resources should balance the needs for national development and the reconstruction of Southern Sudan.

5.2 The Parties agree that a formula for sharing the revenue from oil resources shall be as set forth in this Agreement.

5.3 For the purposes of this Agreement, 'Net revenue from oil' shall be the sum of the net revenue (i) from exports of government oil and (ii) from deliveries of government oil to the refineries.

5.4 An Oil Revenue Stabilisation Account shall be established from government oil net revenue derived from actual export sales above an agreed benchmark price.

5.5 The Parties agree that at least two per cent (2%) of oil revenue shall be allocated to the oil producing states/regions in proportion to output produced in such states/regions.

5.6 After the payment to the Oil Revenue Stabilisation Account and to the oil producing states/regions, fifty per cent of net oil revenue derived from oil producing wells in Southern Sudan shall be allocated to the GOSS as of the beginning of the Pre-Interim Period and the remaining fifty per cent to the National Government and States in Northern Sudan.

5.7 A Future Generation Fund shall be established once national oil production reaches two (2) million barrels per day.

5.8 The Parties agree that all funds/special accounts referred to in this Agreement and future accounts shall be on-budget operations.

6.0 Sharing of Non-Oil Revenue

6.1 The National Government shall be entitled to legislate, raise and collect the taxes listed below and to collect revenue from these sources:
- 6.1.1 National Personal Income Tax;
- 6.1.2 Corporate or Business Profit Tax;
- 6.1.3 Customs Duties and Import Taxes;
- 6.1.4 Seaports and Airports Revenue;
- 6.1.5 Service charges;
- 6.1.6 Oil revenues as set out herein;
- 6.1:7 National Government Enterprises and projects;
- 6.1.8 VAT or GST or other retail taxes on goods and services;
- 6.1.9 Excise Tax;
- 6.1.10 Any other tax as agreed upon in these negotiations;
- 6.1.11 Loans, including borrowing from the Central Bank and the public.

6.2 The GOSS shall be entitled to revenue from the following sources and to raise and collect the taxes listed below:
- 6.2.1 The National revenue allocation to the Government of Southern Sudan and States/Regions from the National Revenue Fund as set forth in section 7.0 of this Agreement;
- 6.2.2 Revenue from any of the sources listed as State/Region revenue sources referred to in paragraph 6.3;
- 6.2.3 The Southern Sudan Reconstruction and Development Fund (SSRDF);
- 6.2.4 Oil revenues as is set out in this Agreement;
- 6.2.5 Southern Sudan Government Taxes, which do not encroach on the exclusive National Government taxing powers or which are contemplated in the Power Sharing Protocol;
- 6.2.6 Service charges of the Government of Southern Sudan;
- 6.2.7 Government of Southern Sudan enterprises and projects;
- 6.2.8 Grants in Aid and Foreign Aid;
- 6.2.9 Taxes and levies on small and medium businesses;
- 6.2.10 Excise taxes on goods within the region deemed to be luxury consumables;
- 6.2.11 Southern Sudan Personal Income Tax;
- 6.2.12 Any other taxes as may be agreed to from time to time;
- 6.2.13 Loans and Borrowing in accordance with the Monetary Policy, Banking, Currency and Borrowing sections of this Agreement.

6.3 The States/Regions shall be entitled to raise and collect the taxes listed below and revenue from the sources listed below:
- 6.3.1 State/Regional land and property tax and royalties;
- 6.3.2 Service charges for state/regional services;
- 6.3.3 Licenses;

6.3.4 State/Regional Personal Income Tax;
6.3.5 Levies on Tourism;
6.3.6 State/Regional share of oil Revenues;
6.3.7 Stamp duties;
6.3.8 Agricultural Taxes;
6.3.10 Grants in Aid and Foreign Aid through the National Government and the GOSS;
6.3.11 Excise taxes;
6.3.12 Border Trade charges or levies in accordance with National Legislation;
6.3.13 Other state/region taxes which do not encroach on national or Southern Sudan Government taxes;
6.3.14 Any other tax as may be agreed to from time to time; and
6.3.15 Loans and borrowing in accordance with the Monetary Policy, Banking, Currency and Borrowing sections of this Agreement.

7.0 **Equalisation and Allocation to the National, Southern Sudan and State/Regional Levels of Government in Respect of Revenue Collected Nationally**
  7.1 All revenues collected nationally for or by the National Government shall be pooled in a National Revenue Fund (NRF) administered by the National Treasury.
  7.2 All the revenues and expenditures of the Government will be on-budget operations and made public.
  7.3 Notwithstanding the provisions of paragraphs 5.6, 7.1 and 13.1, the National Government shall allocate 50 per cent of the national non-oil revenue collected in Southern Sudan to the GOSS to partially meet the development cost and other activities during the Interim Period.
  7.4 As a result of the allocation arrangements in paragraph 7.3 above, the Parties agree to appeal to the international and donor community to help the GOSS by providing post-conflict reconstruction assistance especially at the beginning of the transition.
  7.5 The states/regions and the GOSS shall retain and dispose of such other income raised and collected under their own taxing powers.

8.0 **Fiscal and Financial Allocation and Monitoring Commission (FFAMC)**
  8.1 To ensure transparency and fairness both in regard to the allocation of nationally collected funds to the states/regions and the GOSS, a Fiscal and Financial Allocation and Monitoring Commission (FFAMC) shall be established. Decision-making arrangements of the FFAMC shall be as agreed to by the Parties.
  8.2 The FFAMC shall undertake the following duties and responsibilities:

8.2.1 Monitor and ensure that equalisation grants from the National Revenue Fund are promptly transferred to respective levels of government;

8.2.2 Ensure appropriate utilisation and sharing of financial resources;

8.2.3 Ensure that resources allocated to war affected areas are transferred in accordance with agreed upon formulae; and

8.2.4 Ensure transparency and fairness in the allocation of funds to the GOSS and States/Regions according to established ratios or percentages stipulated in this Agreement.

8.3 The FFAMC shall be composed of representatives from the National Government and the GOSS and States/Regions as follows: (a) three (3) representatives of the National Government; (b) three (3) representatives of the GOSS; and, (c) all Finance Ministers in all States/Regions of Sudan.

8.4 The Chairperson of the FFAMC shall be appointed by the Presidency.

8.5 The FFAMC shall work out its own rules and procedures, which shall be approved by the Presidency.

9.0 **Interstate Commerce**

9.1 There shall be no legal impediment to interstate commerce or the flow of goods and services, capital or labour between the States/Regions.

10.0 **Government Liabilities**

10.1 Any debts/liabilities incurred by any level of government shall be the responsibility of that level of government.

11.0 **Division of Government Assets**

11.1 There shall be a fair and equitable division of government assets. In the event of a dispute, the Parties agree that such dispute shall be referred to a committee comprising a representative of each of the Parties involved in the dispute and a mutually agreed expert.

12.0 **Accounting Standards and Procedures and Fiscal Accountability**

12.1 All levels of government shall comply with generally accepted accounting standards and procedures.

12.2 To ensure the effective operation of such institutions, there shall be independent National and Southern Sudan Audit Chambers, which shall have responsibility for the functions referred to above. Appointments to the Chamber shall be made by the Presidency and confirmed by the National Assembly.

12.3 All levels of government shall hold all income and revenue received by it in public accounts and subject to public scrutiny and accountability.

13.0 **Financing the Transition**
- 13.1 The National Government shall assist, during the Pre-Interim Period, the SPLM/ A in the establishment of the new transitional governments at the State/Regional level and the GOSS
- 13.2. Upon signature of a Comprehensive Peace Agreement, the Parties shall establish a Joint National Transition Team to undertake the following:
- 13.2.1 Prepare budget estimates for the establishment of Governments at the National, Southern Sudan and State/Regional levels.
- 13.2.2 Organise and prepare relevant documents for the donor conference;
- 13.2.3 Develop fund-raising strategies, and assist in the identification of potential sources of funds necessary for a smooth and timely commencement of the Interim Period.

14.0 **Monetary Policy, Banking, Currency and Borrowing**
A. **Monetary Policy, Banking and Currency**
- 14.1. The Parties agree, consistent with the Machakos Protocol of 20th July 2002, to have a dual banking system in Sudan during the Interim Period. An Islamic banking system shall operate in Northern Sudan and conventional banking system shall operate in Southern Sudan.
- 14.2. The Parties agree that conventional banking facilities are urgently needed in Southern Sudan. The Parties therefore agree to establish the Bank of Southern Sudan (BOSS) as a branch of Central Bank of Sudan (CBOS) consistent with paragraph 14.1 above.
- 14.3. The Parties agree to restructure the CBOS so as to reflect the duality of the banking system in Sudan: (i) an Islamic financing window in Northern Sudan under a Deputy Governor of CBOS using Islamic financing instruments to implement the national monetary policy in Northern Sudan; and (ii) the BOSS, headed by a deputy governor of CBOS, to manage the conventional window using conventional financing instruments.
- 14.4. The CBOS shall be responsible for the conduct of monetary policy. All banking institutions shall be subject to the rules and regulations set by the CBOS.
- 14.5. The primary responsibility and mandate of the CBOS shall be ensuring price stability, maintaining stable exchange rates, sound banking system and issuance of currency.
- 14.6. The CBOS shall be fully independent in its pursuit of monetary policy.
- 14.7. The Governor of CBOS and his/her two deputies shall be appointed by the Presidency. The Governor of the CBOS shall appoint other senior officers within the Central Bank.
- 14.8. The Parties agree to establish, during the Pre-Interim Period, an independent Board of Directors (BOD), which shall be responsible to the Presidency on the accountability of the CBOS and shall consist of nine (9) members as follows: (a) the

14.9 The CBOS shall adopt a programme to issue a new currency as soon as is practical during the Interim Period. The design of the new currency shall reflect the cultural diversity of Sudan. Until a new currency has been issued, the circulating currencies in Southern Sudan shall be recognised.

14.10 The BOSS shall be responsible for chartering and supervising financial institutions in Southern Sudan.

14.11 All financial institutions shall be subject to internationally recognised regulatory and prudential standards for Islamic and conventional finance, as set by the CBOS.

14.12 All financial institutions shall be bound to implement monetary policies set by the CBOS.

B. **Borrowing**

14.13. The GOSS and the States/Regions may borrow money based on their respective creditworthiness.

14.14 The GOSS and all sub-national governments shall report financial and fiscal data to the relevant National Government bodies for statistical purposes.

14.15 The GOSS and the states/regions may borrow money from foreign sources based on their respective credit worthiness.

14.16 Foreign borrowing by all sub-national governments shall be done in a manner that does not undermine national macroeconomic policies and shall be consistent with the objective of maintaining external financial viability.

15.0 Reconstruction and Development Funds
A. Southern Sudan Reconstruction and Development Fund (SSRDF)

15.1. There shall be established a Southern Sudan Reconstruction and Development Fund (SSRDF) to solicit, raise and collect funds from domestic and international donors and disburse such funds for the reconstruction and rehabilitation of the infrastructure of the South.

15.2. A monitoring and evaluation system shall be established to ensure accountability, transparency, efficiency, equity and fairness in the utilisation of resources.

15.3. The GOSS shall be responsible for expenditure from the fund and shall be entitled to raise additional funds by way of donation from foreign states, multilateral organisations or other bodies for the purposes of the reconstruction and development of the southern States/Regions.

B. **National Reconstruction and Development Fund (NRDF)**

15.4. There shall be established by the Treasury, a National Reconstruction and Development Fund (NRDF) having the mission of developing the war affected areas and least developed

Appendix

areas outside Southern Sudan and a steering committee with appropriate representation from such areas.

C. **Multi-Donor Trust Funds**
15.5. The Parties recognise the need to establish, during the Pre-Interim Period, two Multi-Donor Trust Funds (MDTFs), one for the National Government and one for the GOSS to support urgent recurrent and investment budget costs under clearly stated criteria of eligible financing components.
15.6. The MDTFs shall commence immediately to support, among other things, priority areas of capacity building and institutional strengthening and quick start/impact programmes identified by the Parties.
15.7. Both funds shall support urgent recurrent and investment budget costs under clearly stated criteria of eligible financing components, and both shall have the right to solicit, raise and collect funds from foreign donors.
15.8. All trust funds shall report the flow of funds to the CBOS.
15.9. To ensure proper accountability for funds disbursed through the MDTFs the Parties shall cause audits to be performed on funds used within six (6) months of the close of the recipient's financial year.
15.10. During the Pre-Interim as well as the Interim Period, funds may be channelled directly to finance activities beneficial to the National Government or the GOSS.
15.11. During the Pre-Interim Period, the flow of foreign funds shall be through special accounts established in the Bank of Sudan for areas outside Southern Sudan and for Southern Sudan in a commercial bank in Southern Sudan until the Bank of Southern Sudan is established and operational.

Chapter IV: The Resolution of the Abyei Conflict*

(Signed at Naivasha, Kenya, on 26th May 2004)

Principles of Agreement on Abyei*

1.1   In General
    1.1.1   Abyei is a bridge between the north and the south, linking the people of Sudan.
    1.1.2   The territory is defined as the area of the nine Ngok Dinka chiefdoms transferred to Kordofan in 1905.
    1.1.3   The Misseriya and other nomadic peoples retain their traditional rights to graze cattle and move across the territory of Abyei.

1.2   **Interim Period**
Upon signing the peace agreement, Abyei will be accorded special administrative status, in which:
    1.2.1   Residents of Abyei will be citizens of both Western Kordofan and Bahr el Ghazal, with representation in the legislatures of both states;
    1.2.2   Abyei will be administered by a local Executive Council, elected by the residents of Abyei. Pending the election of the Executive Council, its initial members will be appointed by the Presidency;
    1.2.3   Net oil revenues from Abyei will be divided six ways during the Interim Period: the National Government, 50%; the GOSS, 42%; Bahr el Ghazal Region, 2%; Western Kordofan, 2%; locally with the Ngok Dinka, 2%; and locally with the Misseriya people, 2%;
    1.2.4   The National Government will provide Abyei with assistance to improve the lives of the peoples of Abyei, including urbanisation and development projects;
    1.25   International monitors will be deployed to Abyei to ensure full implementation of these agreements.

1.3   **End of Interim Period**
Simultaneously with the referendum for Southern Sudan, the residents of Abyei will cast a separate ballot. The proposition voted on in the separate ballot will present the residents of Abyei with the following choices, irrespective of the results of the Southern referendum:
    a)   That Abyei retains its special administrative status in the North;
    b)   That Abyei be part of Bahr el Ghazal.

1.4   The January 1, 1956 line between North and South will be inviolate, except as agreed above.

---

*This is the full text of the proposal entilted "Principles of Agreement on Abyei," presented by US Special Envoy Senator John Danforth to H.E. First Vice-President Ali Osman Mohamed Taha and SPLM/A Chairman Dr. John Garang on the 19th march, 2004. The Parties hereby declare to adopt these principles as the basis for the resoulution of the Abyei Conflict.

Appendix

2.0 **Administrative Structure**
   2.1 Upon signing the Peace Agreement, Abyei Area shall be accorded special administrative status under the institution of the Presidency.
   2.2 Abyei area shall be administered by a local Executive Council, elected by the residents of Abyei.
   2.3 The administration of the Abyei area shall be representative and inclusive of all the residents of the area.
   2.4 The Executive Council shall be composed of the Chief Administrator, his/her Deputy and not more than five heads of departments. The Chief Administrator shall make recommendations to the Presidency regarding the appointments of the heads of departments.
2.5 The Executive Council shall:
   2.5.1 Render necessary services;
   2.5.2 Supervise and promote security and stability in the area;
   2.5.3 Propose development and urbanisation projects for the area to both the Abyei Area Council and to the Presidency;
   2.5.4 Present to the National Government proposals regarding the provision of assistance to improve the lives of the peoples of Abyei;
2.6 The Presidency shall determine the executive, legislative and financial powers and competencies of the special status of Abyei area, having regard to this protocol, other protocols, agreements, and the Comprehensive Peace Agreement.
2.7 In view of the special status of Abyei Area, the Presidency shall apply to the Judiciary to establish courts for Abyei Area as deemed appropriate.

3.0 **Financial Resources**
3.1 Without prejudice to the provisions of the Wealth Sharing Agreement, the net-oil revenue produced in Abyei shall be shared during the Interim Period as follows:
   3.1.1 50% - National Government;
   3.1.2 42% - GOSS;
   3.1.3 2% - Bahr el Ghazal Region;
   3.1.4 2% - Western Kordofan;
   3.1.5 2% - Locally with the Ngok Dinka;
   3.1.6 2% - Locally with the Misseriya people.
3.2 In addition to the above financial resources, Abyei Area shall be entitled to:
   3.2.1 Its share of the national revenue as per the Wealth Sharing Agreement
   3.2.2 Revenues raised in the Abyei area: Income Tax, other taxes and levies;
   3.2.3 Its share of the NRDF;
   3.2.4 An equitable share of SSRDF;
   3.2.5 Allocations from the National Government to cover the cost of establishment of the new administration;
   3.2.6 Donations and grants.

3.3 There shall be established, under the Executive Council, Abyei Resettlement, Construction and Development Fund.

3.4 The National Government shall appeal to the international and donor community to facilitate the return and resettlement of the residents of Abyei Area.

3.5 The financial resources due to Abyei Area shall be deposited in special accounts from which the administration of the Area shall make withdrawals.

4.0 **Public Participation**

4.1 There shall be established Abyei Area Council comprised of not more than twenty members.

4.2 Prior to elections, the Presidency shall appoint the members of the Abyei Area Council.

4.3 The Abyei Area Council shall:

4.3.1 Issue local enactments within the powers of local government and on customary matters;

4.3.2 Approve the budget of the Area; adopt reconstruction, development and urbanisation plans for the Area;

4.3.3 If necessary, recommend to the Presidency the relief of the Chief Administrator or his/her Deputy;

4.3.4 Participate in the promotion of reconciliation efforts in the Area.

5.0 **Determination of Geographic Boundaries**

5.1 There shall be established by the Presidency, Abyei Boundaries Commission (ABC) to define and demarcate the area of the nine Ngok Dinka chiefdoms transferred to Kordofan in 1905, referred to herein as Abyei Area.

5.2 The composition and time frame of the Abyei Boundaries Commission (ABC) shall be determined by the Presidency.

5.3 The Abyei Boundaries Commission (ABC) shall present its final report to the Presidency as soon as it is ready.

6.0 **Residents of the Area**

6.1 The residents of Abyei Area shall be:

(a) The Members of Ngok Dinka community and other Sudanese residing in the area;

(b) Citizens of both Western Kordofan and Bahr el Ghazal with representation in the legislatures of both States as determined by the National Electoral Commission.

7.0 **Security Arrangements**

7.1 There shall be established Abyei Area Security Committee, chaired by the Chief Administrator, and shall comprise of the Deputy Chief Administrator, the Army Commander, the Police Chief and the representative of the Security Organ.

- 7.2 Without prejudice to the Agreement on Security Arrangements, the Parties shall form and deploy one joint battalion in the Area.
- 7.3 International monitors shall also be deployed in the Area through the Interim Period.
- 7.4 International monitors shall be deployed to Abyei to ensure full implementation of these Agreements.

8.0 **Abyei Referendum Commission**
- 8.1 There shall be established an Abyei Referendum Commission to conduct Abyei referendum simultaneously with the referendum of Southern Sudan. The composition of the Commission shall be determined by the Presidency.
- 8.2 The residents of Abyei shall cast a separate ballot. The proposition voted on in the separate ballot shall present the following choices irrespective of the results of the Southern referendum:
    a) That Abyei retain its special administrative status in the North; that Abyei be part of Bahr el Ghazal.
    b) The January 1, 1956 line between North and South shall be inviolate, except as agreed above.

9. Reconciliation Process

Upon signing the Comprehensive Peace Agreement, the Presidency shall, as a matter of urgency, start peace and reconciliation process for Abyei that shall work for harmony and peaceful co-existence in the Area.

Chapter V: Resolution of the Conflict in Southern Kordofan and Blue Nile States

(Signed at Naivasha, Kenya, on 26th May 2004)

1.0 **General Principles**

The Parties agree on the following as the basis for political, administrative, economic and social solutions to the conflict in Southern Kordofan/Nuba Mountains* and Blue Nile:

- 1.1 Human rights and fundamental freedoms shall be guaranteed to all individuals in the State as prescribed in the Interim National Constitution.
- 1.2 The diverse cultural heritage and local languages of the population of the State shall be developed and protected.
- 1.3 Development of human resources and infrastructure shall be the main goal of the State.

2.0 **Definition of the Two Areas**

- 2.1 The boundaries of Southern Kordofan/Nuba Mountains State shall be the same boundaries of former Southern Kordofan Province when Greater Kordofan was sub-divided into two provinces.
- 2.2 For the purpose of this Protocol, Blue Nile State shall be understood as referring to the presently existing Blue Nile State.

3.0 **Popular Consultation**

The Government of Sudan and the Sudan People's Liberation Movement (the Parties), committed to reaching a just, fair and Comprehensive Peace Agreement to end the war in Southern Kordofan/Nuba Mountains and Blue Nile States, agree on the following:

- 3.1 Popular consultation is a democratic right and mechanism to ascertain the views of the people of Southern Kordofan/Nuba Mountains and Blue Nile States on the comprehensive agreement.
- 3.2 That this comprehensive agreement shall be subjected to the will of the people of the two States through their respective democratically elected legislatures.
- 3.3 That the legislatures of the two States shall each establish a Parliamentary Assessment and Evaluation Commission to assess and evaluate the implementation of the agreement in each State.
- 3.4 An independent Commission shall be established by the Presidency to assess and evaluate the implementation of the Comprehensive Peace Agreement in each of the two States.

---

*The name of the State shall be settled before the conclusion of the Peace Agreement by a commitee ling the State formed by the two parties.

3.5 Once this Agreement is endorsed by the people through the legislature of any of the two States as meeting their aspirations, then the agreement becomes the final settlement of the political conflict in that State.

3.6 Should any of the legislatures of the two States decide to rectify any shortcomings in the constitutional, political and administrative arrangements of the Agreement, then such legislature shall engage in negotiations with the National Government with the view of rectifying these shortcomings.

4.0 **Structure of the State Government**
4.1 The State shall have the following structure:
4.2 The State Executive, which shall comprise:
4.2.1 The State Governor;
4.2.2 The State Council of Ministers; and
4.2.3 Local Governments.
4.3 The State Legislature
4.4 The State Judiciary.

5.0 **The State Executive**
5.1 The Governor of the State shall be directly elected by the registered voters of the State in a public adult suffrage.
5.2 The Governor shall appoint the ministers and the commissioners of the state in accordance with the State Interim Constitution.
5.3 The Governor shall exercise the Executive Powers of the State which shall be in respect of the functional areas listed in Schedules A and B, read together with Schedule C and in accordance with the State Interim Constitution.
5.4 The State Council of Ministers shall be accountable to the Governor and the State Legislature in the performance of their duties.
5.5 The State shall have commissioners and elected local councils.
5.6 There shall be State Security Committee to be chaired by the Governor of the State.
5.7 Without prejudice to the provisions of paragraph 5.6 above, the Governor of the State may demand the transfer of the Director of the National Security Branch from the State.
5.8 The State Police Service shall adhere to the national standards and regulations as set forth by National Police Service.
5.9 Police, Prisons, Wildlife and Fire Brigade Officers shall be recruited by the State Service according to the national standards, trained and commissioned nationally and returned to the State for service.
5.10 Without prejudice to the provisions of paragraph 5.9 above, the National Authority may agree with the State Authority to transfer any number of police officers from the State police to the National Police Service whenever necessary.

5.11 The State Authority may request the National Authority to transfer to the State any number of police officers to fill any vacancies in the state.

6.0 The State Legislature

6.1 Members of the State Legislature (SL) shall be elected by the registered voters of the State in accordance with the State Law and in conformity with the electoral provisions as set forth by the National Electoral Commission.

6.2 The SL shall prepare and adopt the State Constitution, provided that it shall conform to the Interim National Constitution.

6.3 The Governor of the State shall sign any law duly approved by the SL, failure to which, after thirty (30) days it shall be deemed to have been signed into law.

6.4 The SL shall legislate for the state within its legislative powers as stipulated in Schedule (A).

6.5 State laws currently applicable in the State shall continue until new legislation is duly enacted by the SL within its competence.

6.6 The SL shall decide its own rules, procedures and committees, and elect its Speaker and other officers.

6.7 The SL may relieve the Governor of the State of hislher functions by a motion supported by two-thirds of its membership.

6.8 Members of the State Legislature and the State Executive shall have such immunities as are provided by law.

7.0 The State Courts

7.1 The structures and powers of the courts of the States shall be subject to the Interim National Constitution.

7.2 The State Constitution shall provide for the establishment of such state courts as are necessary.

7.3 The SL shall provide for the appointment and dismissal of state appointed judges, subject to the State constitution and the approval of the National Judicial Service Commission.

7.4 The SL shall provide for guarantees for the independence and impartiality of the State judiciary.

7.5 The state courts shall have civil and criminal jurisdiction in respect of State and National Laws, save that a right of appeal shall lie to the National Courts in respect of matters brought before or heard under National laws.

7.6 The National Legislature shall determine the civil and criminal procedures to be followed in respect of litigation or prosecution under national laws in accordance with the Interim National Constitution.

8.0 The State Share in the National Wealth

8.1 The National wealth shall be shared equitably between different levels of Government so as to allow enough resources for each level of Government to exercise its constitutional competence.

8.2 The States shall raise and collect taxes and revenues as listed in Schedule (D).

8.3 The State is entitled to two per cent (2%) of the oil produced, as specified in the Wealth Sharing Agreement.

8.4 The state shall be represented in the FFAMC, which shall ensure transparency and fairness in regard to allocation of the share due to the state.

8.5 The general objective of the National Reconstruction and Development Fund (NRDF) is to develop the war affected areas and least developed areas in the Sudan.

8.6 The Parties agree to allocate seventy-five per cent (75%) of the total fund to the war-affected areas, particularly to Southern Kordofan/Nuba Mountains and Blue Nile States.

8.7 The allocation of funds among the areas affected shall be determined during the Pre-Interim Period by the Joint National Transition Team (JNTT).

8.8 The FFAMC shall allocate current transfers to Southern Kordofan/Nuba Mountains, Blue Nile and other war-affected areas and least developed areas according to the following criteria:-
  8.8.1 Population;
  8.8.2 Minimum expenditure responsibilities;
  8.8.3 Human Development Index / social indicators;
  8.8.4 Geographical area (cost disability factor);
  8.8.5 Fiscal effort (internal revenue effort); and
  8.8.6 The effect of war factor.

8.9 In addition to the budgetary allocations and the two states' share in the NRDF, the President shall allocate an amount of money to each of the two states.

8.10 The Parties agree to appeal to the donor community to provide technical assistance to the FFAMC to develop comprehensive equalisation criteria.

8.11. The states shall hold all income and revenue received in audited public accounts and shall comply with the regulations and auditing standards set by the Chamber of the Auditor General, who may audit the state's accounts.

8.12. There shall be no impediment to interstate commerce or the flow of goods and services, capital or labour to and from the State.

8.13 Any debts/liabilities incurred by any level of government shall be the responsibility of that level of government.

8.14 There shall be a fair and equitable division of government assets.

8.15 There shall be accounting standards, procedures and fiscal accountability institutions operating in accordance with generally accepted accounting standards.

9.0 **State Land Commission**
 9.1 The regulation of the land tenure, usage and exercise of rights in land shall be a concurrent competency exercised by the National and State Governments.
 9.2 Rights in land owned by the National Government within the State shall be exercised through the appropriate or designated level of government.
 9.3. There shall be established a State Land Commission in the two respective States.
 9.4. The State Land Commission shall be composed of persons from the State concerned.
 9.5. The State Land Commission shall exercise all the powers of the National Land Commission at the State level.
 9.6 The State Land Commission shall be competent to review existing land leases and contracts and examine the criteria for the present land allocations and recommend the introduction of such necessary changes.
 9.7 The National Land Commission and the State Land Commission shall cooperate and coordinate their activities and may agree as follows:
  9.7.1 To exchange information and decisions of each Commission;
 9.7.2 That certain functions of the National Land Commission may be carried out through the State Land Commission; and
 9.7.3 On the way in which any conflict between the findings or recommendations of each Commission may be resolved.
 9.8. In case of conflict between the findings and recommendations of the National Land Commission and the State Land Commission that cannot be resolved, the matter shall be referred to the Constitutional Court for adjudication.

10.0 **Security Arrangements**
 10.1 Without prejudice to the Agreement on the Security Arrangements and the right of Sudan Armed Forces (SAF) Command to deploy forces all over North Sudan as it deems fit, SAF troop levels in Southern Kordofan/Nuba Mountains and Blue Nile during the Interim Period shall be determined by the Presidency.

11.0 **Pre-Election Arrangements**
 11.1. As part of pre-election arrangements, the Parties agree on the following:
 11.1.1. The Executive and Legislature in the two states shall be allocated as follows:
  (a) 55% - to the NCP
  (b) 45% - to the SPLM.
 11.1.2. There shall be rotational Governorship in the two states with each Party holding the Office of Governor for half of the pre-election period.

11.1.3 No one Party is to hold the Governorship in both states at the same time.
11.1.4 The office of Deputy Governor is to be allocated to the Party that is not presently occupying the Office of Governor.
11.1.5 The Parties are to decide, upon the signature of the Comprehensive Peace Agreement, the time and order in which each party assumes the Governorship in each state.
11.2 Pending general elections, and as part of affirmative action, the Parties agree that Southern Kordofan/Nuba Mountains and Blue Nile States shall be adequately represented in national institutions targeting a percentage not less than the ratio of their population size.

Schedules (see complete version)
Schedule A: The Exclusive Executive and Legislative Competencies of the Two States
Schedule B: Concurrent Powers
Schedule C: Residue Powers
Schedule D: State Revenue Sources

Chapter VI: Security Arrangements

(Signed at Naivasha, Kenya, on 25th September, 2003)

1. **Status of the Two Armed Forces**
   a) In the context of a united Sudan, the Parties agree to the formation of the future army of Sudan that shall be composed from the SAP and the SPLA.
   b) As part of a peace agreement and in order to end the war, the Parties agree that the two forces, the SAP and the SPLA shall remain separate during the Interim Period, and further agree that both forces shall be considered and treated equally as Sudan's National Armed Forces during the Interim Period taking into consideration 1 (c) below.
   c) The parties agree to the principles of proportional downsizing of the forces on both sides, at a suitable time, following the completion of the comprehensive ceasefire arrangements.
   d) The national Armed Forces shall have no internal law and order mandate except in constitutionally specified emergencies.

2. **Ceasefire**
   The parties agree to an internationally monitored ceasefire, which shall come into effect from the date of signature of a Comprehensive Peace Agreement. Details of the Ceasefire Agreement shall be worked out by the two parties together with the IGAD mediators and international experts.

3. **Redeployment**
   a) The two forces shall be disengaged, separated, encamped and redeployed as will be detailed in the Comprehensive Ceasefire Agreement.
   b) Except for those deployed in the Joint/Integrated Units (JIUs), the rest of the forces of SAP currently deployed in the south shall be redeployed North of the South/North border of 1/1/1956 under international monitoring and assistance within and up to two and one half years ($2^1/_2$) from the beginning of the Pre-Interim Period.
   c) Except for those deployed in the Joint/Integrated Units, the rest of SPLA forces currently deployed in Nuba Mountains and Southern Blue Nile shall be redeployed South of the South/North border of 1/1/1956 as soon as the JIUs are formed and deployed under international monitoring and assistance.
   d) The SPLM/A undertakes that the demobilised Southern Sudanese from those currently serving in SAF in Southern Sudan shall be absorbed into various institutions of the Government of Southern Sudan along with demobilised SPLA soldiers.
   e) The parties agree to implement the DDR programmes for the benefit of all those who will be affected by the reduction, demobilisation and downsizing of the forces as agreed in 1(c), 3(d) and 7(b).

4.0 Joint/Integrated Units (JIUs)

There shall be formed Joint/Integrated Units consisting of equal numbers from the SAF and the Sudan People's Liberation Army (SPLA) during the Interim Period. The JIUs shall constitute a nucleus of a post referendum army of Sudan, should the result of the referendum confirm unity, otherwise they would be dissolved and the component parts integrated into their respective forces.

4.1 Elaboration on JIUs

a) *Their character:*
   They should have a new character based on a common doctrine.
b) *Their Functions:*
   I.   They will be a symbol of national unity during the Interim Period.
   II. They will be a symbol of sovereignty during the Interim Period.
   III. They will participate in the defence of the country together with the two forces.
   IV. They will provide a nucleus of a post-Interim Period future army of the Sudan should the vote of referendum confirm unity.
   V.   They shall be involved in the reconstruction of the country.
c) *Size and Deployment*
   The size and deployment of the JIUs throughout the Interim Period shall be as indicated below:
   I.   Southern Sudan: 24,000
   II. Nuba Mountains: 6,000
   III. Southern Blue Nile: 6,000
   IV. Khartoum: 3,000
   V.   Eastern Sudan: (a) the redeployment of SPLA forces from Eastern Sudan to South of the South/North border of 1/1/1956 shall be completed within one year from-the beginning of the Pre-Interim Period; and (b) the parties shall discuss the issue of establishing Joint/Integrated Units.

5. Command and Control of The Two Forces

1. The Parties agree to establish a Joint Defence Board (JDB) under the Presidency, and shall comprise the Chiefs of Staff of the two forces, their deputies and any number of senior officers to be agreed to by the parties. It shall take its decisions by consensus and it shall be chaired alternately by the respective Chiefs of Staff.
2. Functions of JDB

The JDB shall perform the following functions:
a) Coordination between the two forces.
b) Command of the JIUs

6. Common Military Doctrine

The parties shall develop a common military doctrine as a basis for the JIUs, as well as a basis for a post-Interim Period army of the Sudan. The parties shall develop this common doctrine within one year from the beginning of the Interim Period. During the Interim Period, the training of the SPLA (in the South), the SAP (in the North) and the JIUs (in both North and South) will be based on this common doctrine.

7. **Status of Other Armed Groups (OAGs) in The Country**
   a) No armed group allied to either party shall be allowed to operate outside the two forces.
   b) The Parties agree that those mentioned in 7(a) who have the desire and qualify shall be incorporated into the organised forces of either Party (Army, Police, Prisons arid Wildlife forces), while the rest shall be reintegrated into the civil service and civil society institutions.
   c) The parties agree to address the status of other armed groups in the country with the view of achieving comprehensive peace and stability in the country and to realise full inclusiveness in the transition process.

8. **National Security Organs and Police forces**
   Structures and arrangements affecting all law enforcement organs, especially the Police and National Security Organs shall be dealt with as part of the power sharing arrangements, and tied where is necessary to the appropriate level of the executive.

www.ingramcontent.com/pod-product-compliance
Lightning Source LLC
Chambersburg PA
CBHW031551300426
44111CB00006BA/267